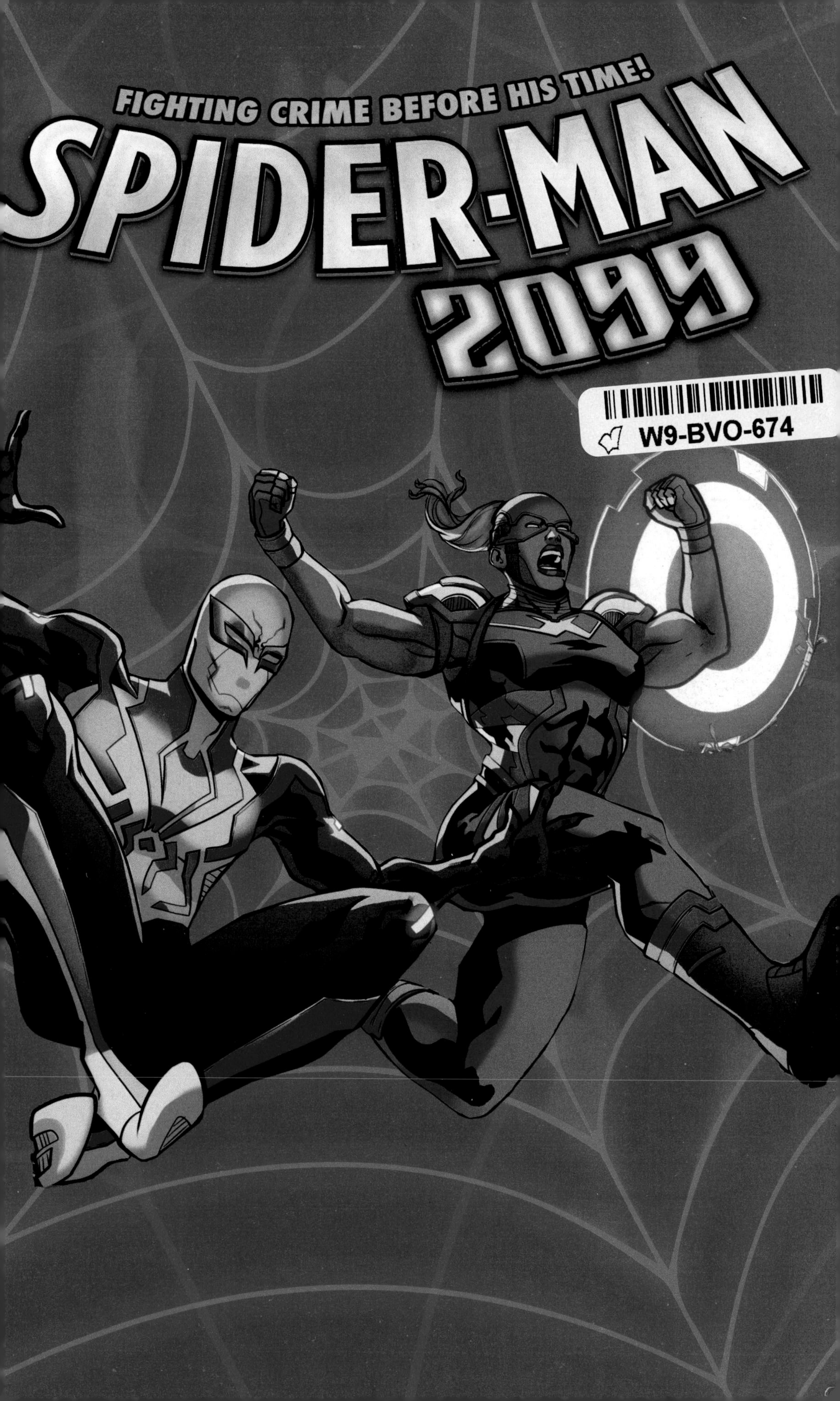
FIGHTING CRIME BEFORE HIS TIME!
SPIDER-MAN
2099

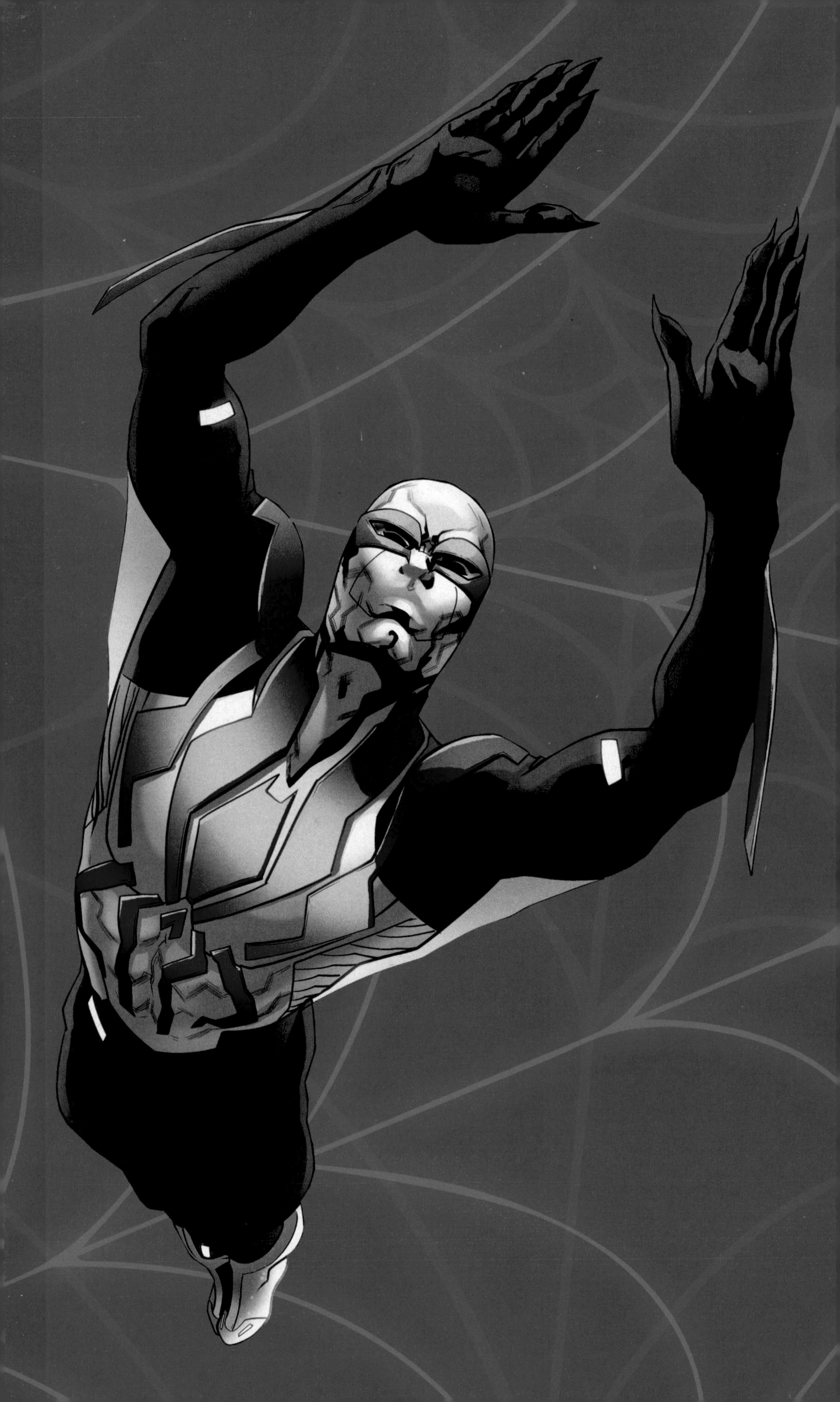

FIGHTING CRIME BEFORE HIS TIME!

SPIDER-MAN 2099

APOCALYPSE SOON

PETER DAVID
writer

WILL SLINEY
artist

RACHELLE ROSENBERG
colorist

VC's CORY PETIT
letterer

FRANCESCO MATTINA
cover art

CHARLES BEACHAM
editor

MARK PANICCIA
senior editor

SPIDER-MAN created by STAN LEE & STEVE DITKO

collection editor JENNIFER GRÜNWALD
assistant editor CAITLIN O'CONNELL
associate managing editor KATERI WOODY
editor, special projects MARK D. BEAZLEY
vp production & special projects JEFF YOUNGQUIST
svp print, sales & marketing DAVID GABRIEL

editor in chief AXEL ALONSO
chief creative officer JOE QUESADA
president DAN BUCKLEY
executive producer ALAN FINE

SPIDER-MAN 2099 VOL. 6: APOCALYPSE SOON. Contains material originally published in magazine form as SPIDER-MAN 2099 #17-21. First printing 2017. ISBN# 978-1-302-90282-7. Published by MARVEL WORLDWIDE, INC., a subsidiary of MARVEL ENTERTAINMENT, LLC. OFFICE OF PUBLICATION: 135 West 50th Street, New York, NY 10020.

Printed in the U.S.A. DAN BUCKLEY, President, Marvel Entertainment; JOE QUESADA, Chief Creative Officer; TOM BREVOORT, SVP of Publishing; DAVID BOGART, SVP of Business Affairs & Operations, Publishing & Partnership; C.B. CEBULSKI, VP of Brand Management & Development, Asia; DAVID GABRIEL, SVP of Sales & Marketing, Publishing; JEFF YOUNGQUIST, VP of Production & Special Projects; DAN CARR, Executive Director of Publishing Technology; ALEX MORALES, Director of Publishing Operations; SUSAN CRESPI, Production Manager; STAN LEE, Chairman Emeritus. For information regarding advertising in Marvel Comics or on Marvel.com, please contact Vit DeBellis, Integrated Sales Manager, at vdebellis@marvel.com. For Marvel subscription inquiries, please call 888-511-5480. **Manufactured between 7/7/2017 and 8/7/2017 by QUAD/GRAPHICS WASECA, WASECA, MN, USA.**

10 9 8 7 6 5 4 3 2 1

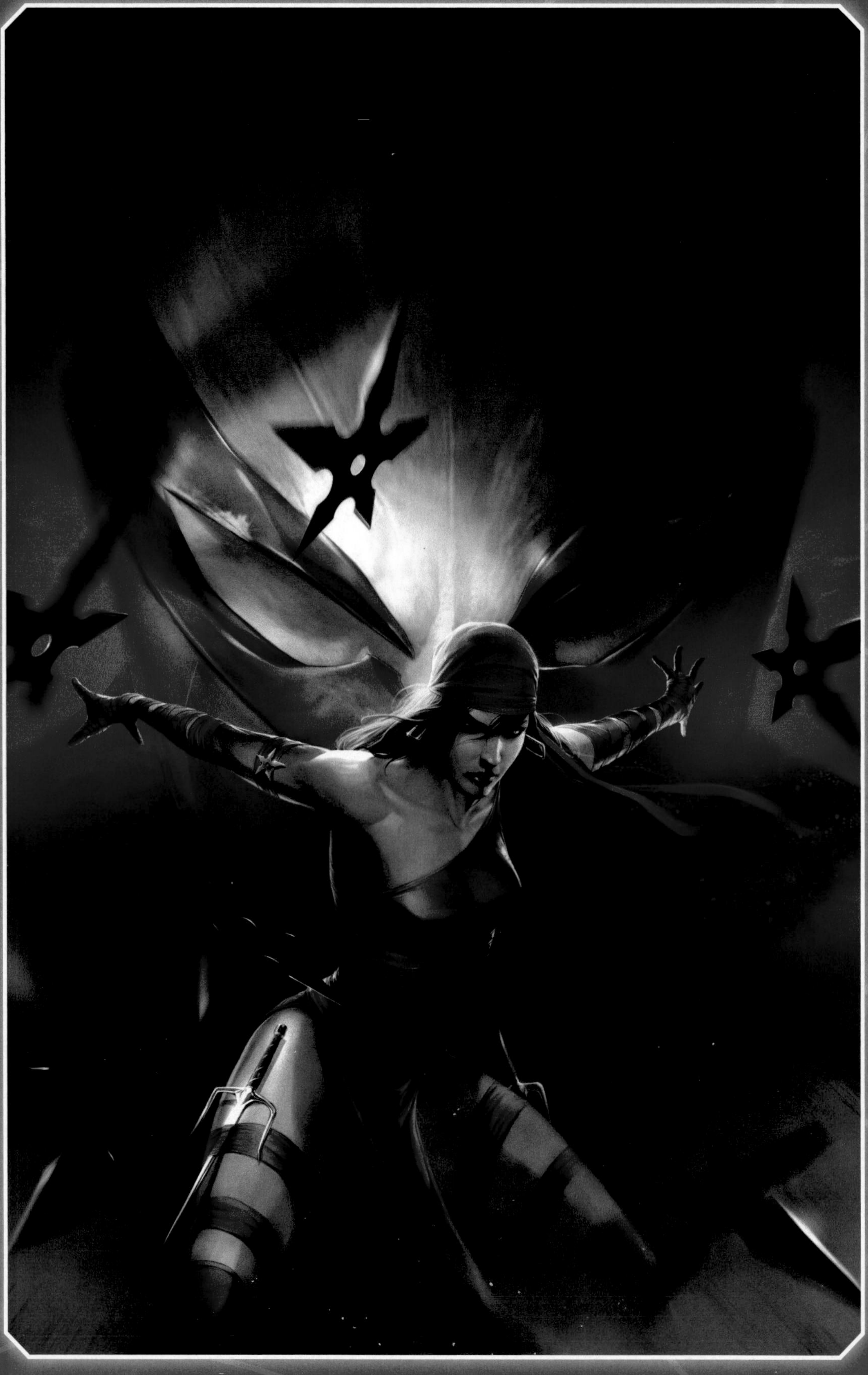

MIGUEL O'HARA WAS A YOUNG GENETICS GENIUS EMPLOYED AT THE MEGACORPORATION ALCHEMAX IN THE FUTURE CITY OF NUEVA YORK! ONE OF HIS EXPERIMENTS--TO REPLICATE THE POWERS OF THE PRESENT-DAY SPIDER-MAN--WAS TURNED AGAINST HIM AND REWROTE HIS DNA TO MAKE IT 50 PERCENT SPIDER! AFTER LEARNING HOW TO USE HIS AMAZING NEW ABILITIES, MIGUEL BECAME...

SPIDER-MAN 2099

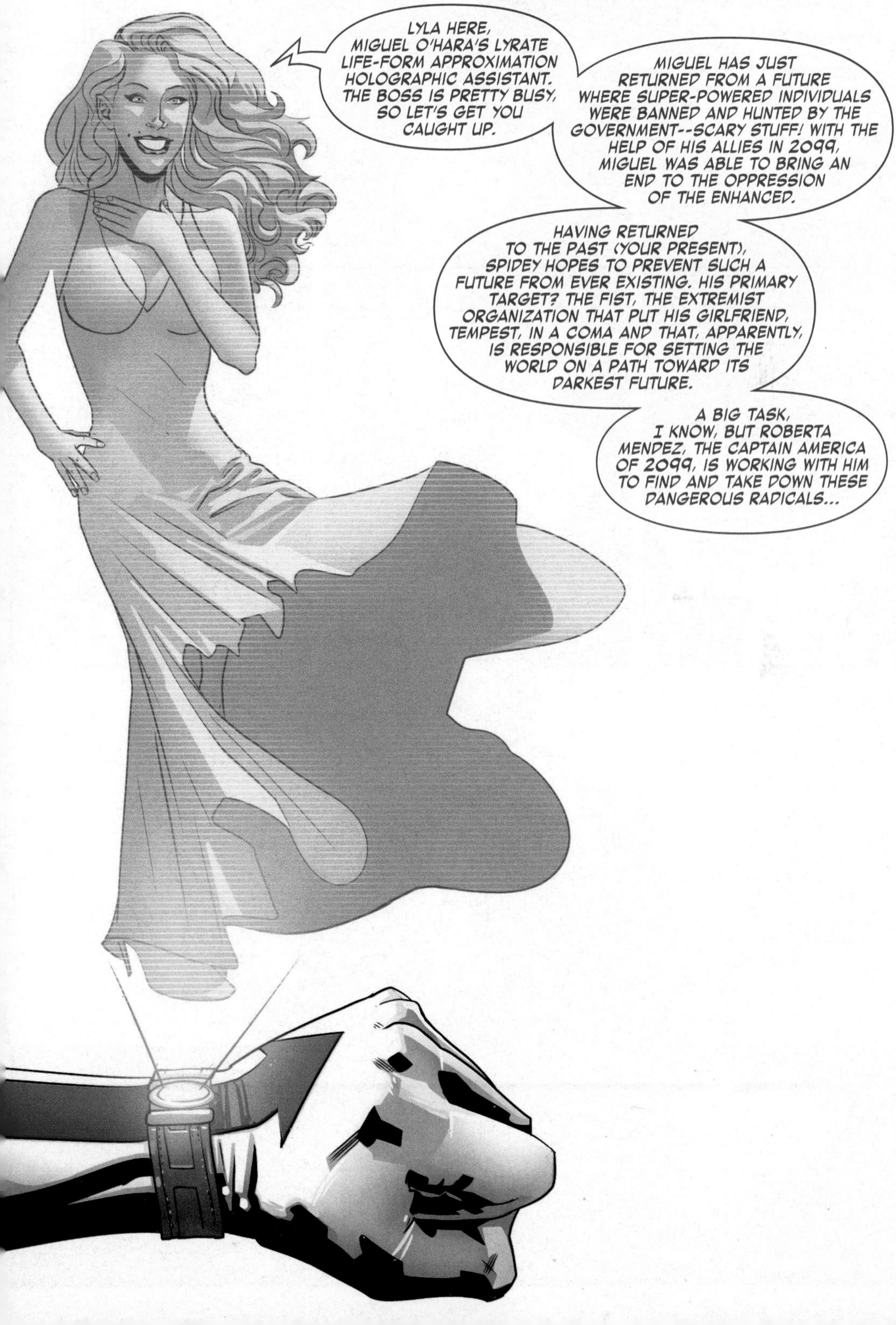
LYLA HERE, MIGUEL O'HARA'S LYRATE LIFE-FORM APPROXIMATION HOLOGRAPHIC ASSISTANT. THE BOSS IS PRETTY BUSY, SO LET'S GET YOU CAUGHT UP.
MIGUEL HAS JUST RETURNED FROM A FUTURE WHERE SUPER-POWERED INDIVIDUALS WERE BANNED AND HUNTED BY THE GOVERNMENT--SCARY STUFF! WITH THE HELP OF HIS ALLIES IN 2099, MIGUEL WAS ABLE TO BRING AN END TO THE OPPRESSION OF THE ENHANCED.
HAVING RETURNED TO THE PAST (YOUR PRESENT), SPIDEY HOPES TO PREVENT SUCH A FUTURE FROM EVER EXISTING. HIS PRIMARY TARGET? THE FIST, THE EXTREMIST ORGANIZATION THAT PUT HIS GIRLFRIEND, TEMPEST, IN A COMA AND THAT, APPARENTLY, IS RESPONSIBLE FOR SETTING THE WORLD ON A PATH TOWARD ITS DARKEST FUTURE.
A BIG TASK, I KNOW, BUT ROBERTA MENDEZ, THE CAPTAIN AMERICA OF 2099, IS WORKING WITH HIM TO FIND AND TAKE DOWN THESE DANGEROUS RADICALS...

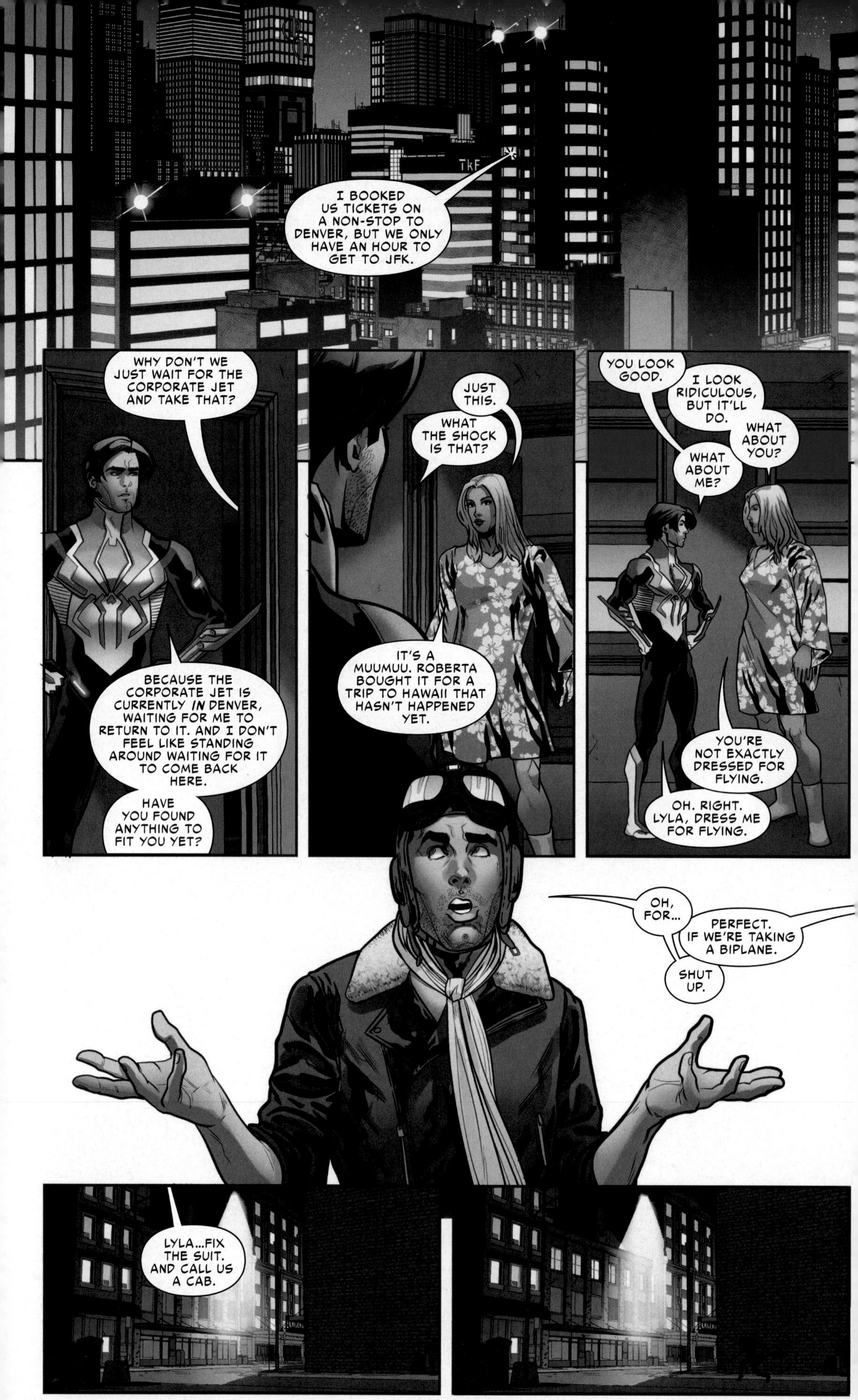

I BOOKED US TICKETS ON A NON-STOP TO DENVER, BUT WE ONLY HAVE AN HOUR TO GET TO JFK.
WHY DON'T WE JUST WAIT FOR THE CORPORATE JET AND TAKE THAT?
BECAUSE THE CORPORATE JET IS CURRENTLY *IN* DENVER, WAITING FOR ME TO RETURN TO IT. AND I DON'T FEEL LIKE STANDING AROUND WAITING FOR IT TO COME BACK HERE.
HAVE YOU FOUND ANYTHING TO FIT YOU YET?
JUST THIS.
WHAT THE SHOCK IS THAT?
IT'S A MUUMUU. ROBERTA BOUGHT IT FOR A TRIP TO HAWAII THAT HASN'T HAPPENED YET.
YOU LOOK GOOD.
I LOOK RIDICULOUS, BUT IT'LL DO.
WHAT ABOUT YOU?
WHAT ABOUT ME?
YOU'RE NOT EXACTLY DRESSED FOR FLYING.
OH. RIGHT. LYLA, DRESS ME FOR FLYING.
OH, FOR...
PERFECT. IF WE'RE TAKING A BIPLANE.
SHUT UP.
LYLA...FIX THE SUIT. AND CALL US A CAB.

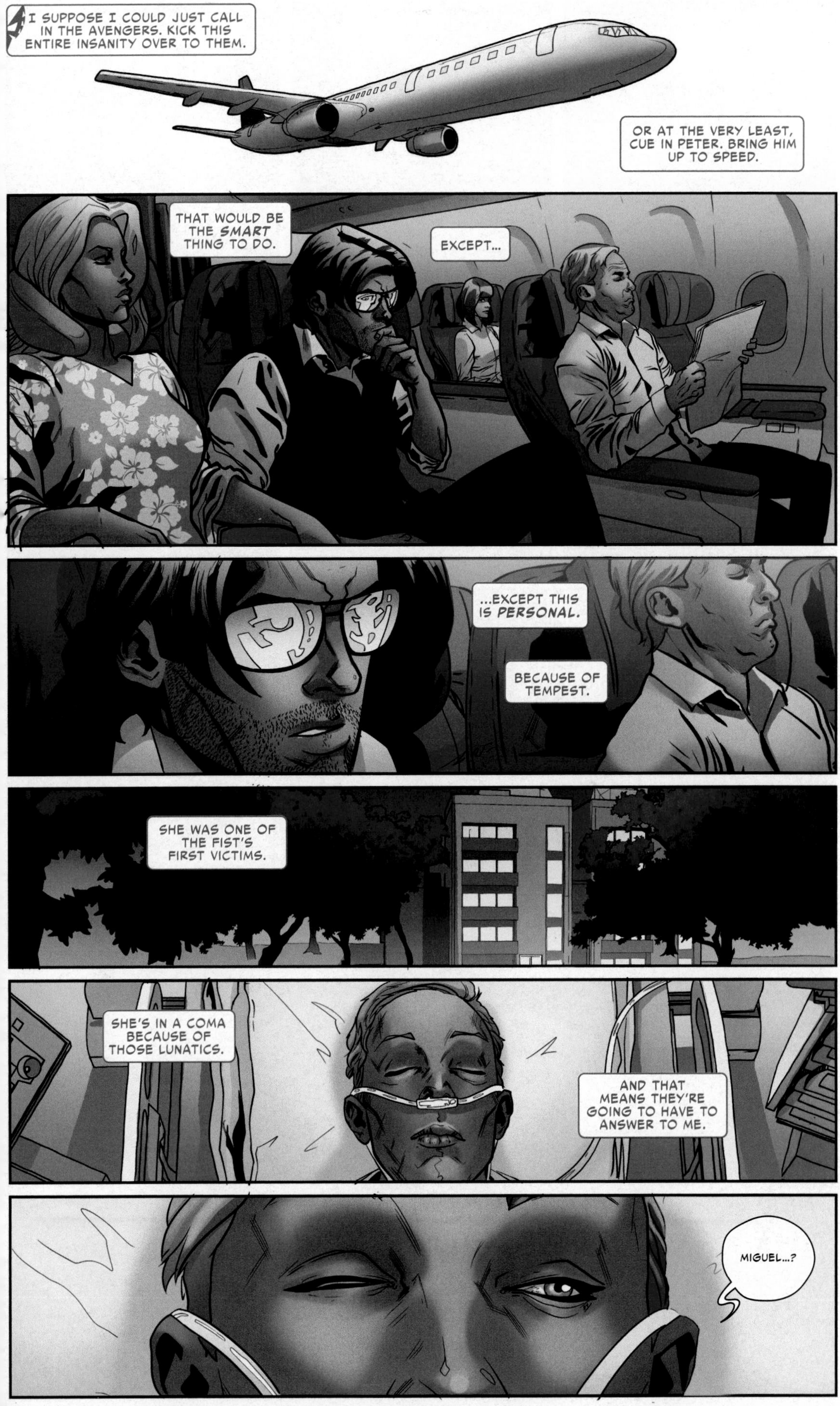
I SUPPOSE I COULD JUST CALL IN THE AVENGERS. KICK THIS ENTIRE INSANITY OVER TO THEM.
OR AT THE VERY LEAST, CUE IN PETER. BRING HIM UP TO SPEED.
THAT WOULD BE THE *SMART* THING TO DO.
EXCEPT...
...EXCEPT THIS IS *PERSONAL*.
BECAUSE OF TEMPEST.
SHE WAS ONE OF THE FIST'S FIRST VICTIMS.
SHE'S IN A COMA BECAUSE OF THOSE LUNATICS.
AND THAT MEANS THEY'RE GOING TO HAVE TO ANSWER TO ME.
MIGUEL...?

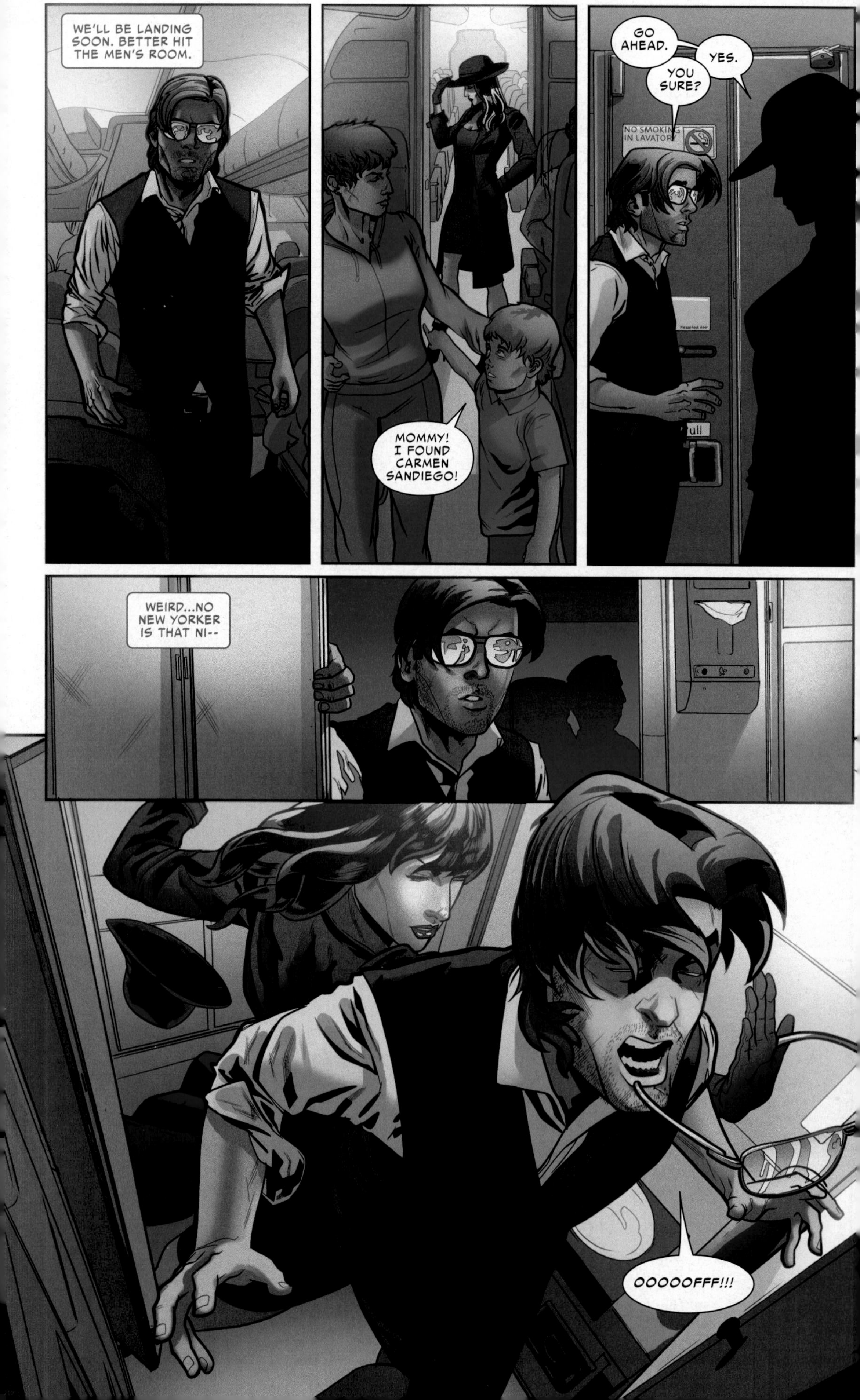
WE'LL BE LANDING SOON. BETTER HIT THE MEN'S ROOM.
MOMMY! I FOUND CARMEN SANDIEGO!
GO AHEAD.
YES.
YOU SURE?
NO SMOKING IN LAVATORY
WEIRD...NO NEW YORKER IS THAT NI--
OOOOOFFF!!!

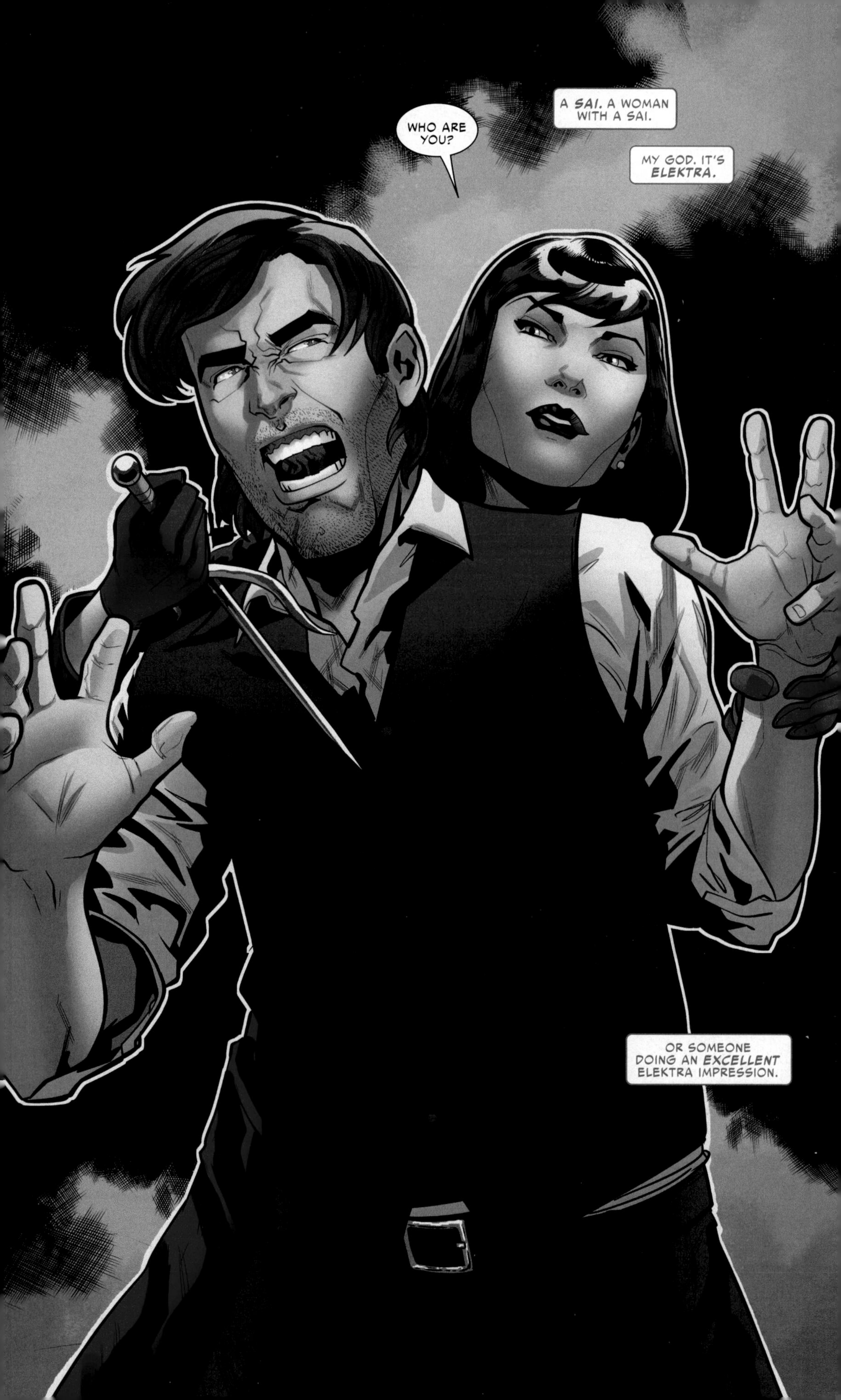
WHO ARE YOU?
A SAI. A WOMAN WITH A SAI.
MY GOD. IT'S ELEKTRA.
OR SOMEONE DOING AN EXCELLENT ELEKTRA IMPRESSION.

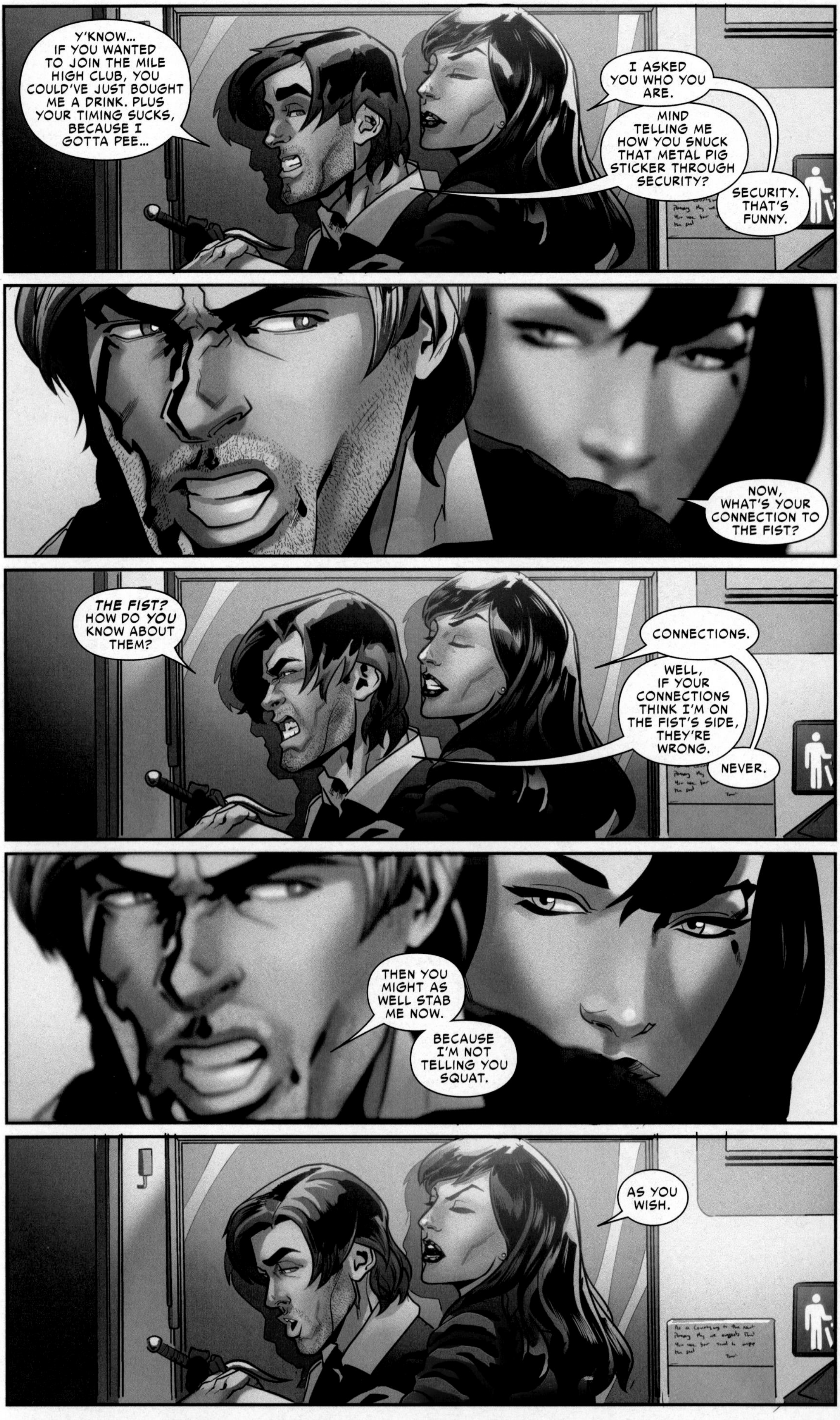
Y'KNOW... IF YOU WANTED TO JOIN THE MILE HIGH CLUB, YOU COULD'VE JUST BOUGHT ME A DRINK. PLUS YOUR TIMING SUCKS, BECAUSE I GOTTA PEE...
I ASKED YOU WHO YOU ARE.
MIND TELLING ME HOW YOU SNUCK THAT METAL PIG STICKER THROUGH SECURITY?
SECURITY. THAT'S FUNNY.
NOW, WHAT'S YOUR CONNECTION TO THE FIST?
THE FIST? HOW DO *YOU* KNOW ABOUT THEM?
CONNECTIONS.
WELL, IF YOUR CONNECTIONS THINK I'M ON THE FIST'S SIDE, THEY'RE WRONG.
NEVER.
THEN YOU MIGHT AS WELL STAB ME NOW.
BECAUSE I'M NOT TELLING YOU SQUAT.
AS YOU WISH.

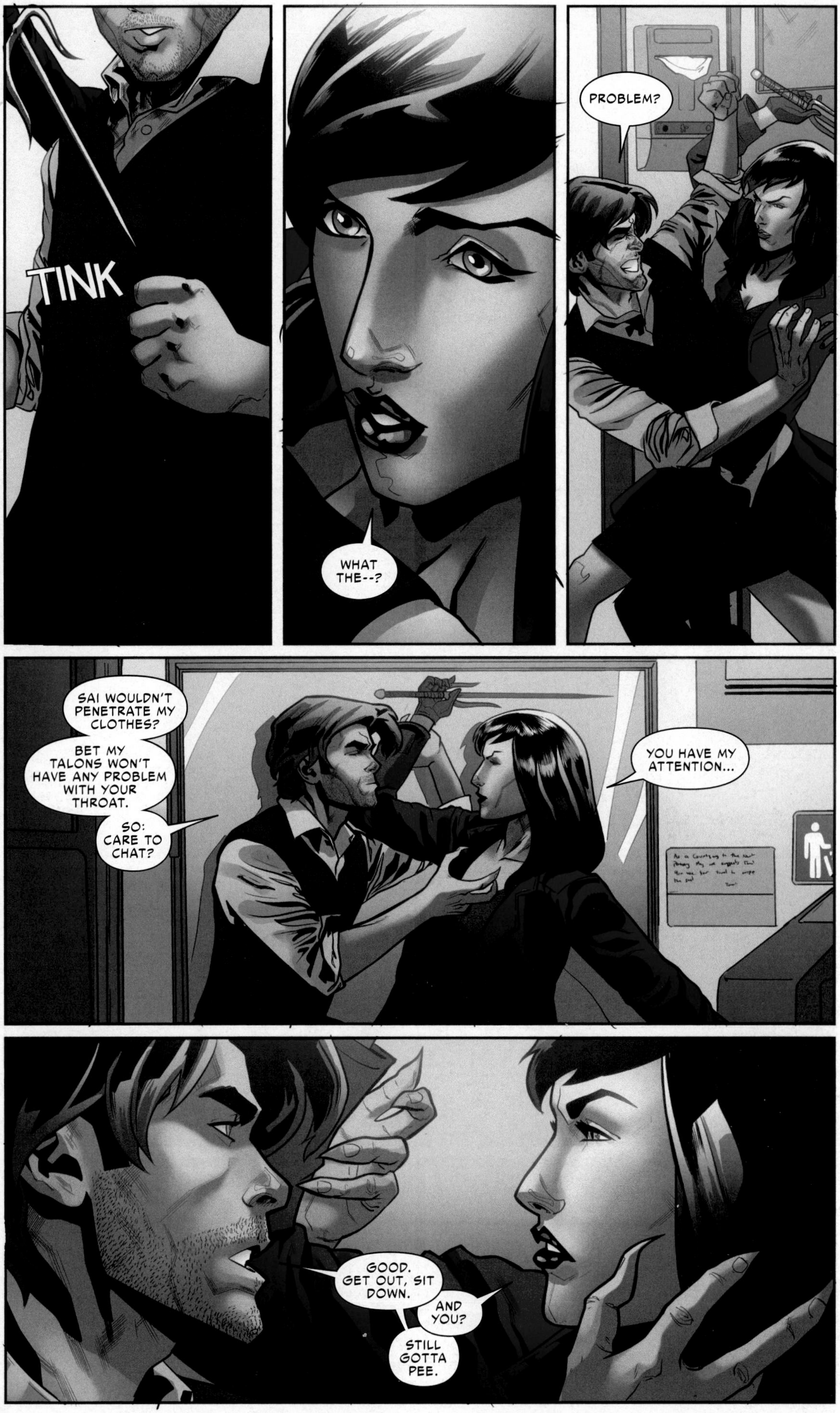
TINK
WHAT THE--?
PROBLEM?
SAI WOULDN'T PENETRATE MY CLOTHES?
BET MY TALONS WON'T HAVE ANY PROBLEM WITH YOUR THROAT.
SO: CARE TO CHAT?
YOU HAVE MY ATTENTION...
GOOD. GET OUT, SIT DOWN.
AND YOU?
STILL GOTTA PEE.

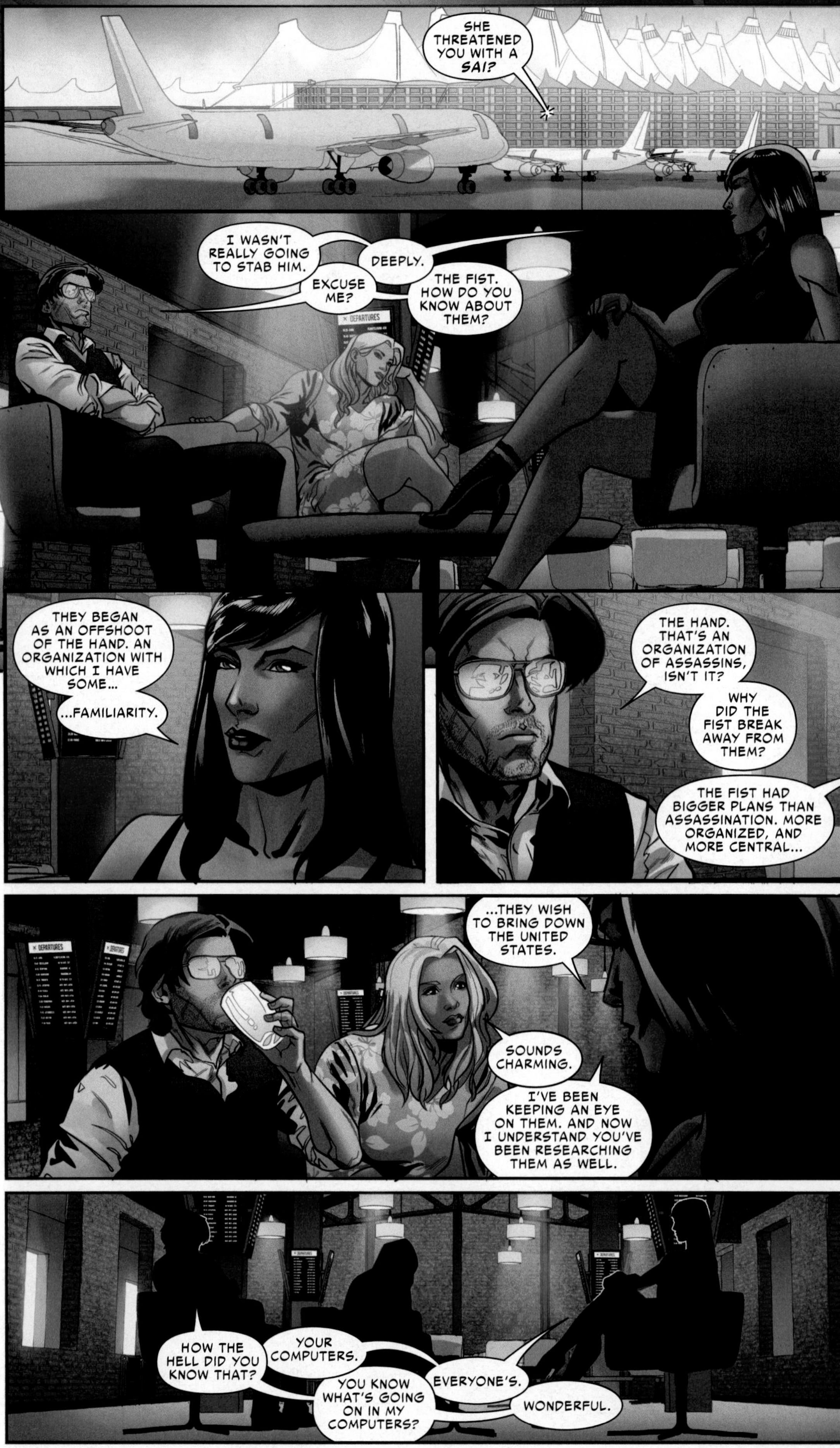
SHE THREATENED YOU WITH A SAI?
I WASN'T REALLY GOING TO STAB HIM.
DEEPLY.
EXCUSE ME?
THE FIST. HOW DO YOU KNOW ABOUT THEM?
THEY BEGAN AS AN OFFSHOOT OF THE HAND. AN ORGANIZATION WITH WHICH I HAVE SOME...
...FAMILIARITY.
THE HAND. THAT'S AN ORGANIZATION OF ASSASSINS, ISN'T IT?
WHY DID THE FIST BREAK AWAY FROM THEM?
THE FIST HAD BIGGER PLANS THAN ASSASSINATION. MORE ORGANIZED, AND MORE CENTRAL...
...THEY WISH TO BRING DOWN THE UNITED STATES.
SOUNDS CHARMING.
I'VE BEEN KEEPING AN EYE ON THEM. AND NOW I UNDERSTAND YOU'VE BEEN RESEARCHING THEM AS WELL.
HOW THE HELL DID YOU KNOW THAT?
YOUR COMPUTERS.
EVERYONE'S.
YOU KNOW WHAT'S GOING ON IN MY COMPUTERS?
WONDERFUL.

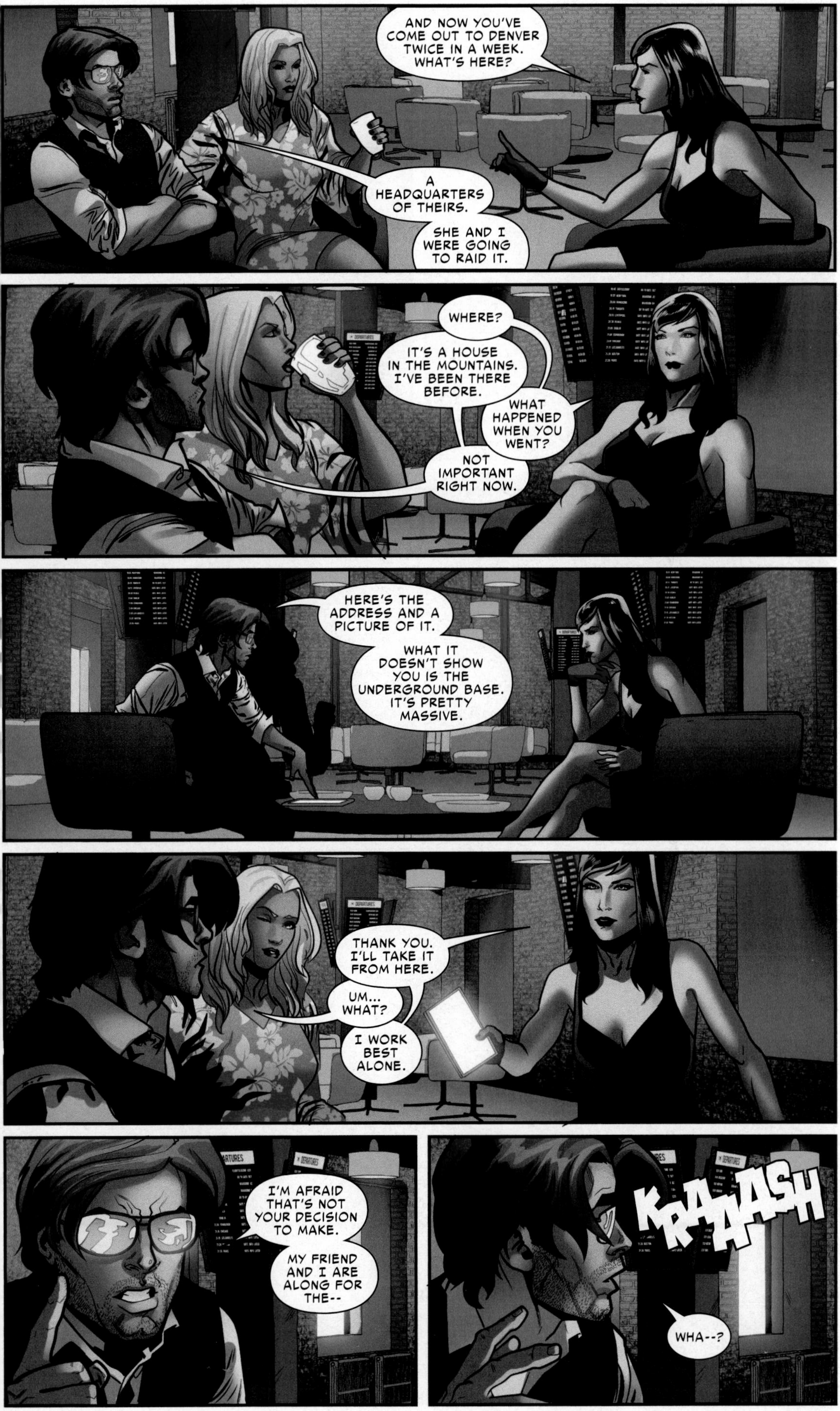

AND NOW YOU'VE COME OUT TO DENVER TWICE IN A WEEK. WHAT'S HERE?
A HEADQUARTERS OF THEIRS.
SHE AND I WERE GOING TO RAID IT.
WHERE?
IT'S A HOUSE IN THE MOUNTAINS. I'VE BEEN THERE BEFORE.
WHAT HAPPENED WHEN YOU WENT?
NOT IMPORTANT RIGHT NOW.
HERE'S THE ADDRESS AND A PICTURE OF IT.
WHAT IT DOESN'T SHOW YOU IS THE UNDERGROUND BASE. IT'S PRETTY MASSIVE.
THANK YOU. I'LL TAKE IT FROM HERE.
UM... WHAT?
I WORK BEST ALONE.
I'M AFRAID THAT'S NOT YOUR DECISION TO MAKE.
MY FRIEND AND I ARE ALONG FOR THE--
KRAAASH
WHA--?

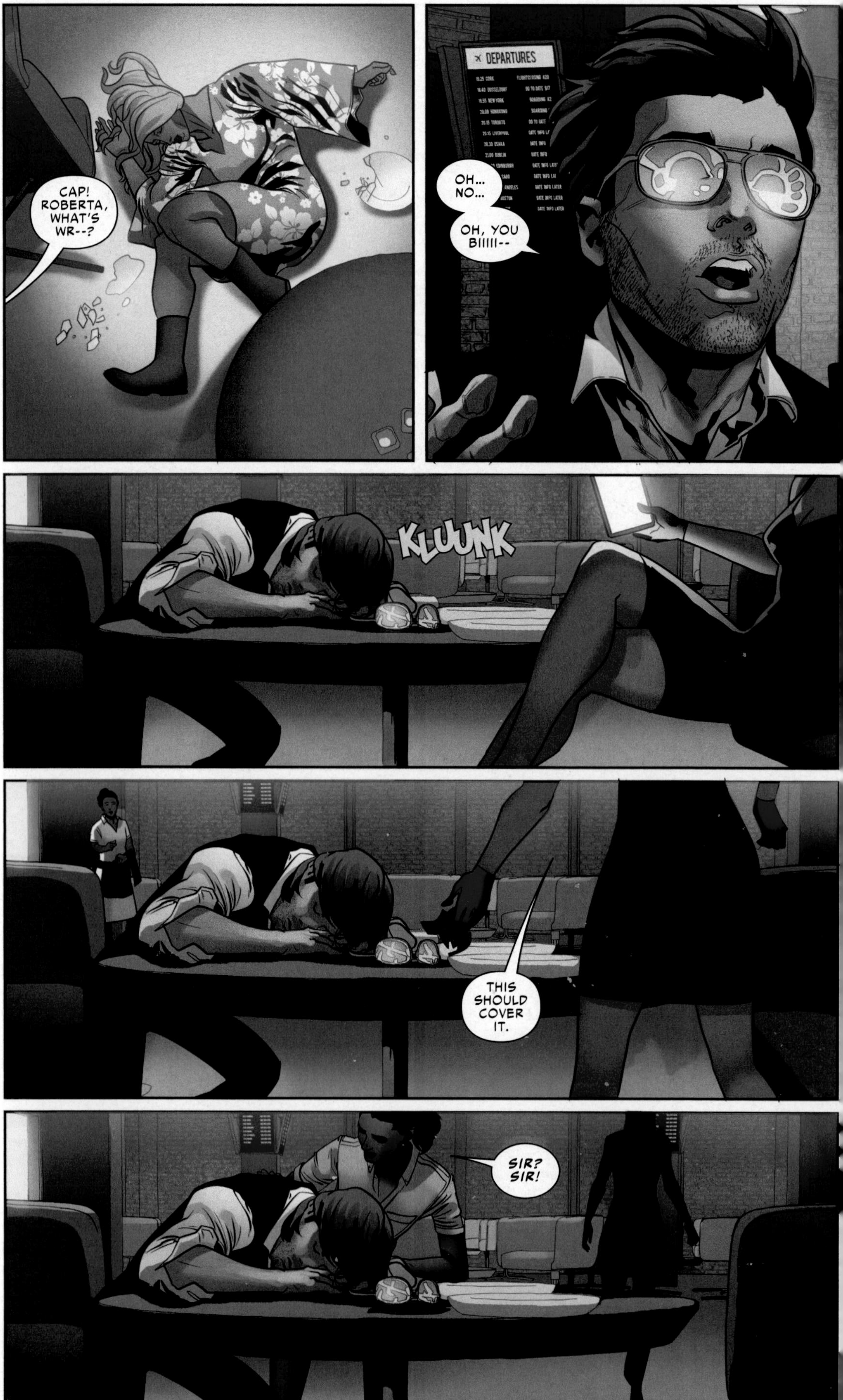

CAP! ROBERTA, WHAT'S WR--?
DEPARTURES
OH... NO...
OH, YOU BIIIII--
KLUUNK
THIS SHOULD COVER IT.
SIR? SIR!

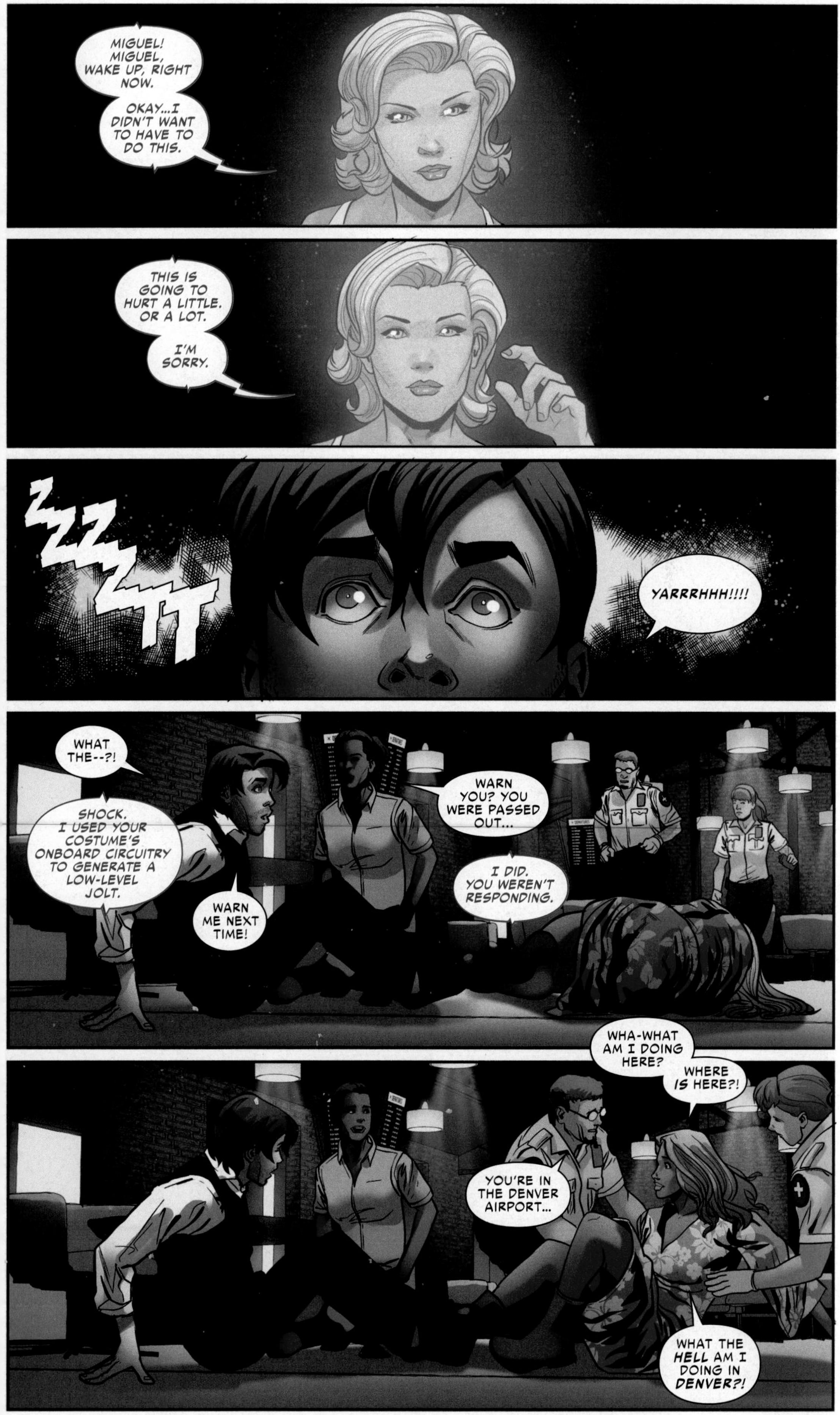
MIGUEL! MIGUEL, WAKE UP, RIGHT NOW.
OKAY...I DIDN'T WANT TO HAVE TO DO THIS.
THIS IS GOING TO HURT A LITTLE. OR A LOT.
I'M SORRY.
ZZZZTT
YARRRHHH!!!!
WHAT THE--?!
SHOCK. I USED YOUR COSTUME'S ONBOARD CIRCUITRY TO GENERATE A LOW-LEVEL JOLT.
WARN ME NEXT TIME!
WARN YOU? YOU WERE PASSED OUT...
I DID. YOU WEREN'T RESPONDING.
WHA-WHAT AM I DOING HERE?
WHERE *IS* HERE?!
YOU'RE IN THE DENVER AIRPORT...
WHAT THE ***HELL*** AM I DOING IN ***DENVER***?!

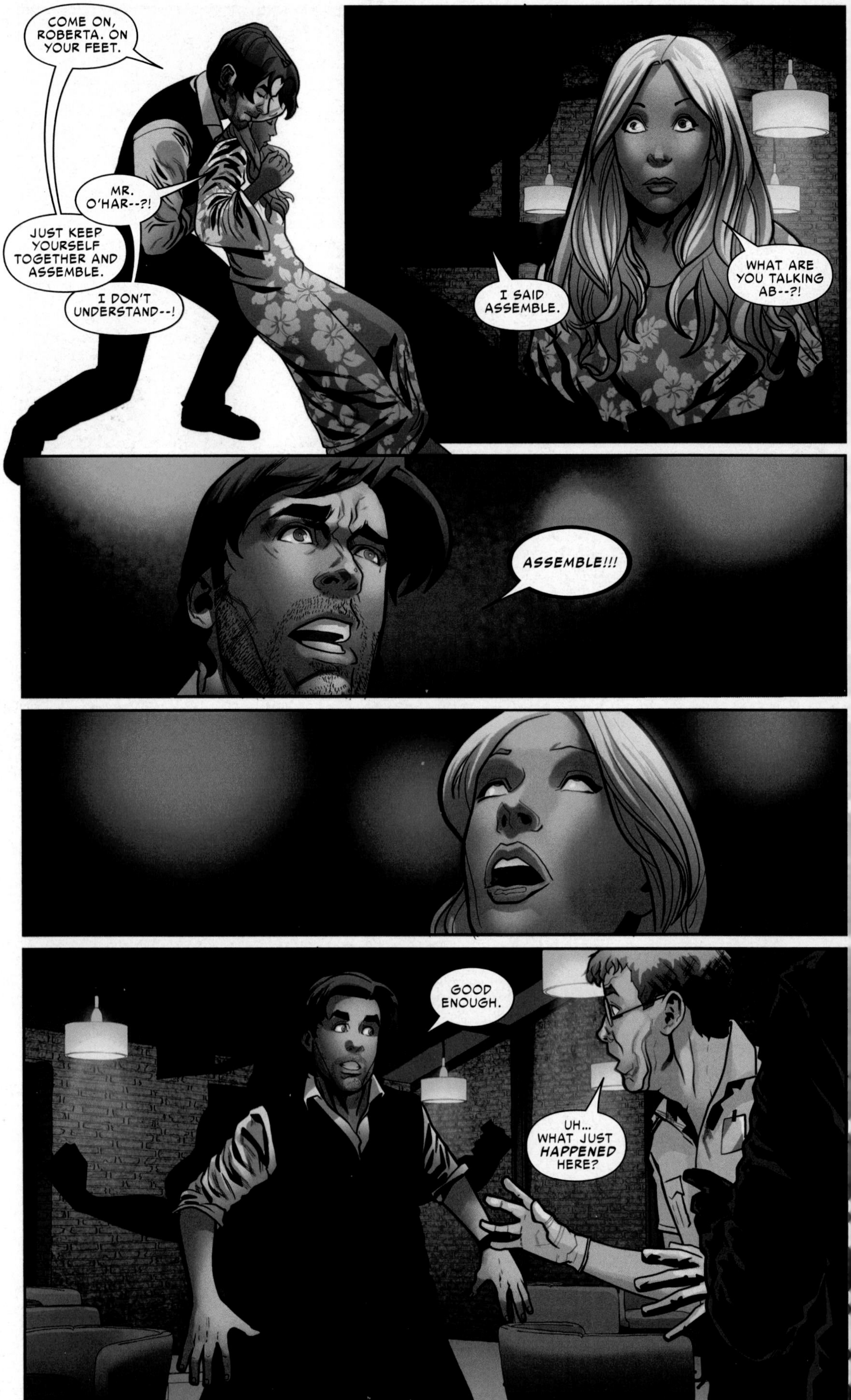
COME ON, ROBERTA. ON YOUR FEET.
MR. O'HAR--?!
JUST KEEP YOURSELF TOGETHER AND ASSEMBLE.
I DON'T UNDERSTAND--!
I SAID ASSEMBLE.
WHAT ARE YOU TALKING AB--?!
ASSEMBLE!!!
GOOD ENOUGH.
UH... WHAT JUST HAPPENED HERE?

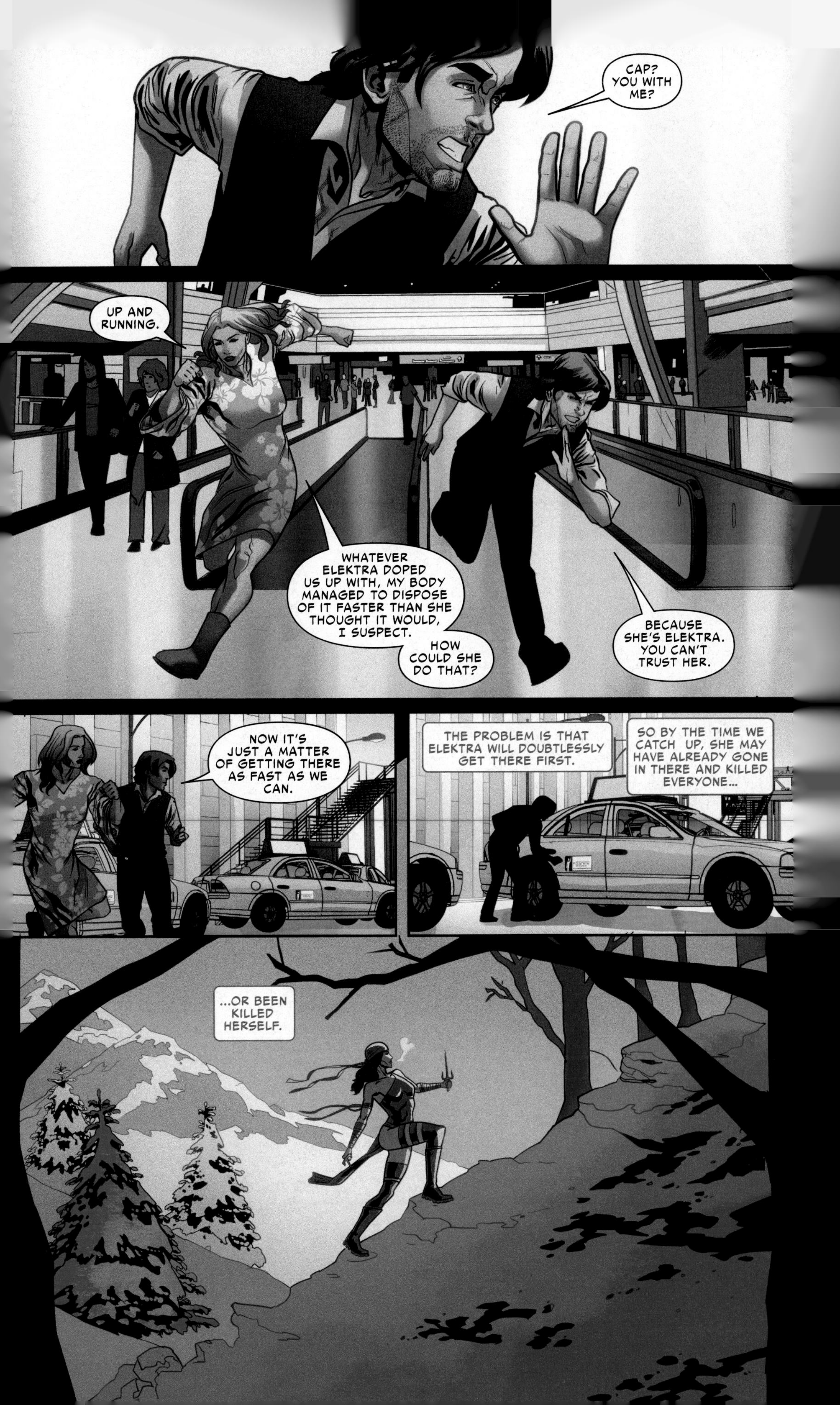
CAP? YOU WITH ME?
UP AND RUNNING.
WHATEVER ELEKTRA DOPED US UP WITH, MY BODY MANAGED TO DISPOSE OF IT FASTER THAN SHE THOUGHT IT WOULD, I SUSPECT.
HOW COULD SHE DO THAT?
BECAUSE SHE'S ELEKTRA. YOU CAN'T TRUST HER.
NOW IT'S JUST A MATTER OF GETTING THERE AS FAST AS WE CAN.
THE PROBLEM IS THAT ELEKTRA WILL DOUBTLESSLY GET THERE FIRST.
SO BY THE TIME WE CATCH UP, SHE MAY HAVE ALREADY GONE IN THERE AND KILLED EVERYONE...
...OR BEEN KILLED HERSELF.

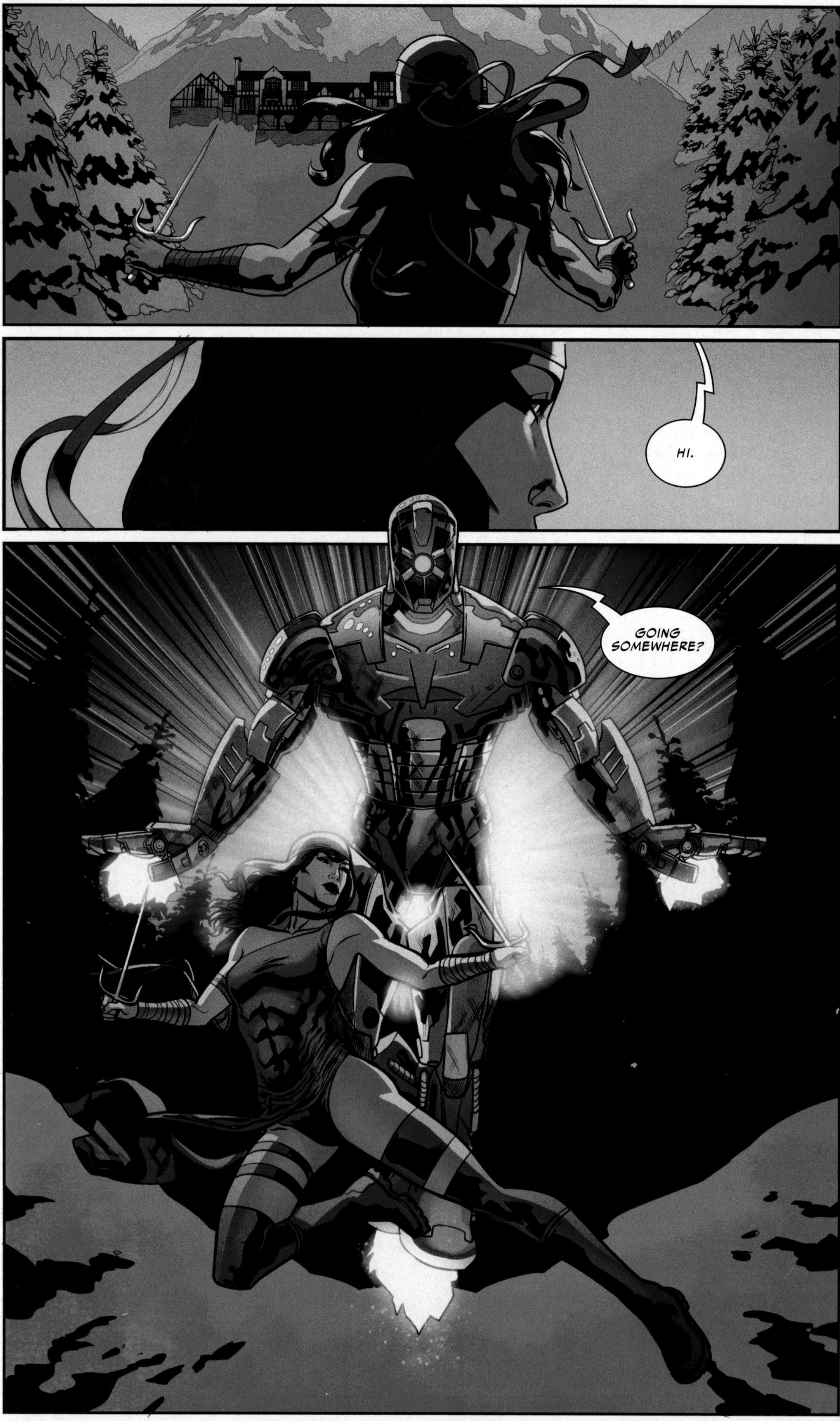
HI.
GOING SOMEWHERE?

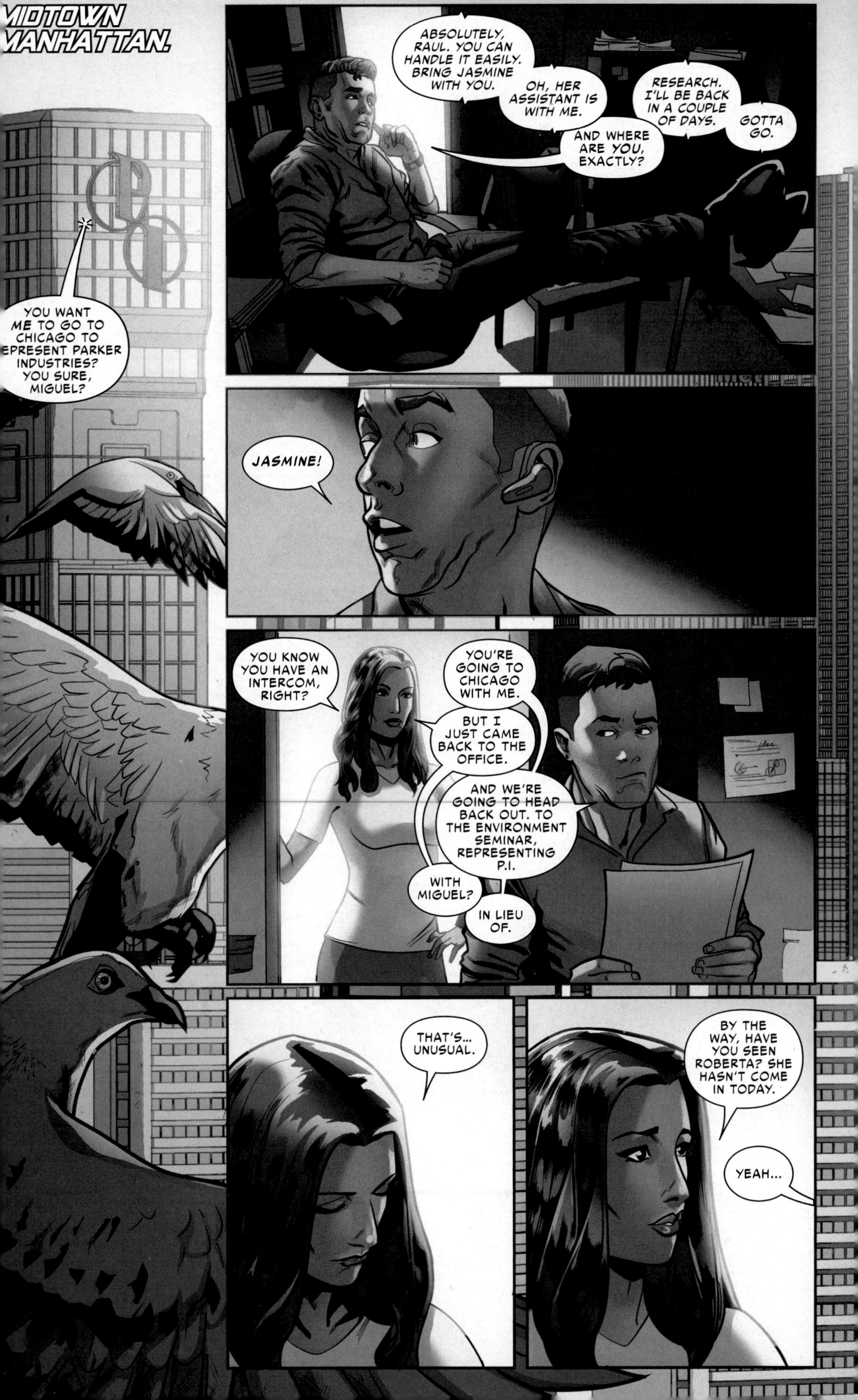
MIDTOWN MANHATTAN.
YOU WANT ME TO GO TO CHICAGO TO REPRESENT PARKER INDUSTRIES? YOU SURE, MIGUEL?
ABSOLUTELY, RAUL. YOU CAN HANDLE IT EASILY. BRING JASMINE WITH YOU.
OH, HER ASSISTANT IS WITH ME.
AND WHERE ARE YOU, EXACTLY?
RESEARCH. I'LL BE BACK IN A COUPLE OF DAYS.
GOTTA GO.
JASMINE!
YOU KNOW YOU HAVE AN INTERCOM, RIGHT?
YOU'RE GOING TO CHICAGO WITH ME.
BUT I JUST CAME BACK TO THE OFFICE.
AND WE'RE GOING TO HEAD BACK OUT. TO THE ENVIRONMENT SEMINAR, REPRESENTING P.I.
WITH MIGUEL?
IN LIEU OF.
THAT'S... UNUSUAL.
BY THE WAY, HAVE YOU SEEN ROBERTA? SHE HASN'T COME IN TODAY.
YEAH...

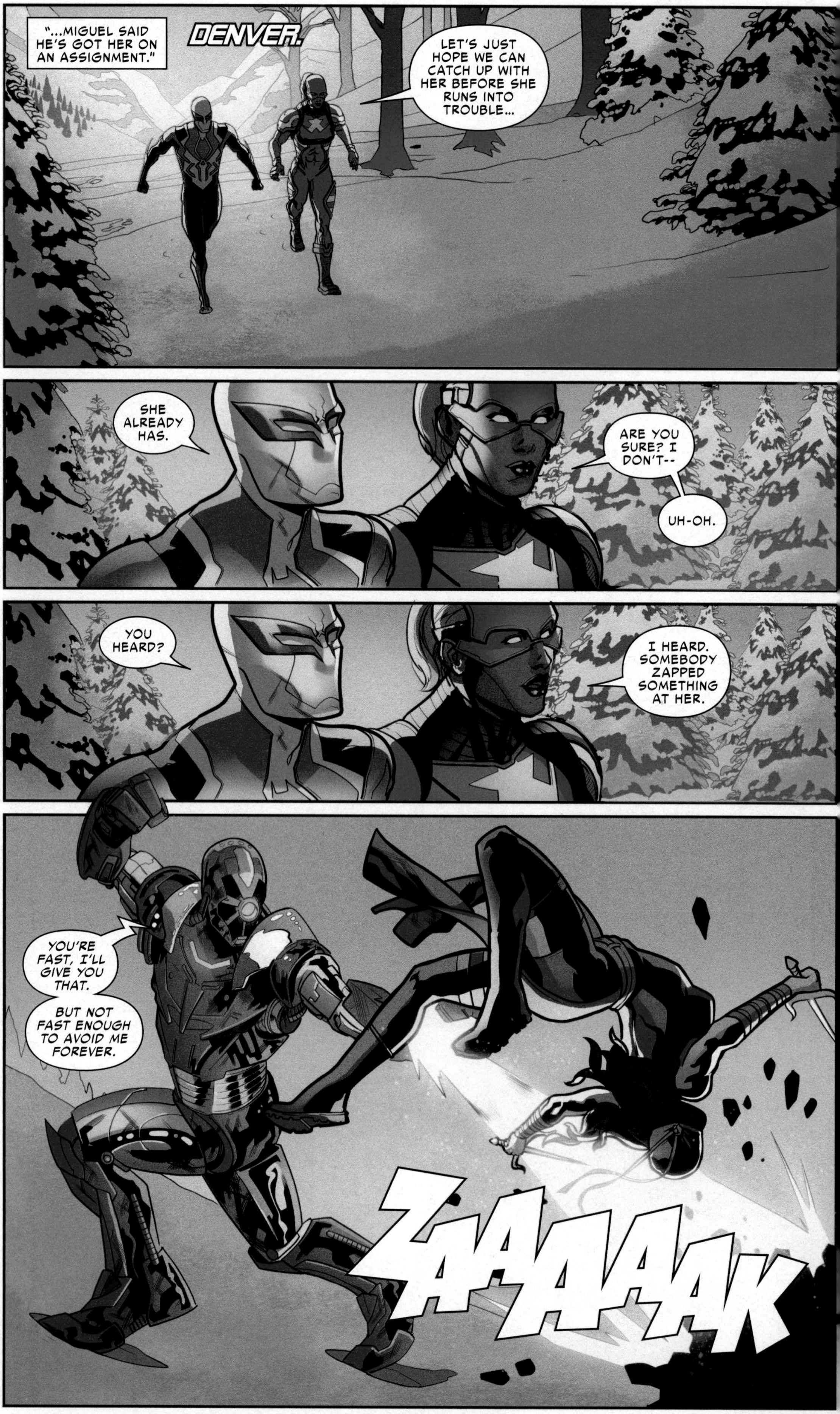

"...MIGUEL SAID HE'S GOT HER ON AN ASSIGNMENT."
DENVER.
LET'S JUST HOPE WE CAN CATCH UP WITH HER BEFORE SHE RUNS INTO TROUBLE...
SHE ALREADY HAS.
ARE YOU SURE? I DON'T--
UH-OH.
YOU HEARD?
I HEARD. SOMEBODY ZAPPED SOMETHING AT HER.
YOU'RE FAST, I'LL GIVE YOU THAT.
BUT NOT FAST ENOUGH TO AVOID ME FOREVER.
ZAAAAAK

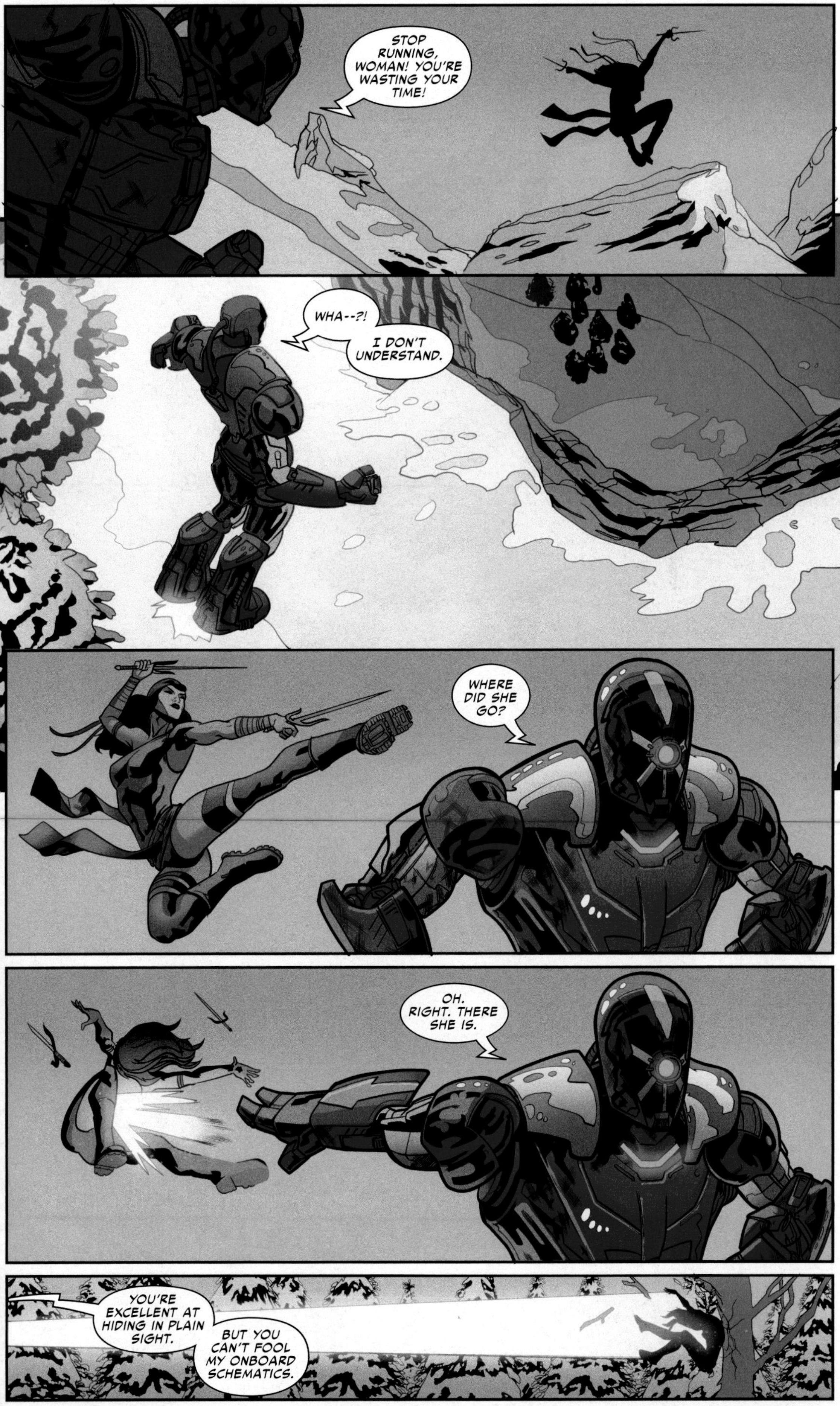
STOP RUNNING, WOMAN! YOU'RE WASTING YOUR TIME!
WHA--?!
I DON'T UNDERSTAND.
WHERE DID SHE GO?
OH. RIGHT. THERE SHE IS.
YOU'RE EXCELLENT AT HIDING IN PLAIN SIGHT.
BUT YOU CAN'T FOOL MY ONBOARD SCHEMATICS.

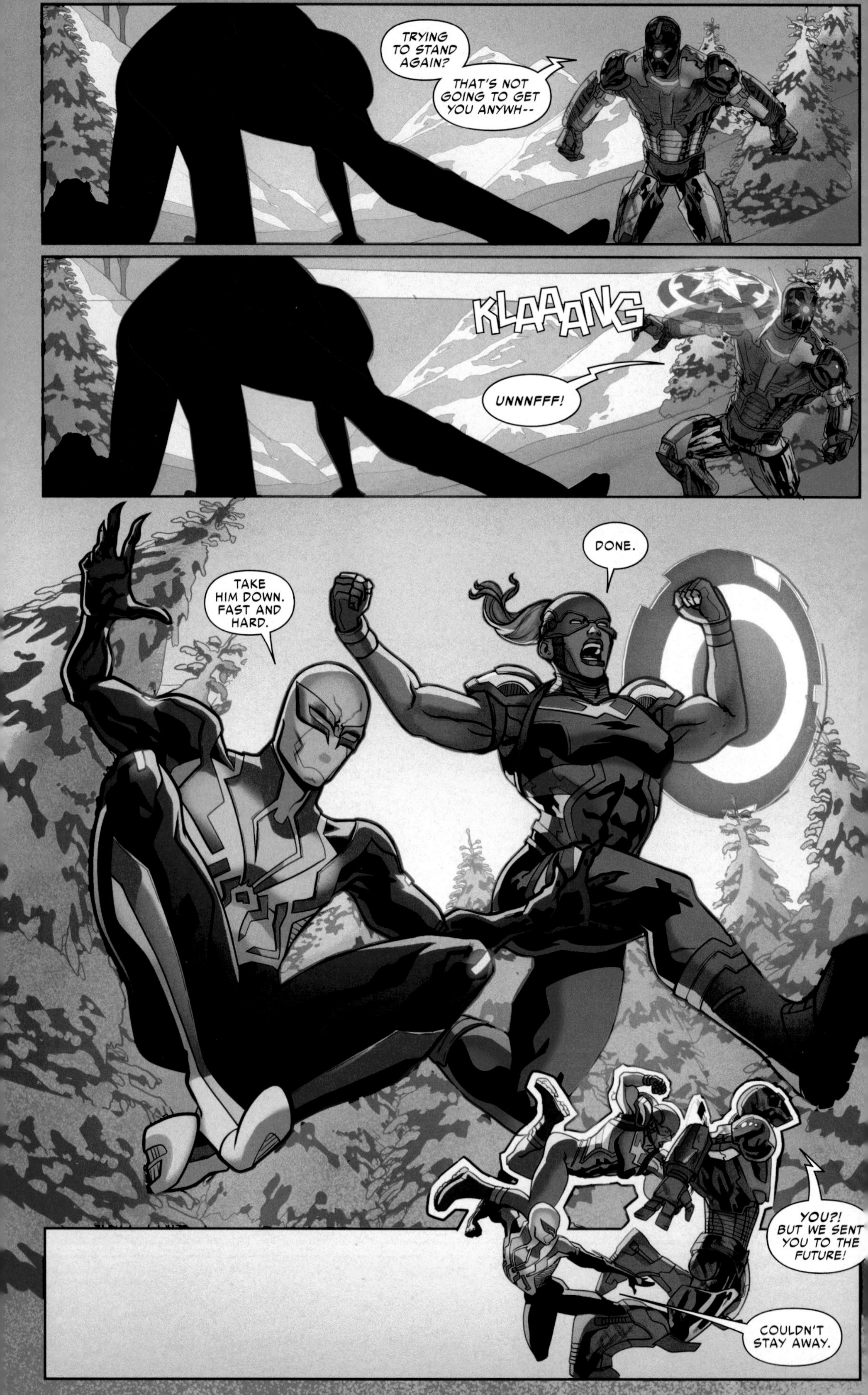

TRYING TO STAND AGAIN?
THAT'S NOT GOING TO GET YOU ANYWH--
KLAAANG
UNNNFFF!
TAKE HIM DOWN. FAST AND HARD.
DONE.
YOU?! BUT WE SENT YOU TO THE FUTURE!
COULDN'T STAY AWAY.

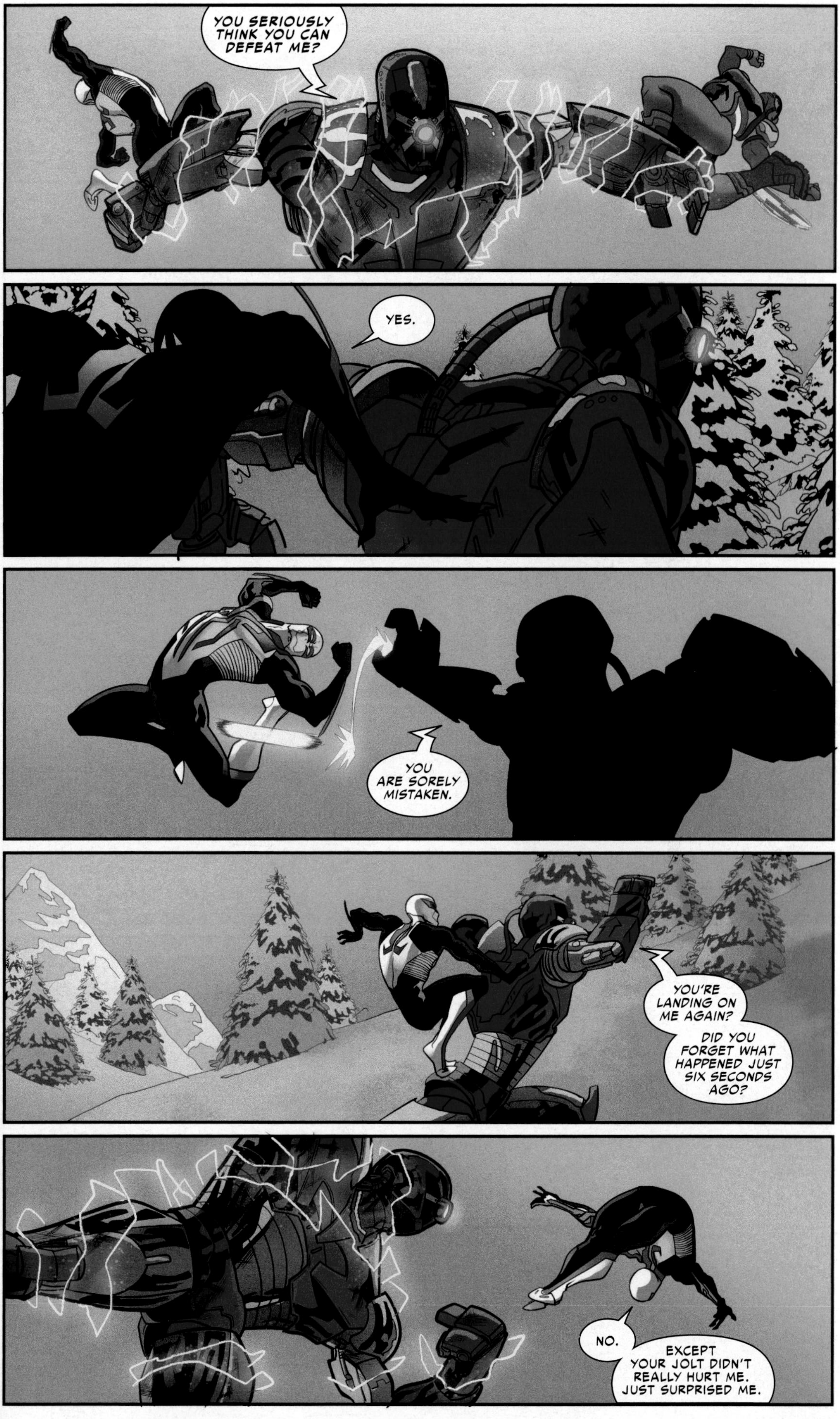
YOU SERIOUSLY THINK YOU CAN DEFEAT ME?
YES.
YOU ARE SORELY MISTAKEN.
YOU'RE LANDING ON ME AGAIN?
DID YOU FORGET WHAT HAPPENED JUST SIX SECONDS AGO?
NO.
EXCEPT YOUR JOLT DIDN'T REALLY HURT ME. JUST SURPRISED ME.

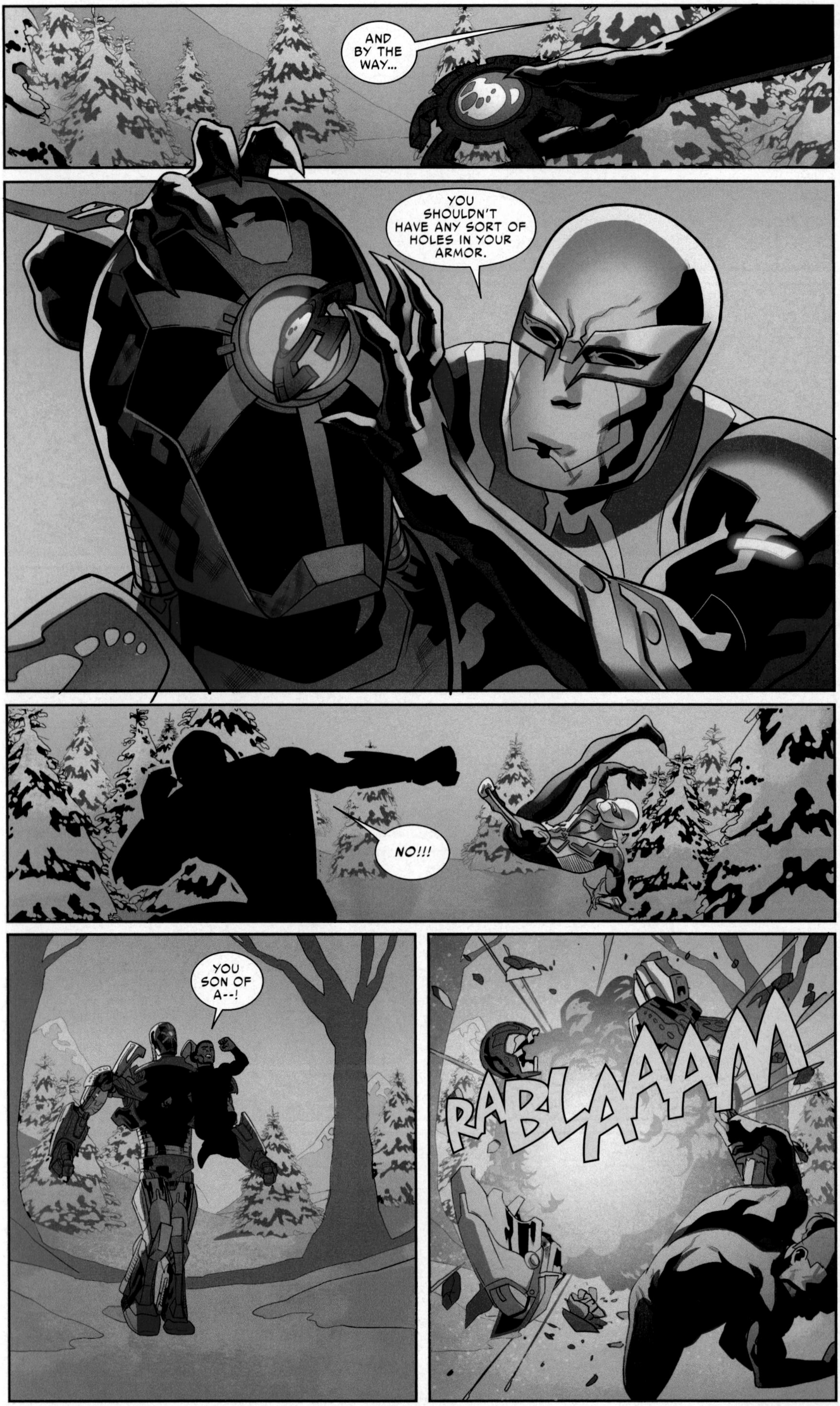
AND BY THE WAY...
YOU SHOULDN'T HAVE ANY SORT OF HOLES IN YOUR ARMOR.
NO!!!
YOU SON OF A--!
RABLAAAM

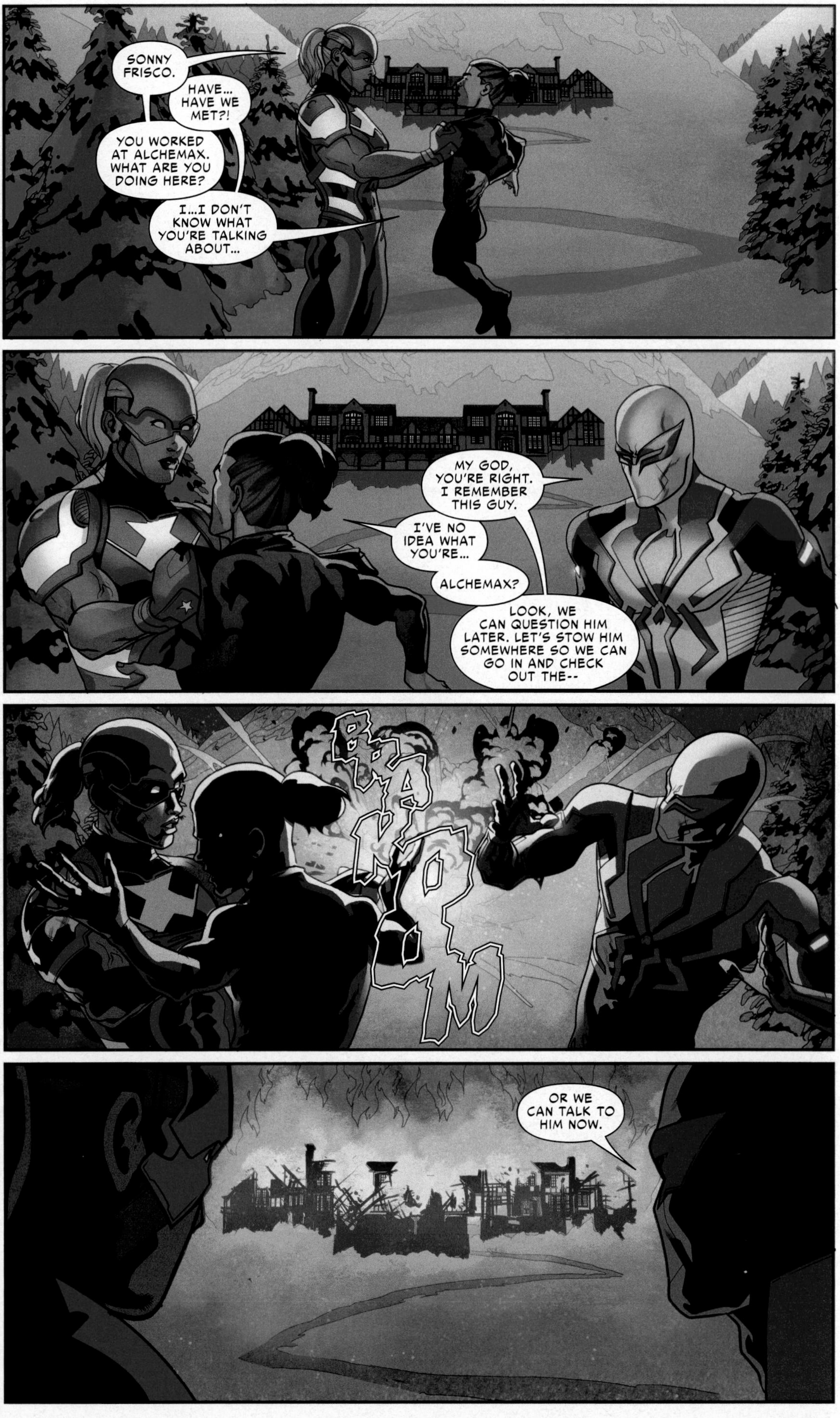
SONNY FRISCO.
HAVE... HAVE WE MET?!
YOU WORKED AT ALCHEMAX. WHAT ARE YOU DOING HERE?
I...I DON'T KNOW WHAT YOU'RE TALKING ABOUT...
MY GOD, YOU'RE RIGHT. I REMEMBER THIS GUY.
I'VE NO IDEA WHAT YOU'RE...
ALCHEMAX?
LOOK, WE CAN QUESTION HIM LATER. LET'S STOW HIM SOMEWHERE SO WE CAN GO IN AND CHECK OUT THE--
BRAKOOM
OR WE CAN TALK TO HIM NOW.

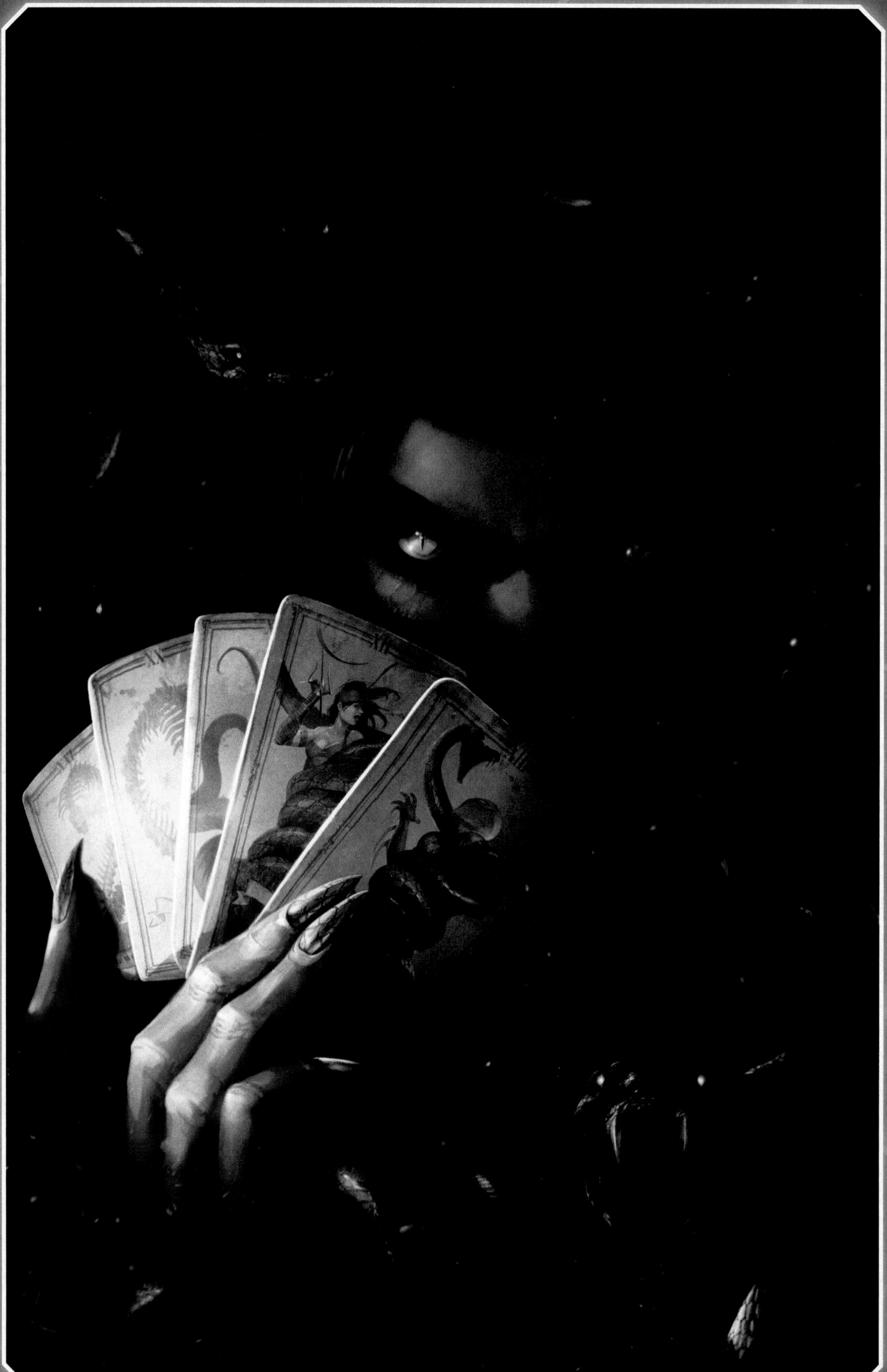

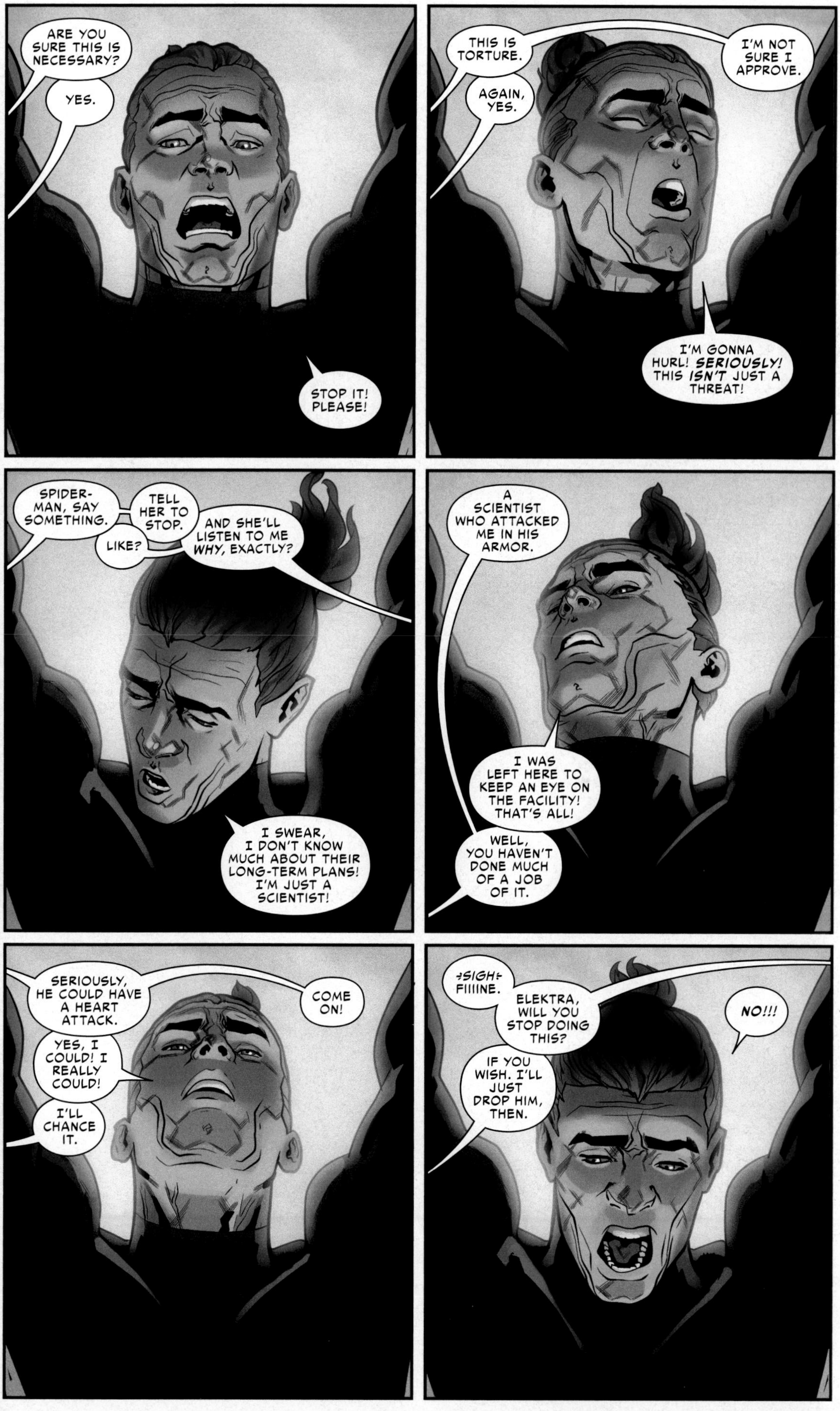
ARE YOU SURE THIS IS NECESSARY?
YES.
STOP IT! PLEASE!
THIS IS TORTURE.
I'M NOT SURE I APPROVE.
AGAIN, YES.
I'M GONNA HURL! SERIOUSLY! THIS ISN'T JUST A THREAT!
SPIDER-MAN, SAY SOMETHING.
LIKE?
TELL HER TO STOP.
AND SHE'LL LISTEN TO ME WHY, EXACTLY?
I SWEAR, I DON'T KNOW MUCH ABOUT THEIR LONG-TERM PLANS! I'M JUST A SCIENTIST!
A SCIENTIST WHO ATTACKED ME IN HIS ARMOR.
I WAS LEFT HERE TO KEEP AN EYE ON THE FACILITY! THAT'S ALL!
WELL, YOU HAVEN'T DONE MUCH OF A JOB OF IT.
SERIOUSLY, HE COULD HAVE A HEART ATTACK.
COME ON!
YES, I COULD! I REALLY COULD!
I'LL CHANCE IT.
SIGH FIIIINE.
ELEKTRA, WILL YOU STOP DOING THIS?
NO!!!
IF YOU WISH. I'LL JUST DROP HIM, THEN.

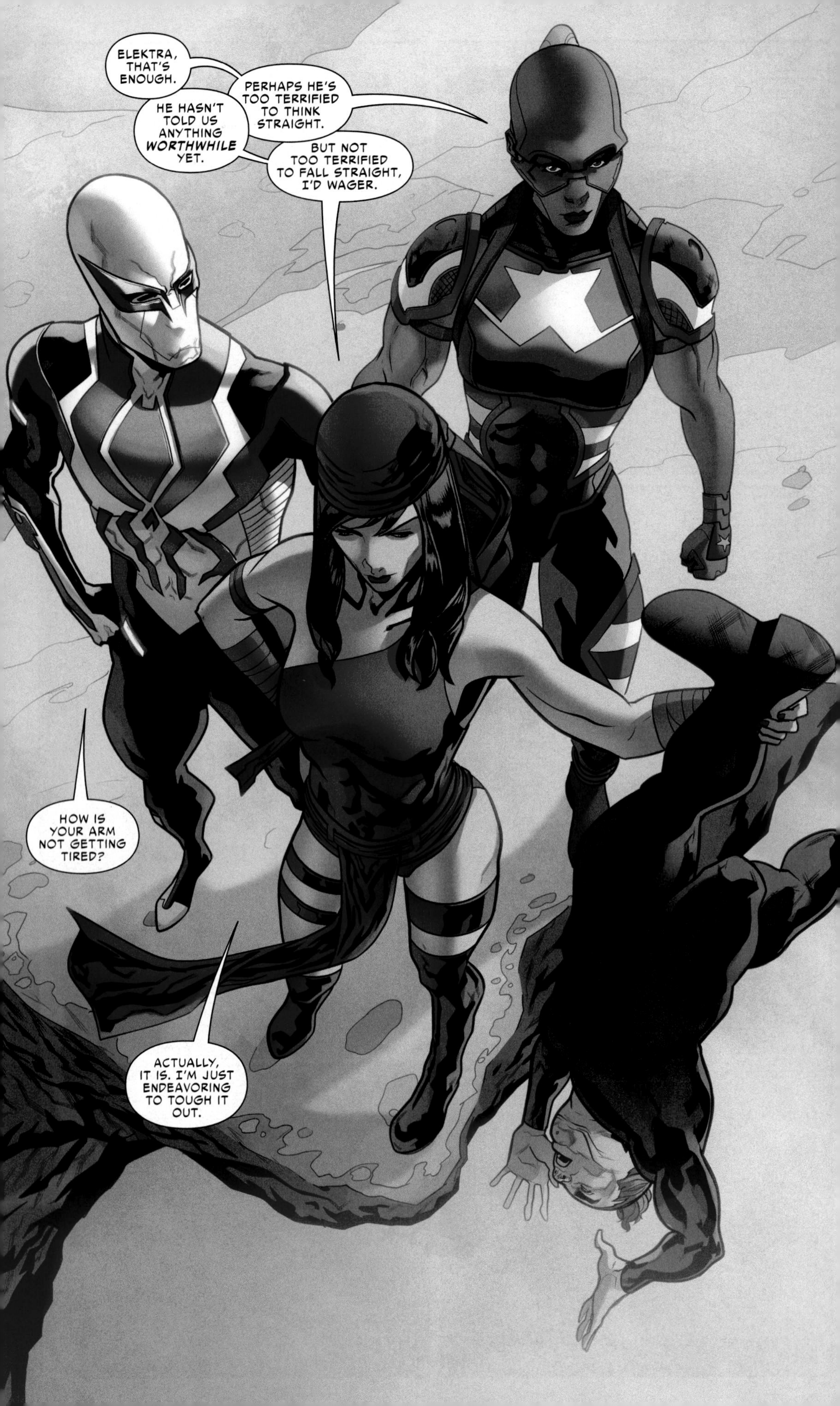
ELEKTRA, THAT'S ENOUGH.
HE HASN'T TOLD US ANYTHING *WORTHWHILE* YET.
PERHAPS HE'S TOO TERRIFIED TO THINK STRAIGHT.
BUT NOT TOO TERRIFIED TO FALL STRAIGHT, I'D WAGER.
HOW IS YOUR ARM NOT GETTING TIRED?
ACTUALLY, IT IS. I'M JUST ENDEAVORING TO TOUGH IT OUT.

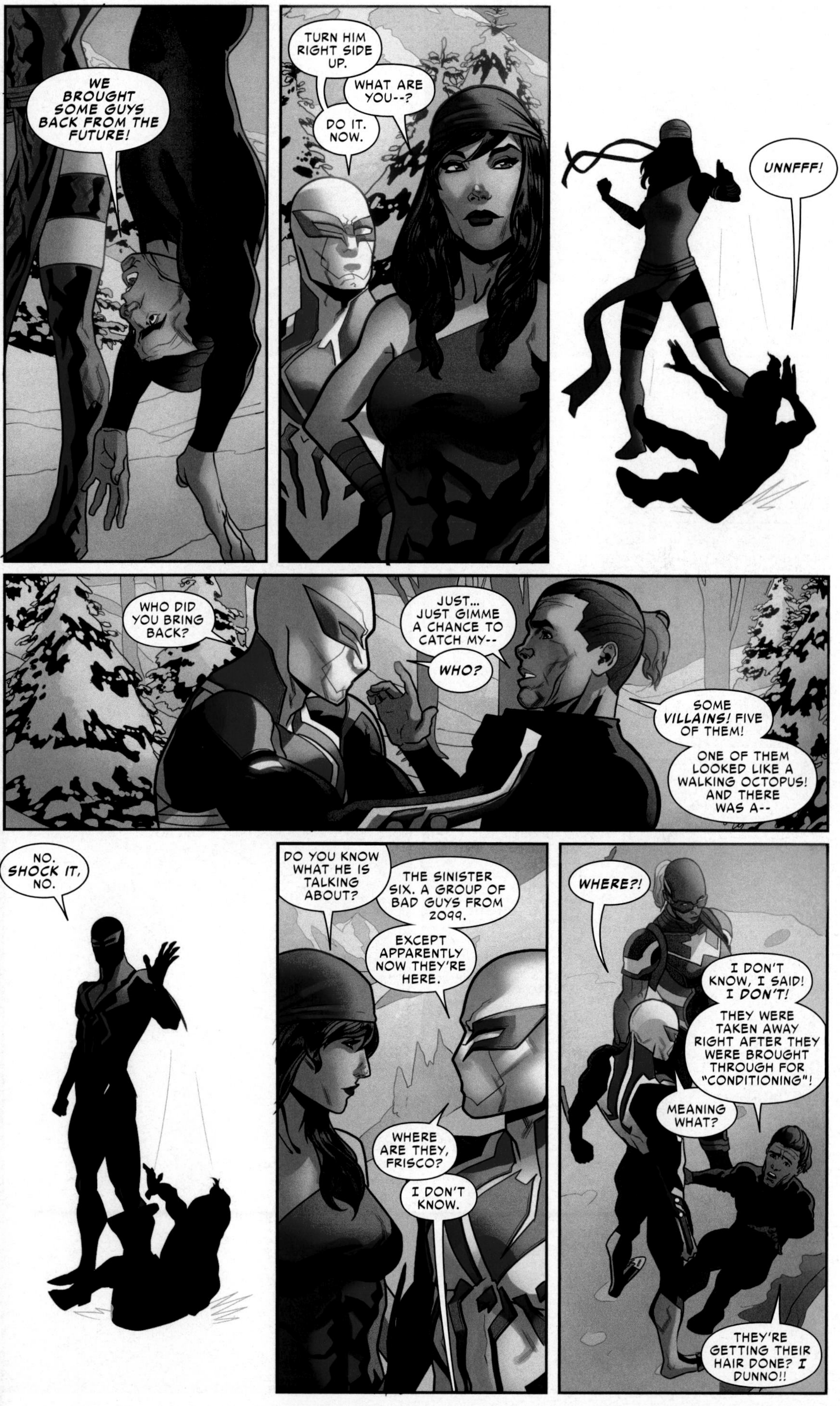
WE BROUGHT SOME GUYS BACK FROM THE FUTURE!
TURN HIM RIGHT SIDE UP.
WHAT ARE YOU--?
DO IT. NOW.
UNNFFF!
WHO DID YOU BRING BACK?
JUST... JUST GIMME A CHANCE TO CATCH MY--
WHO?
SOME VILLAINS! FIVE OF THEM!
ONE OF THEM LOOKED LIKE A WALKING OCTOPUS! AND THERE WAS A--
NO. SHOCK IT, NO.
DO YOU KNOW WHAT HE IS TALKING ABOUT?
THE SINISTER SIX. A GROUP OF BAD GUYS FROM 2099.
EXCEPT APPARENTLY NOW THEY'RE HERE.
WHERE ARE THEY, FRISCO?
I DON'T KNOW.
WHERE?!
I DON'T KNOW, I SAID! I DON'T!
THEY WERE TAKEN AWAY RIGHT AFTER THEY WERE BROUGHT THROUGH FOR "CONDITIONING"!
MEANING WHAT?
THEY'RE GETTING THEIR HAIR DONE? I DUNNO!!

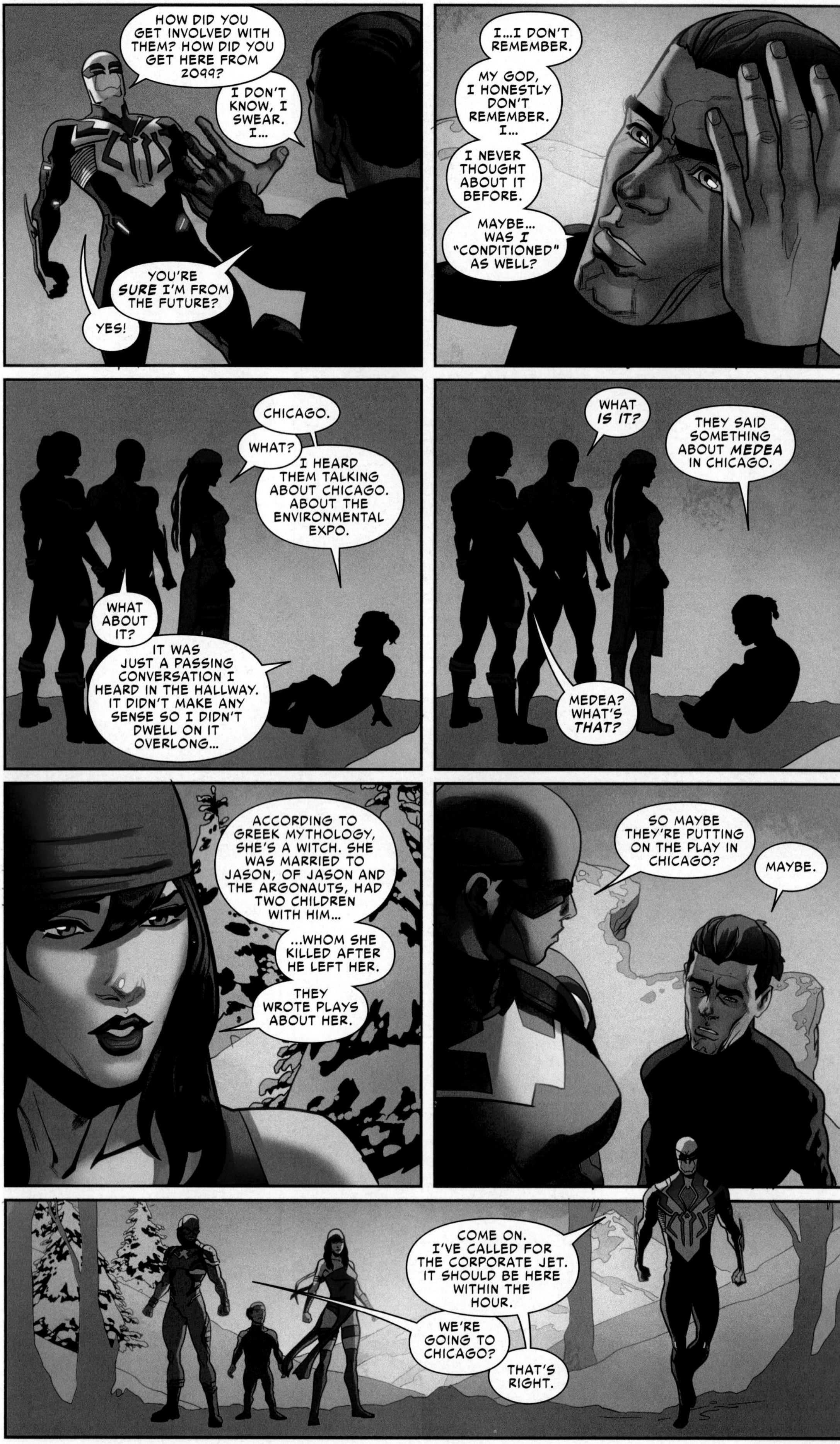
HOW DID YOU GET INVOLVED WITH THEM? HOW DID YOU GET HERE FROM 2099?
I DON'T KNOW, I SWEAR. I...
YOU'RE SURE I'M FROM THE FUTURE?
YES!
I...I DON'T REMEMBER.
MY GOD, I HONESTLY DON'T REMEMBER. I...
I NEVER THOUGHT ABOUT IT BEFORE.
MAYBE... WAS I "CONDITIONED" AS WELL?
CHICAGO.
WHAT?
I HEARD THEM TALKING ABOUT CHICAGO. ABOUT THE ENVIRONMENTAL EXPO.
WHAT ABOUT IT?
IT WAS JUST A PASSING CONVERSATION I HEARD IN THE HALLWAY. IT DIDN'T MAKE ANY SENSE SO I DIDN'T DWELL ON IT OVERLONG...
WHAT IS IT?
THEY SAID SOMETHING ABOUT MEDEA IN CHICAGO.
MEDEA? WHAT'S THAT?
ACCORDING TO GREEK MYTHOLOGY, SHE'S A WITCH. SHE WAS MARRIED TO JASON, OF JASON AND THE ARGONAUTS, HAD TWO CHILDREN WITH HIM...
...WHOM SHE KILLED AFTER HE LEFT HER.
THEY WROTE PLAYS ABOUT HER.
SO MAYBE THEY'RE PUTTING ON THE PLAY IN CHICAGO?
MAYBE.
COME ON. I'VE CALLED FOR THE CORPORATE JET. IT SHOULD BE HERE WITHIN THE HOUR.
WE'RE GOING TO CHICAGO?
THAT'S RIGHT.

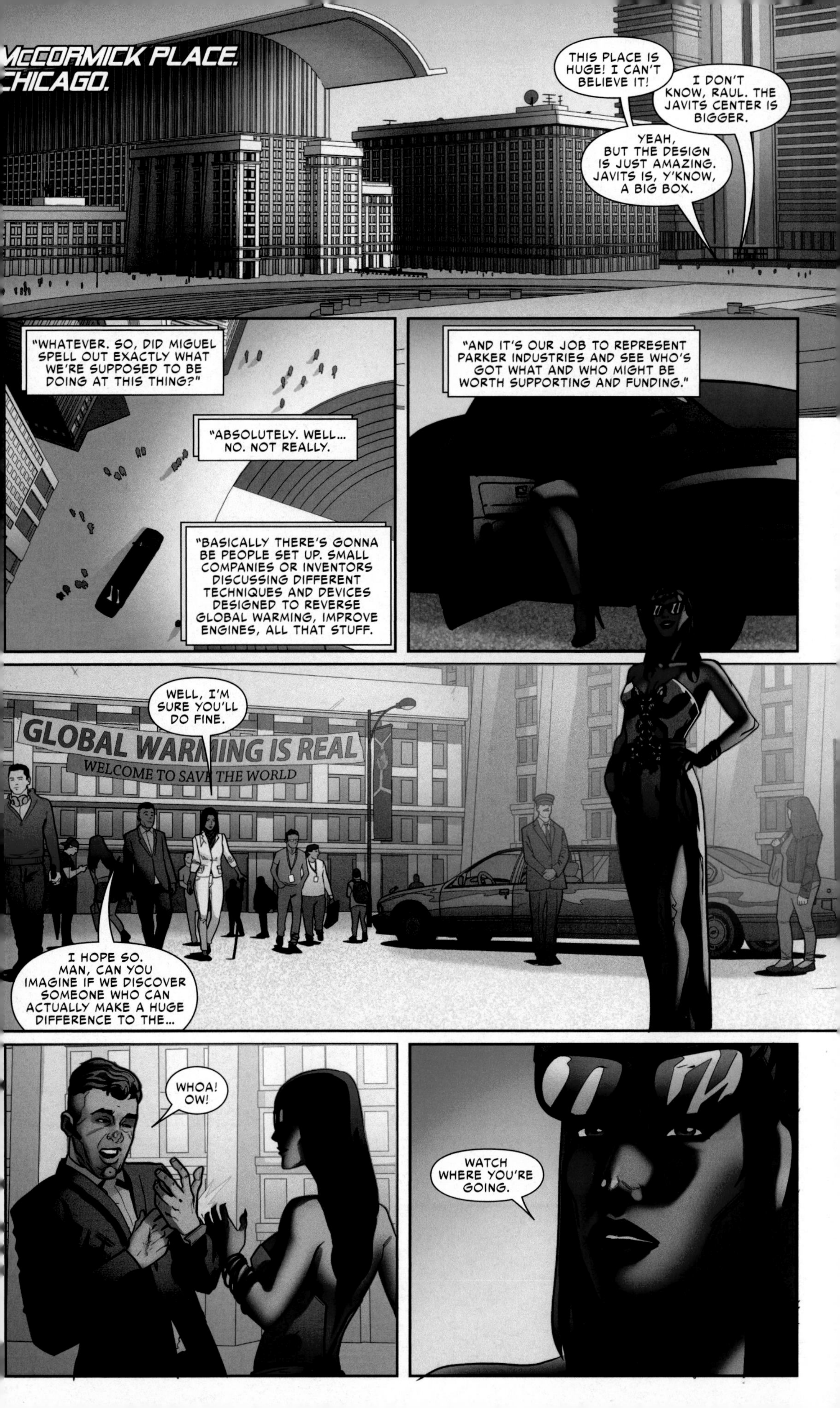
McCORMICK PLACE. CHICAGO.
THIS PLACE IS HUGE! I CAN'T BELIEVE IT!
I DON'T KNOW, RAUL. THE JAVITS CENTER IS BIGGER.
YEAH, BUT THE DESIGN IS JUST AMAZING. JAVITS IS, Y'KNOW, A BIG BOX.
"WHATEVER. SO, DID MIGUEL SPELL OUT EXACTLY WHAT WE'RE SUPPOSED TO BE DOING AT THIS THING?"
"ABSOLUTELY. WELL... NO. NOT REALLY.
"BASICALLY THERE'S GONNA BE PEOPLE SET UP. SMALL COMPANIES OR INVENTORS DISCUSSING DIFFERENT TECHNIQUES AND DEVICES DESIGNED TO REVERSE GLOBAL WARMING, IMPROVE ENGINES, ALL THAT STUFF.
"AND IT'S OUR JOB TO REPRESENT PARKER INDUSTRIES AND SEE WHO'S GOT WHAT AND WHO MIGHT BE WORTH SUPPORTING AND FUNDING."
GLOBAL WARMING IS REAL
WELCOME TO SAVE THE WORLD
WELL, I'M SURE YOU'LL DO FINE.
I HOPE SO. MAN, CAN YOU IMAGINE IF WE DISCOVER SOMEONE WHO CAN ACTUALLY MAKE A HUGE DIFFERENCE TO THE...
WHOA! OW!
WATCH WHERE YOU'RE GOING.

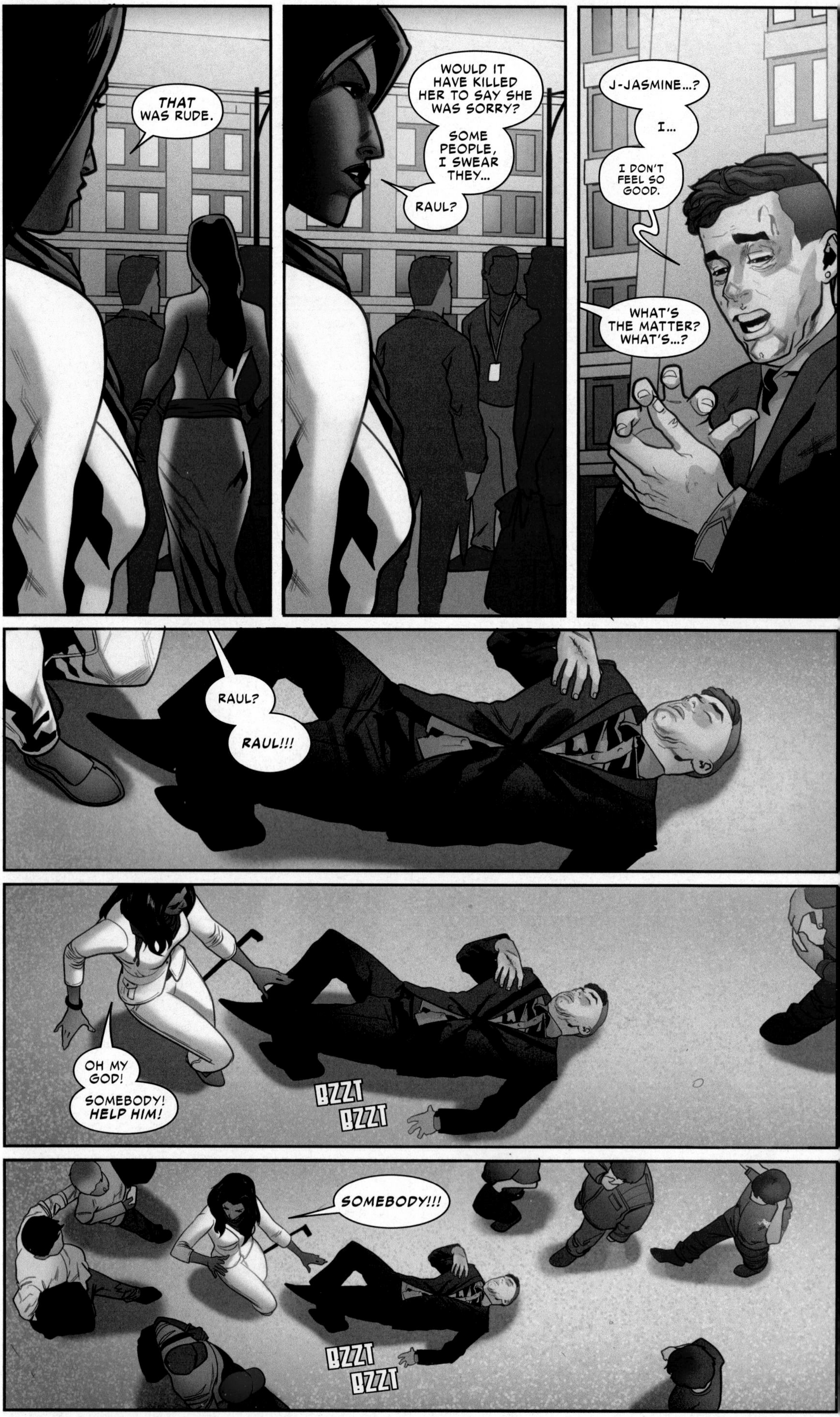
THAT WAS RUDE.
WOULD IT HAVE KILLED HER TO SAY SHE WAS SORRY?
SOME PEOPLE, I SWEAR THEY...
RAUL?
J-JASMINE...?
I...
I DON'T FEEL SO GOOD.
WHAT'S THE MATTER? WHAT'S...?
RAUL?
RAUL!!!
OH MY GOD!
SOMEBODY! HELP HIM!
BZZT
BZZT
SOMEBODY!!!
BZZT
BZZT

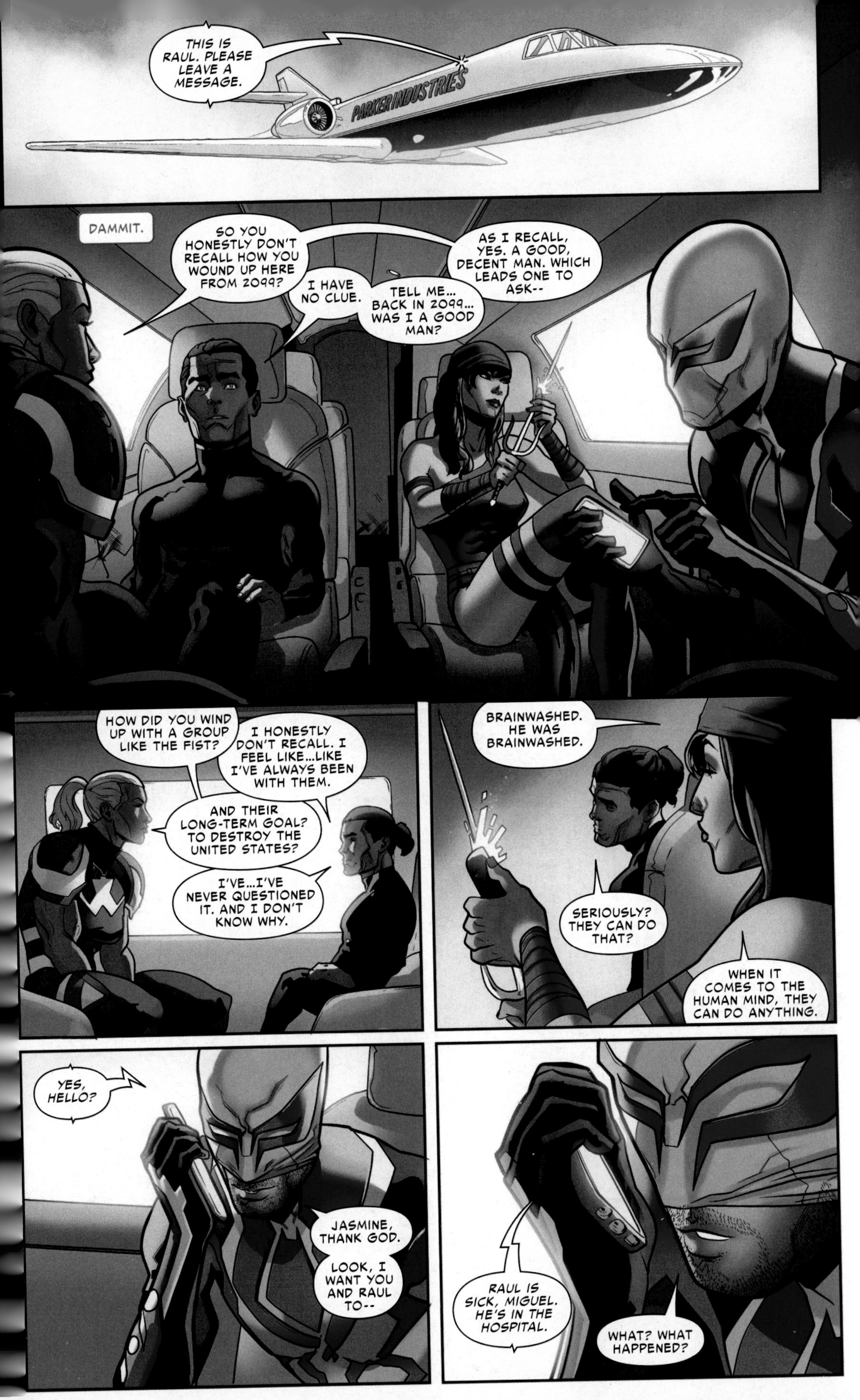
THIS IS RAUL. PLEASE LEAVE A MESSAGE.
PARKER INDUSTRIES
DAMMIT.
SO YOU HONESTLY DON'T RECALL HOW YOU WOUND UP HERE FROM 2099?
I HAVE NO CLUE.
TELL ME... BACK IN 2099... WAS I A GOOD MAN?
AS I RECALL, YES. A GOOD, DECENT MAN. WHICH LEADS ONE TO ASK--
HOW DID YOU WIND UP WITH A GROUP LIKE THE FIST?
I HONESTLY DON'T RECALL. I FEEL LIKE...LIKE I'VE ALWAYS BEEN WITH THEM.
AND THEIR LONG-TERM GOAL? TO DESTROY THE UNITED STATES?
I'VE...I'VE NEVER QUESTIONED IT. AND I DON'T KNOW WHY.
BRAINWASHED. HE WAS BRAINWASHED.
SERIOUSLY? THEY CAN DO THAT?
WHEN IT COMES TO THE HUMAN MIND, THEY CAN DO ANYTHING.
YES, HELLO?
JASMINE, THANK GOD.
LOOK, I WANT YOU AND RAUL TO--
RAUL IS SICK, MIGUEL. HE'S IN THE HOSPITAL.
WHAT? WHAT HAPPENED?

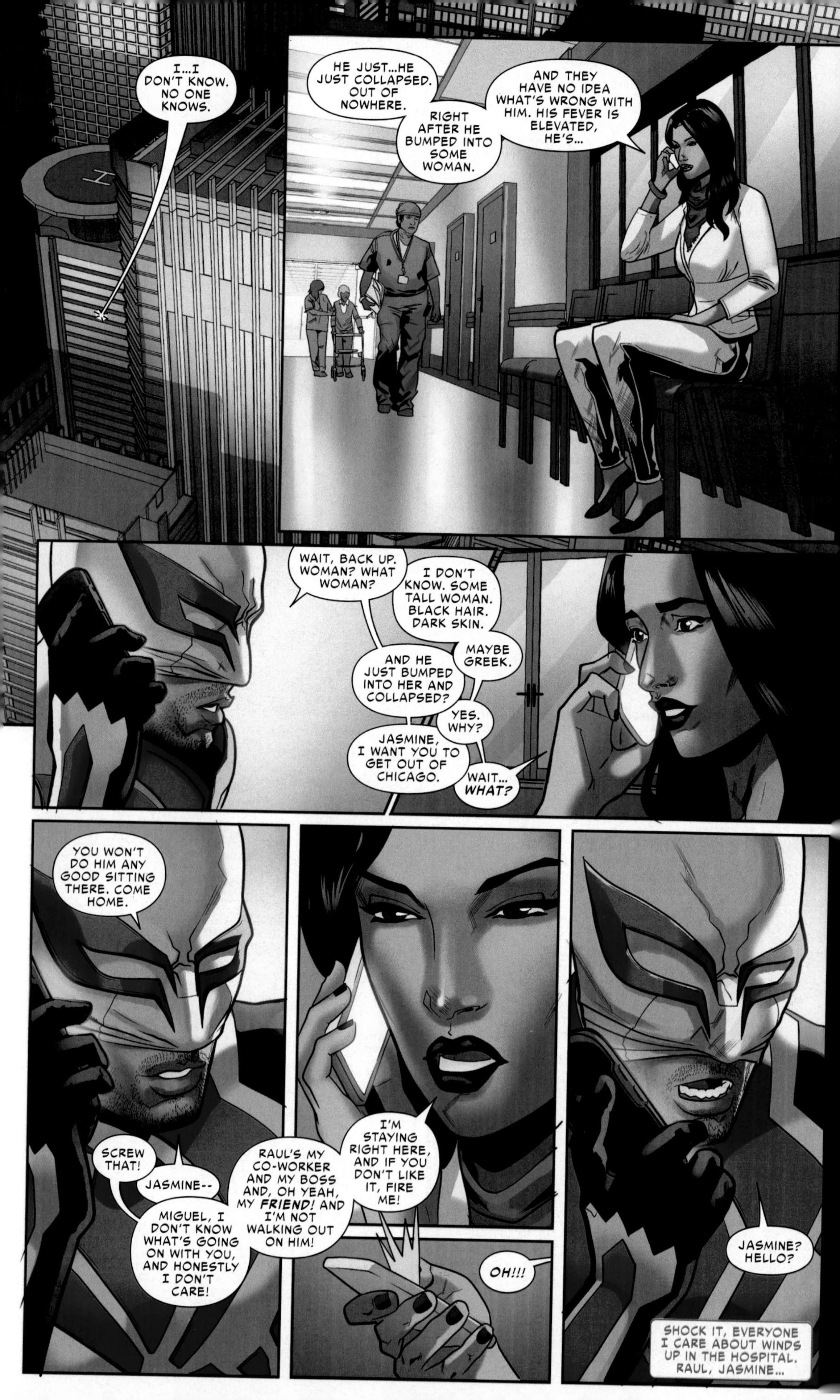

I...I DON'T KNOW. NO ONE KNOWS.
HE JUST...HE JUST COLLAPSED. OUT OF NOWHERE.
RIGHT AFTER HE BUMPED INTO SOME WOMAN.
AND THEY HAVE NO IDEA WHAT'S WRONG WITH HIM. HIS FEVER IS ELEVATED, HE'S...
WAIT, BACK UP. WOMAN? WHAT WOMAN?
I DON'T KNOW. SOME TALL WOMAN. BLACK HAIR. DARK SKIN.
MAYBE GREEK.
AND HE JUST BUMPED INTO HER AND COLLAPSED?
YES. WHY?
JASMINE, I WANT YOU TO GET OUT OF CHICAGO.
WAIT... *WHAT?*
YOU WON'T DO HIM ANY GOOD SITTING THERE. COME HOME.
SCREW THAT!
JASMINE--
MIGUEL, I DON'T KNOW WHAT'S GOING ON WITH YOU, AND HONESTLY I DON'T CARE!
RAUL'S MY CO-WORKER AND MY BOSS AND, OH YEAH, MY *FRIEND!* AND I'M NOT WALKING OUT ON HIM!
I'M STAYING RIGHT HERE, AND IF YOU DON'T LIKE IT, FIRE ME!
OH!!!
JASMINE? HELLO?
SHOCK IT, EVERYONE I CARE ABOUT WINDS UP IN THE HOSPITAL. RAUL, JASMINE...

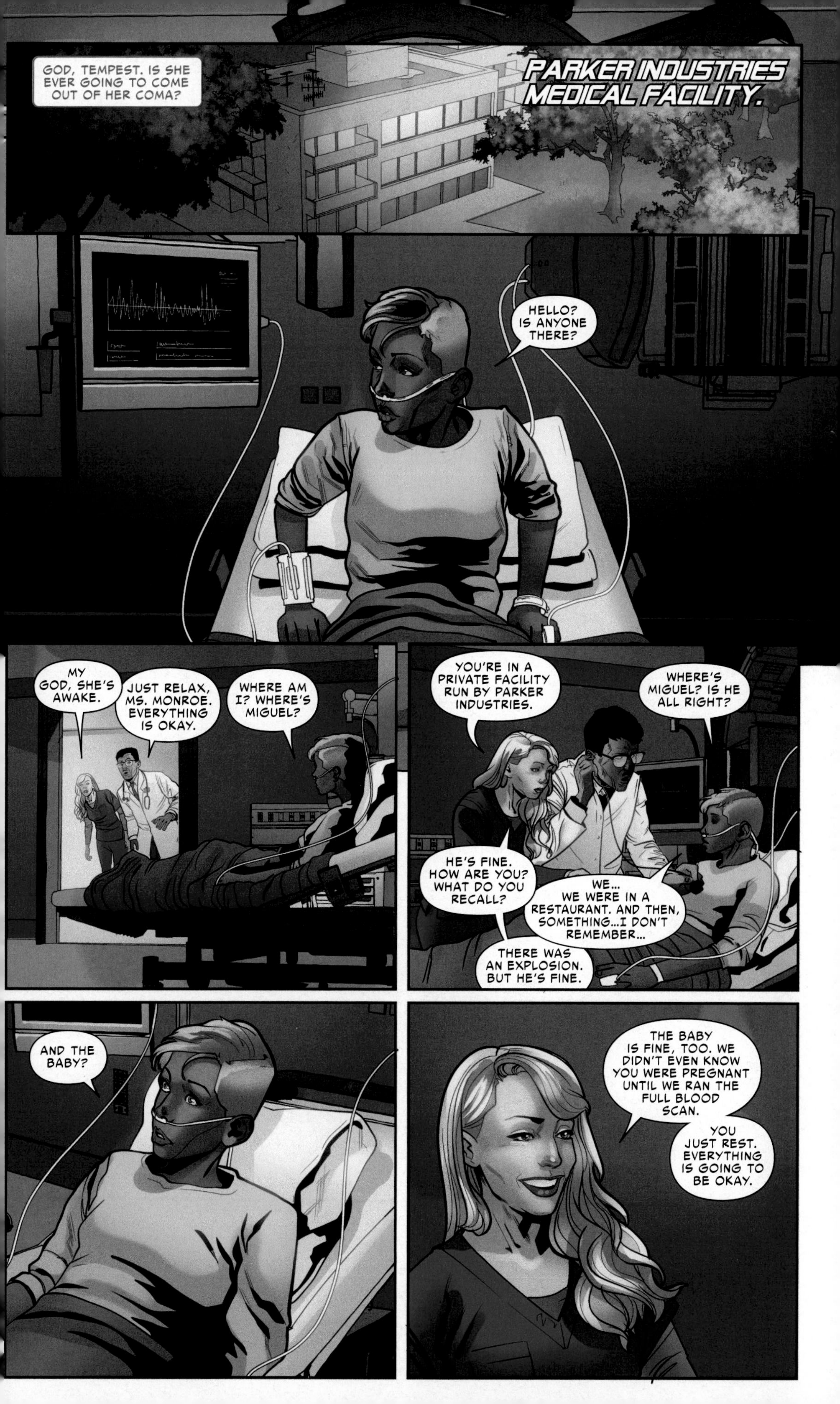
GOD, TEMPEST. IS SHE EVER GOING TO COME OUT OF HER COMA?
PARKER INDUSTRIES MEDICAL FACILITY.
HELLO? IS ANYONE THERE?
MY GOD, SHE'S AWAKE.
JUST RELAX, MS. MONROE. EVERYTHING IS OKAY.
WHERE AM I? WHERE'S MIGUEL?
YOU'RE IN A PRIVATE FACILITY RUN BY PARKER INDUSTRIES.
WHERE'S MIGUEL? IS HE ALL RIGHT?
HE'S FINE. HOW ARE YOU? WHAT DO YOU RECALL?
WE... WE WERE IN A RESTAURANT. AND THEN, SOMETHING...I DON'T REMEMBER...
THERE WAS AN EXPLOSION. BUT HE'S FINE.
AND THE BABY?
THE BABY IS FINE, TOO. WE DIDN'T EVEN KNOW YOU WERE PREGNANT UNTIL WE RAN THE FULL BLOOD SCAN.
YOU JUST REST. EVERYTHING IS GOING TO BE OKAY.

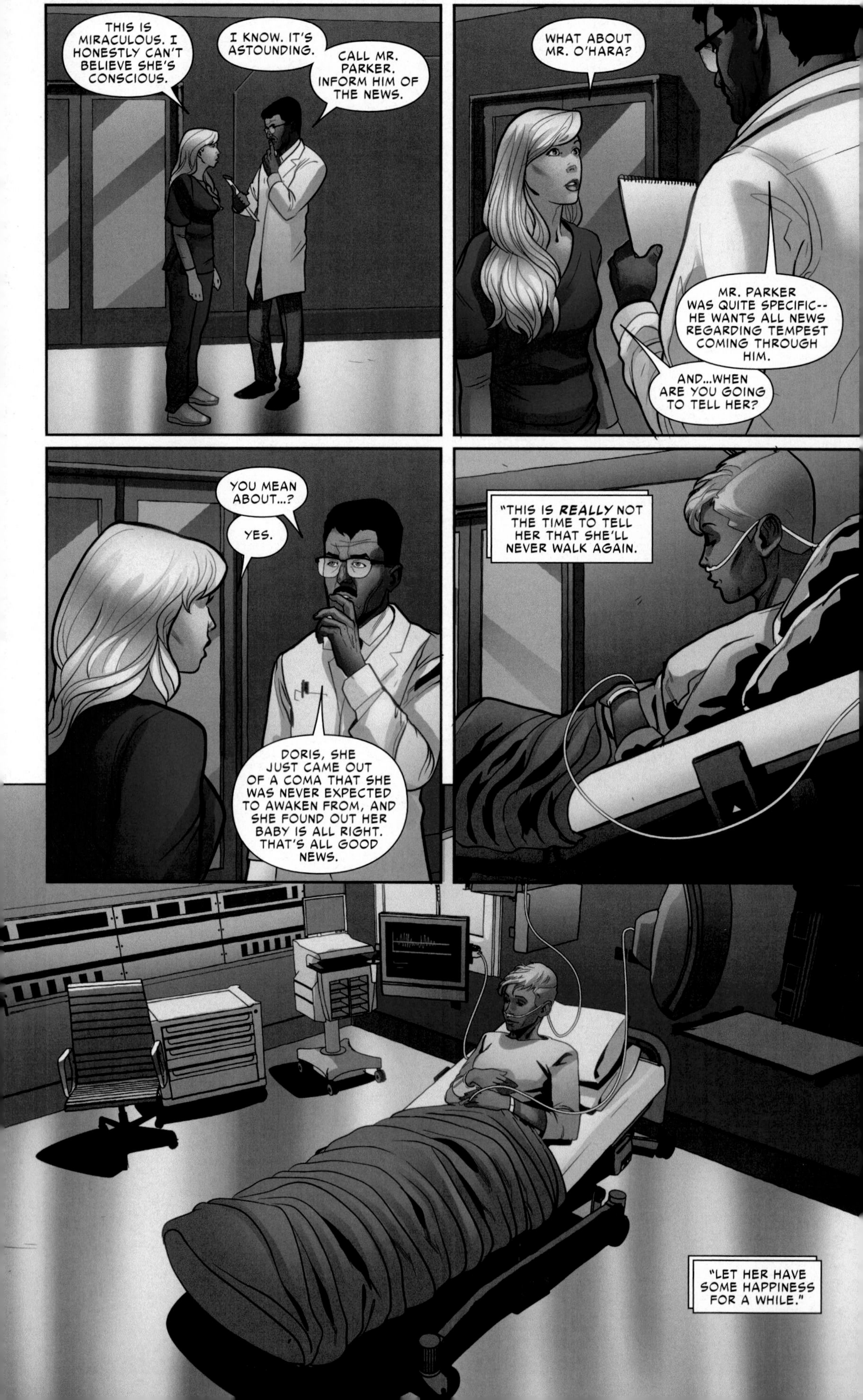
THIS IS MIRACULOUS. I HONESTLY CAN'T BELIEVE SHE'S CONSCIOUS.
I KNOW. IT'S ASTOUNDING.
CALL MR. PARKER. INFORM HIM OF THE NEWS.
WHAT ABOUT MR. O'HARA?
MR. PARKER WAS QUITE SPECIFIC--HE WANTS ALL NEWS REGARDING TEMPEST COMING THROUGH HIM.
AND...WHEN ARE YOU GOING TO TELL HER?
YOU MEAN ABOUT...?
YES.
DORIS, SHE JUST CAME OUT OF A COMA THAT SHE WAS NEVER EXPECTED TO AWAKEN FROM, AND SHE FOUND OUT HER BABY IS ALL RIGHT. THAT'S ALL GOOD NEWS.
"THIS IS ***REALLY*** NOT THE TIME TO TELL HER THAT SHE'LL NEVER WALK AGAIN.
"LET HER HAVE SOME HAPPINESS FOR A WHILE."

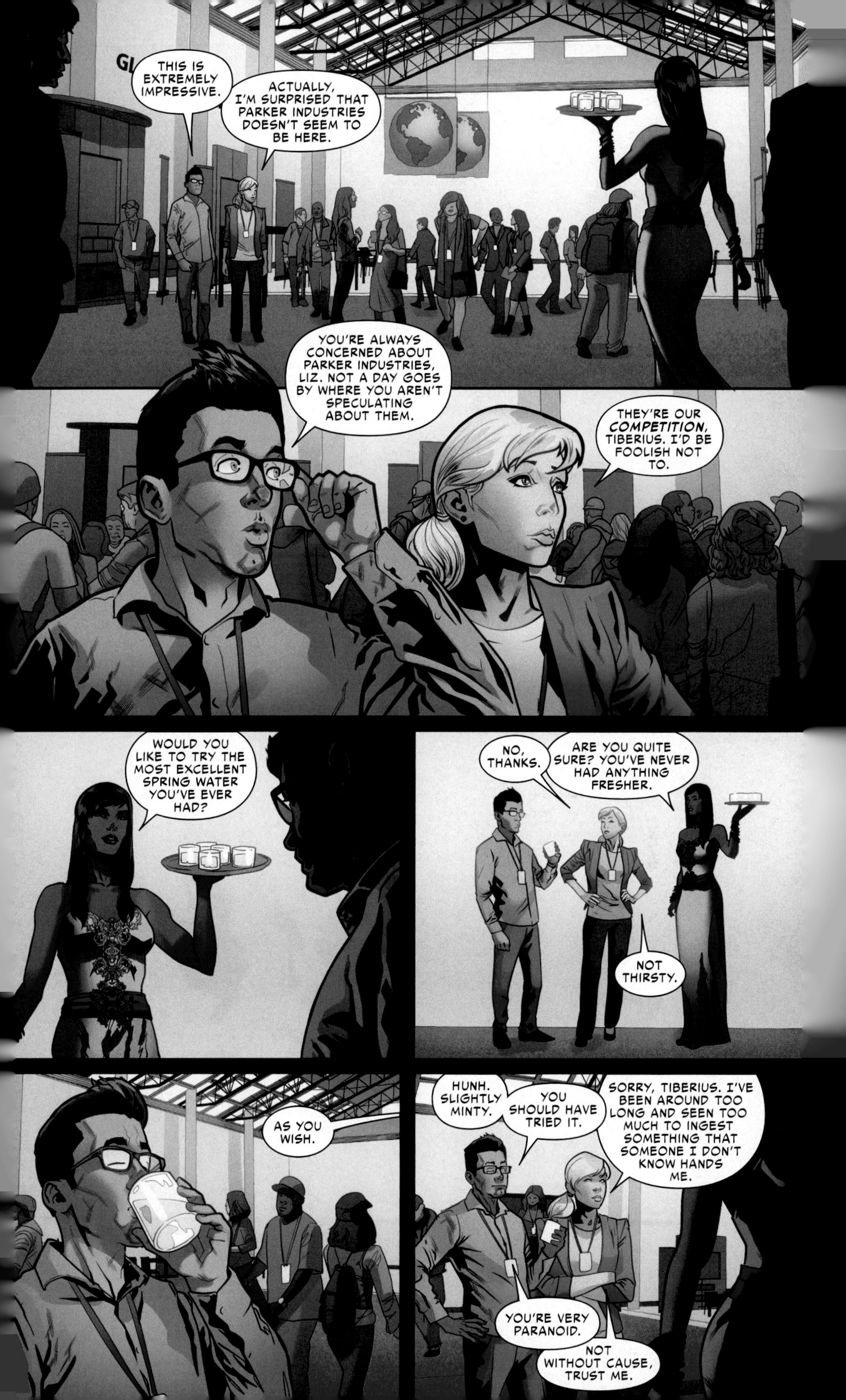
THIS IS EXTREMELY IMPRESSIVE.
ACTUALLY, I'M SURPRISED THAT PARKER INDUSTRIES DOESN'T SEEM TO BE HERE.
YOU'RE ALWAYS CONCERNED ABOUT PARKER INDUSTRIES, LIZ. NOT A DAY GOES BY WHERE YOU AREN'T SPECULATING ABOUT THEM.
THEY'RE OUR *COMPETITION*, TIBERIUS. I'D BE FOOLISH NOT TO.
WOULD YOU LIKE TO TRY THE MOST EXCELLENT SPRING WATER YOU'VE EVER HAD?
NO, THANKS.
ARE YOU QUITE SURE? YOU'VE NEVER HAD ANYTHING FRESHER.
NOT THIRSTY.
AS YOU WISH.
HUNH. SLIGHTLY MINTY.
YOU SHOULD HAVE TRIED IT.
SORRY, TIBERIUS. I'VE BEEN AROUND TOO LONG AND SEEN TOO MUCH TO INGEST SOMETHING THAT SOMEONE I DON'T KNOW HANDS ME.
YOU'RE VERY PARANOID.
NOT WITHOUT CAUSE, TRUST ME.

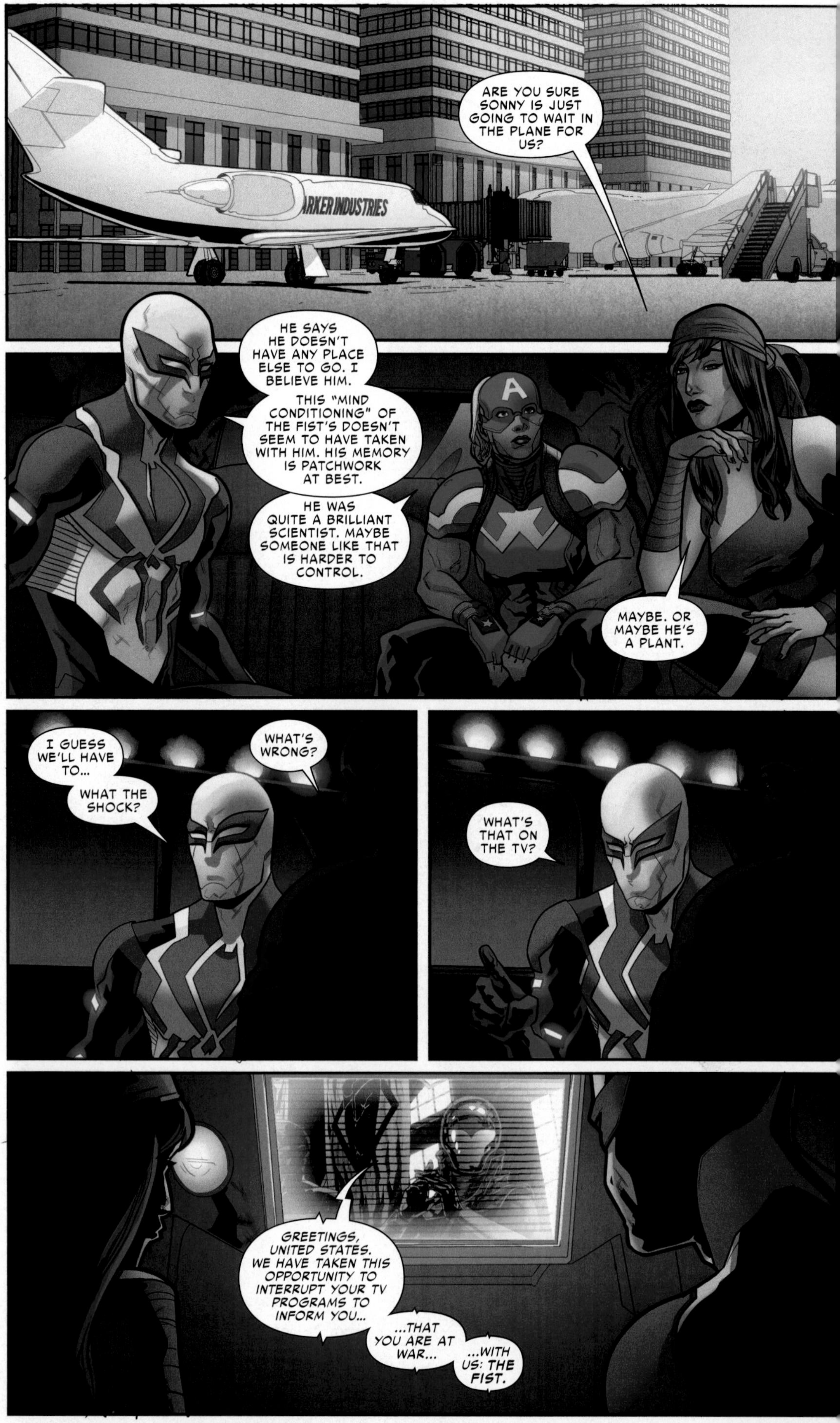
ARE YOU SURE SONNY IS JUST GOING TO WAIT IN THE PLANE FOR US?
ARKER INDUSTRIES
HE SAYS HE DOESN'T HAVE ANY PLACE ELSE TO GO. I BELIEVE HIM.
THIS "MIND CONDITIONING" OF THE FIST'S DOESN'T SEEM TO HAVE TAKEN WITH HIM. HIS MEMORY IS PATCHWORK AT BEST.
HE WAS QUITE A BRILLIANT SCIENTIST. MAYBE SOMEONE LIKE THAT IS HARDER TO CONTROL.
MAYBE. OR MAYBE HE'S A PLANT.
I GUESS WE'LL HAVE TO...
WHAT THE SHOCK?
WHAT'S WRONG?
WHAT'S THAT ON THE TV?
GREETINGS, UNITED STATES. WE HAVE TAKEN THIS OPPORTUNITY TO INTERRUPT YOUR TV PROGRAMS TO INFORM YOU...
...THAT YOU ARE AT WAR...
...WITH US: THE FIST.

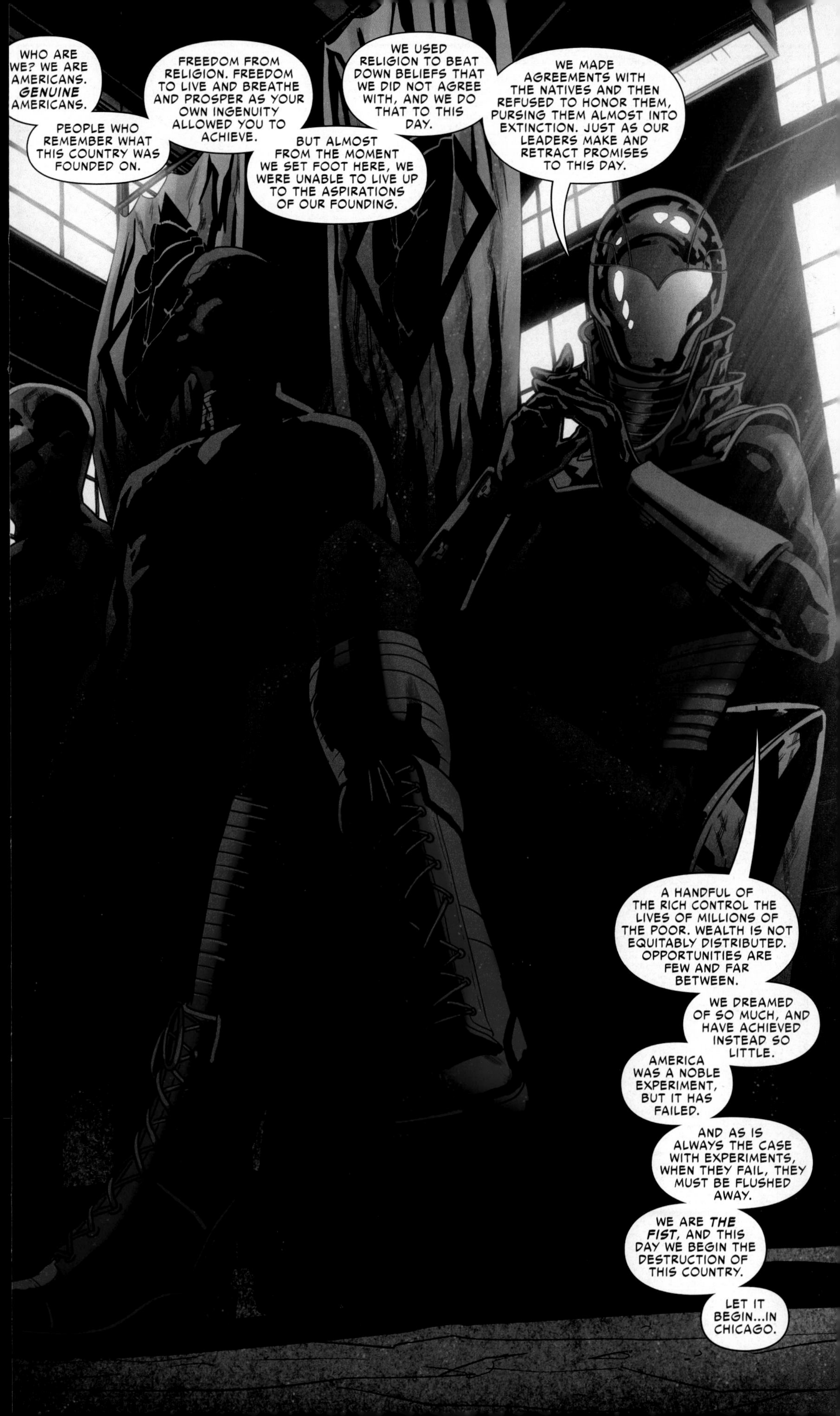
WHO ARE WE? WE ARE AMERICANS. *GENUINE* AMERICANS.
PEOPLE WHO REMEMBER WHAT THIS COUNTRY WAS FOUNDED ON.
FREEDOM FROM RELIGION. FREEDOM TO LIVE AND BREATHE AND PROSPER AS YOUR OWN INGENUITY ALLOWED YOU TO ACHIEVE.
BUT ALMOST FROM THE MOMENT WE SET FOOT HERE, WE WERE UNABLE TO LIVE UP TO THE ASPIRATIONS OF OUR FOUNDING.
WE USED RELIGION TO BEAT DOWN BELIEFS THAT WE DID NOT AGREE WITH, AND WE DO THAT TO THIS DAY.
WE MADE AGREEMENTS WITH THE NATIVES AND THEN REFUSED TO HONOR THEM, PURSING THEM ALMOST INTO EXTINCTION. JUST AS OUR LEADERS MAKE AND RETRACT PROMISES TO THIS DAY.
A HANDFUL OF THE RICH CONTROL THE LIVES OF MILLIONS OF THE POOR. WEALTH IS NOT EQUITABLY DISTRIBUTED. OPPORTUNITIES ARE FEW AND FAR BETWEEN.
WE DREAMED OF SO MUCH, AND HAVE ACHIEVED INSTEAD SO LITTLE.
AMERICA WAS A NOBLE EXPERIMENT, BUT IT HAS FAILED.
AND AS IS ALWAYS THE CASE WITH EXPERIMENTS, WHEN THEY FAIL, THEY MUST BE FLUSHED AWAY.
WE ARE *THE FIST*, AND THIS DAY WE BEGIN THE DESTRUCTION OF THIS COUNTRY.
LET IT BEGIN...IN CHICAGO.

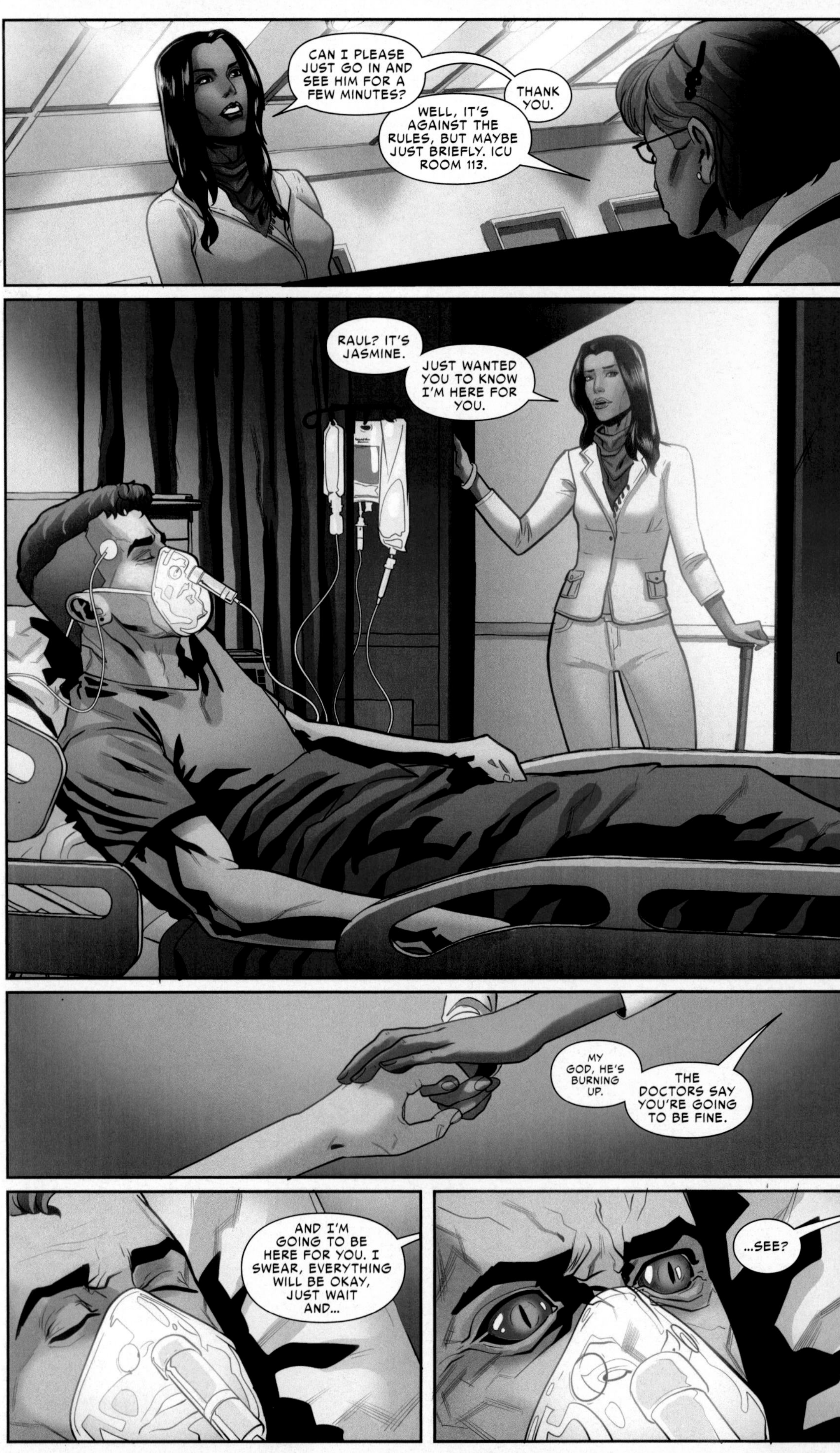
CAN I PLEASE JUST GO IN AND SEE HIM FOR A FEW MINUTES?
WELL, IT'S AGAINST THE RULES, BUT MAYBE JUST BRIEFLY. ICU ROOM 113.
THANK YOU.
RAUL? IT'S JASMINE.
JUST WANTED YOU TO KNOW I'M HERE FOR YOU.
MY GOD, HE'S BURNING UP.
THE DOCTORS SAY YOU'RE GOING TO BE FINE.
AND I'M GOING TO BE HERE FOR YOU. I SWEAR, EVERYTHING WILL BE OKAY, JUST WAIT AND...
...SEE?

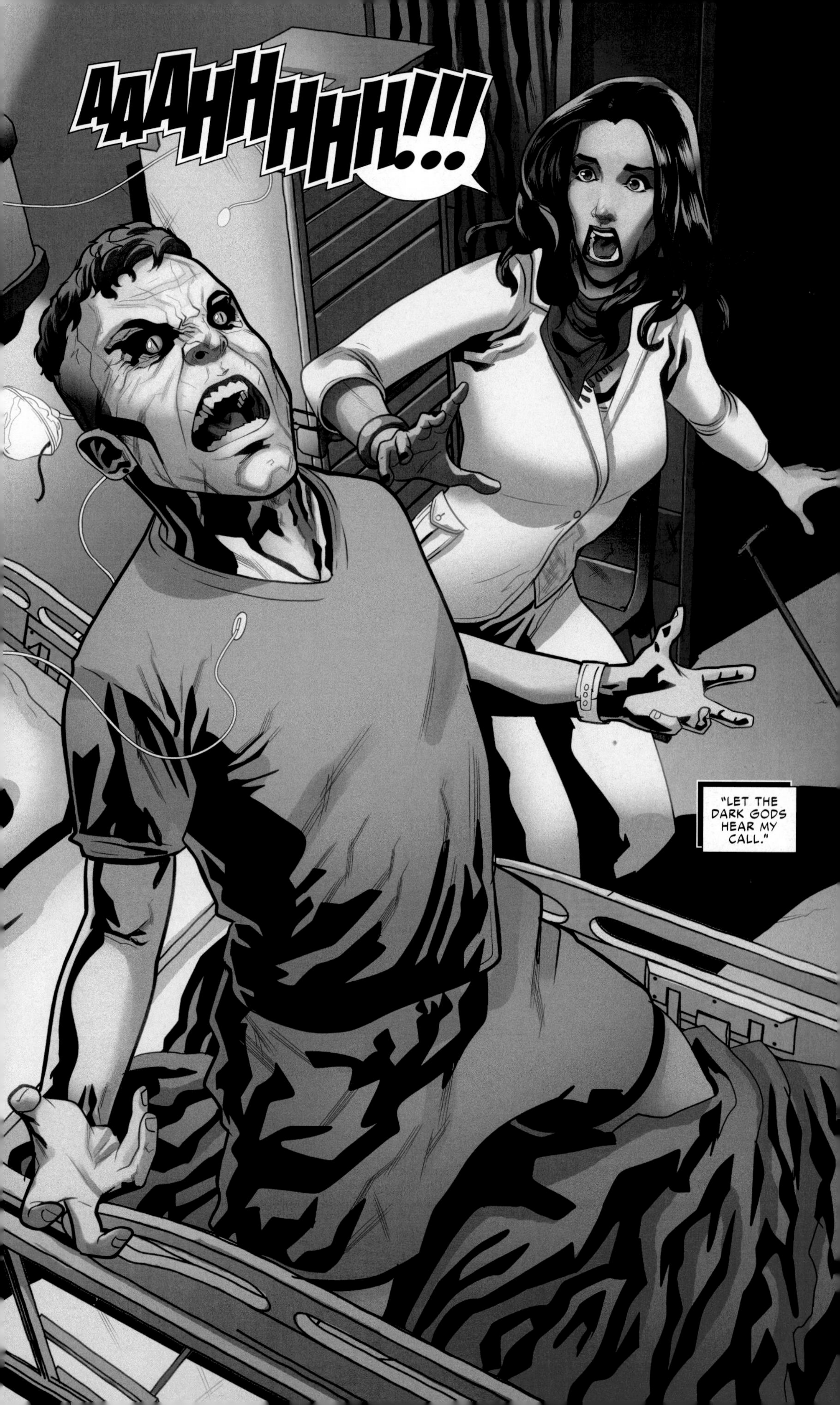
AAAHHHHH!!!
"LET THE DARK GODS HEAR MY CALL."

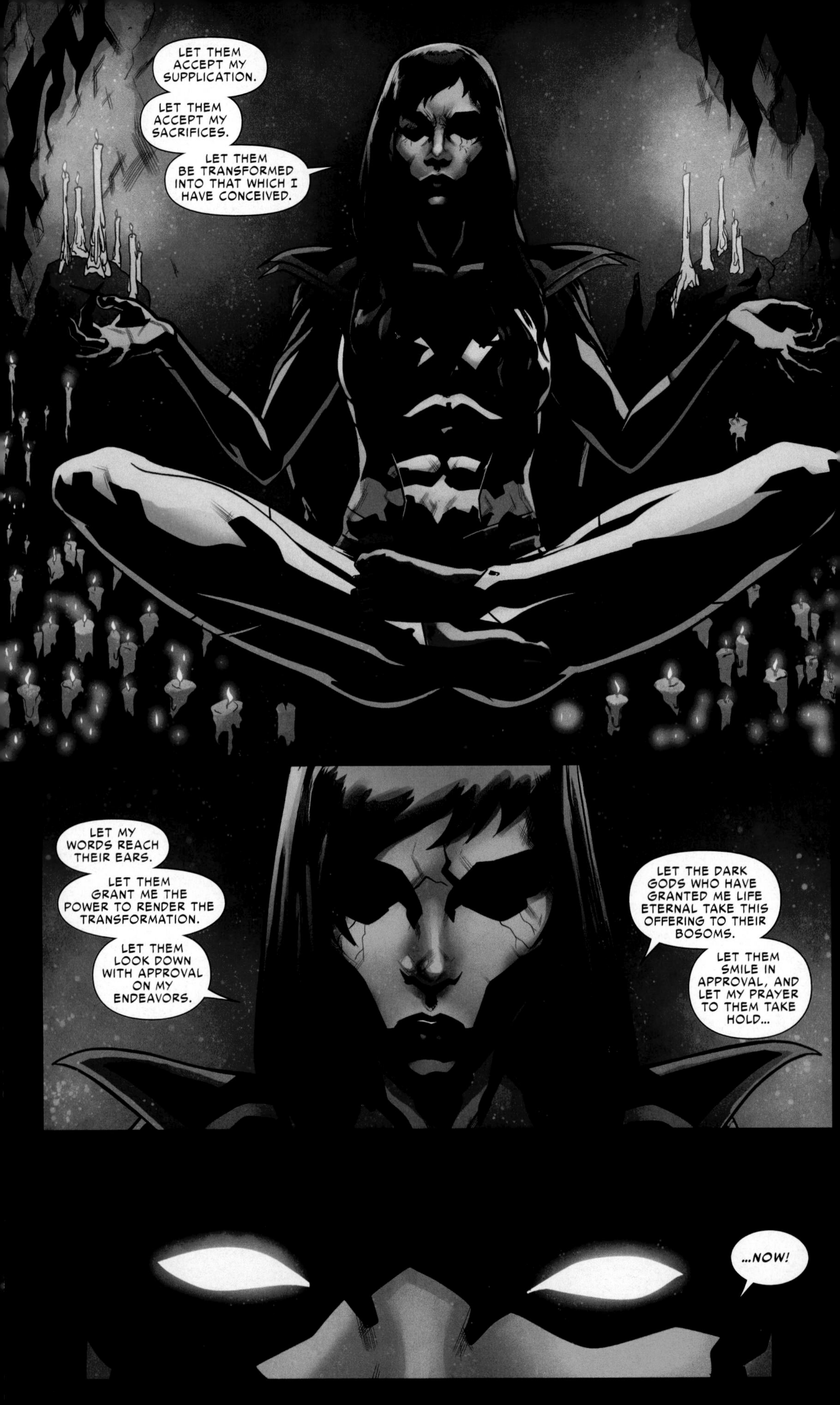
LET THEM ACCEPT MY SUPPLICATION.
LET THEM ACCEPT MY SACRIFICES.
LET THEM BE TRANSFORMED INTO THAT WHICH I HAVE CONCEIVED.
LET MY WORDS REACH THEIR EARS.
LET THEM GRANT ME THE POWER TO RENDER THE TRANSFORMATION.
LET THEM LOOK DOWN WITH APPROVAL ON MY ENDEAVORS.
LET THE DARK GODS WHO HAVE GRANTED ME LIFE ETERNAL TAKE THIS OFFERING TO THEIR BOSOMS.
LET THEM SMILE IN APPROVAL, AND LET MY PRAYER TO THEM TAKE HOLD...
...NOW!

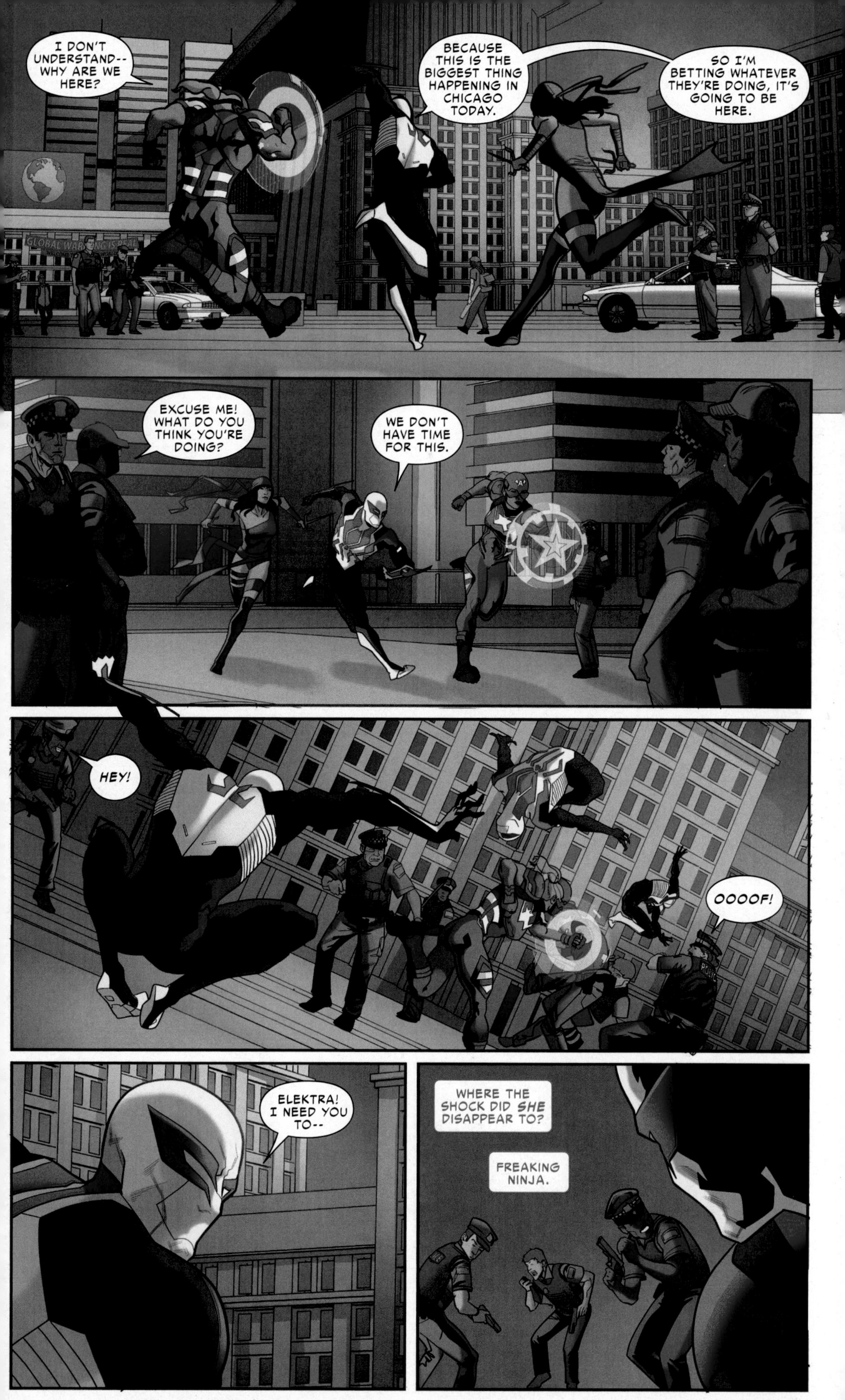
I DON'T UNDERSTAND-- WHY ARE WE HERE?
BECAUSE THIS IS THE BIGGEST THING HAPPENING IN CHICAGO TODAY.
SO I'M BETTING WHATEVER THEY'RE DOING, IT'S GOING TO BE HERE.
GLOBAL WARMING IS REAL
EXCUSE ME! WHAT DO YOU THINK YOU'RE DOING?
WE DON'T HAVE TIME FOR THIS.
HEY!
OOOOF!
POLICE
ELEKTRA! I NEED YOU TO--
WHERE THE SHOCK DID SHE DISAPPEAR TO?
FREAKING NINJA.

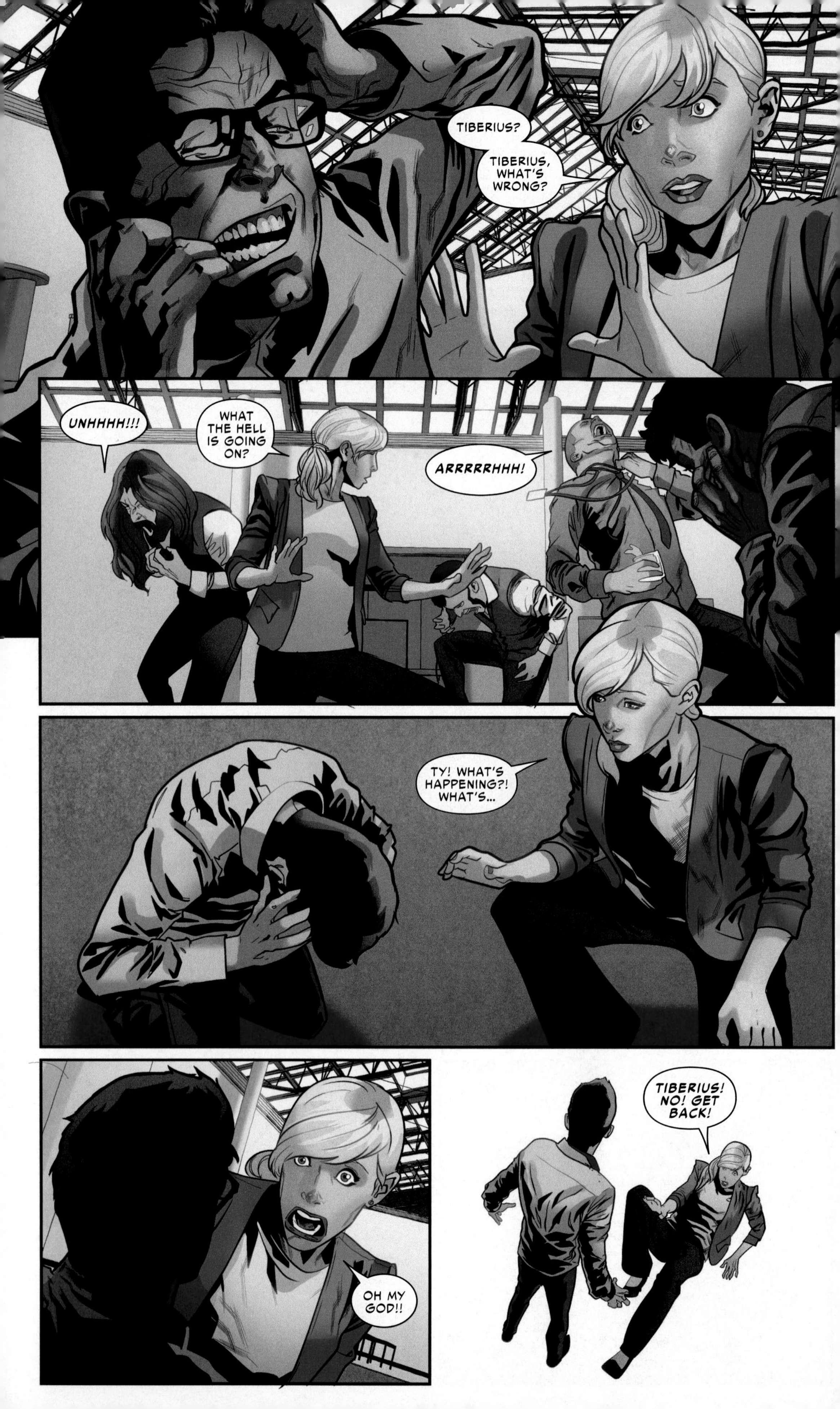
TIBERIUS?
TIBERIUS, WHAT'S WRONG?
UNHHHH!!!
WHAT THE HELL IS GOING ON?
ARRRRRHHH!
TY! WHAT'S HAPPENING?! WHAT'S...
OH MY GOD!!
TIBERIUS! NO! GET BACK!

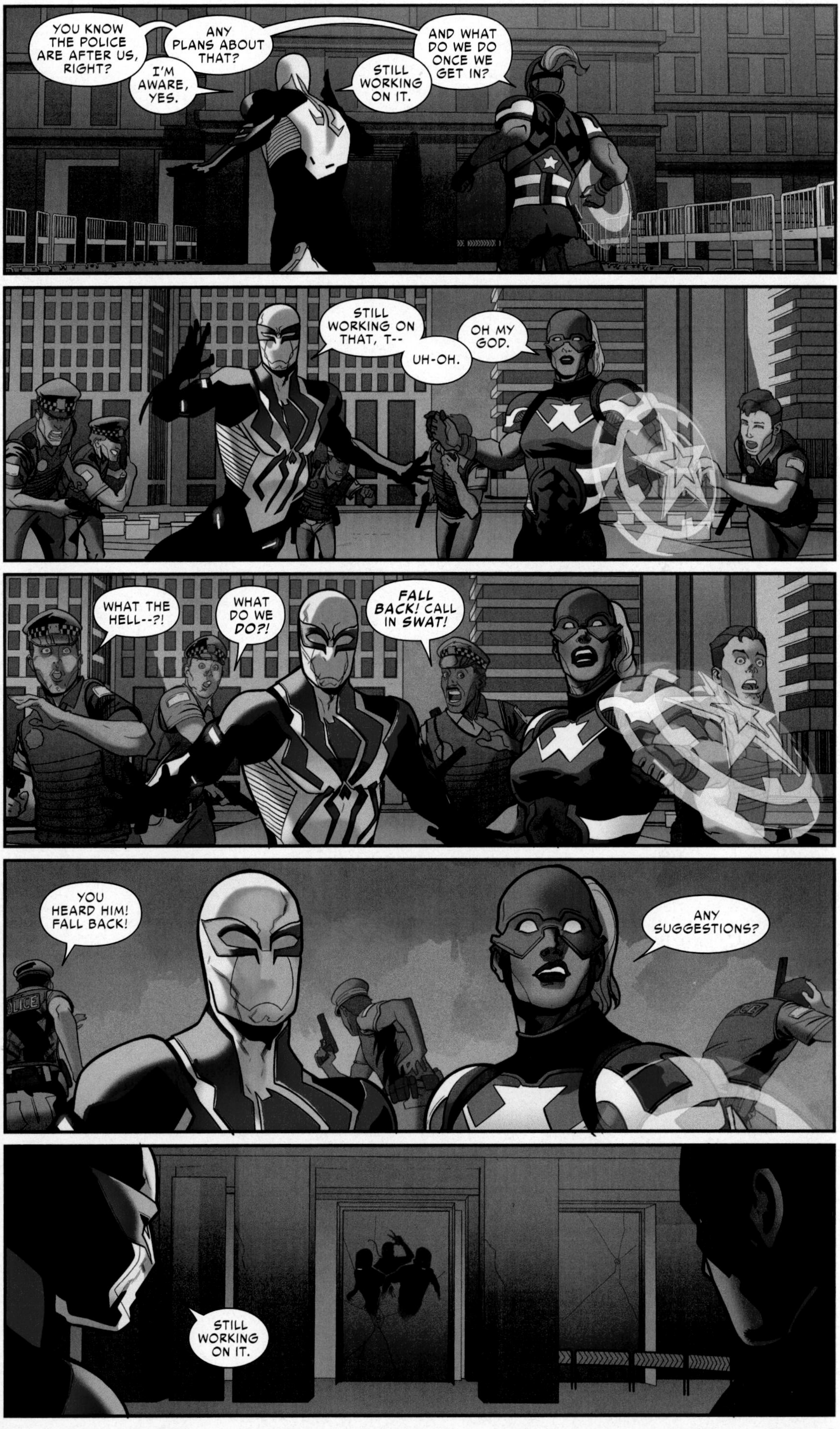

YOU KNOW THE POLICE ARE AFTER US, RIGHT?
I'M AWARE, YES.
ANY PLANS ABOUT THAT?
STILL WORKING ON IT.
AND WHAT DO WE DO ONCE WE GET IN?
STILL WORKING ON THAT, T--
UH-OH.
OH MY GOD.
WHAT THE HELL--?!
WHAT DO WE DO?!
FALL BACK! CALL IN SWAT!
YOU HEARD HIM! FALL BACK!
ANY SUGGESTIONS?
STILL WORKING ON IT.

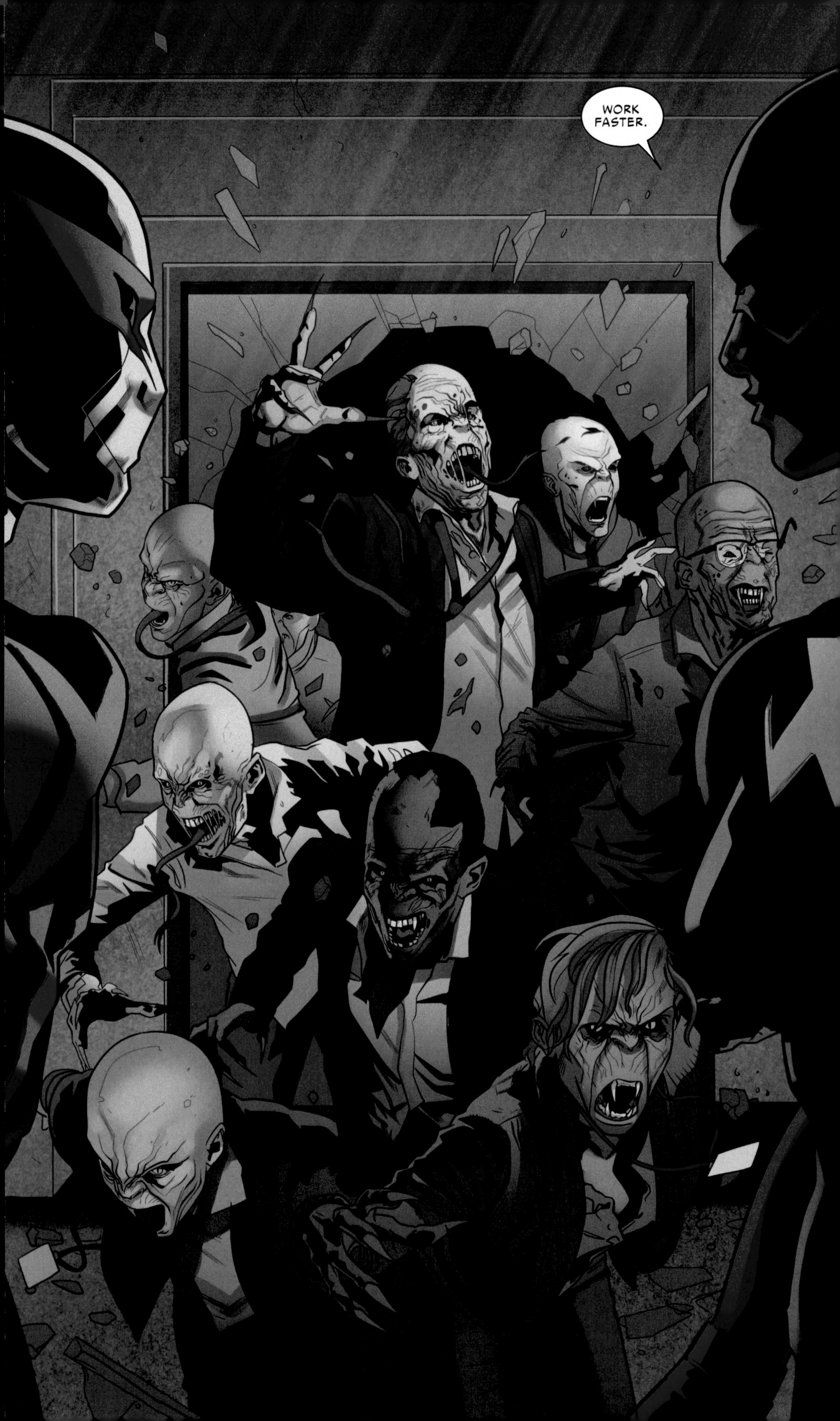
WORK FASTER.

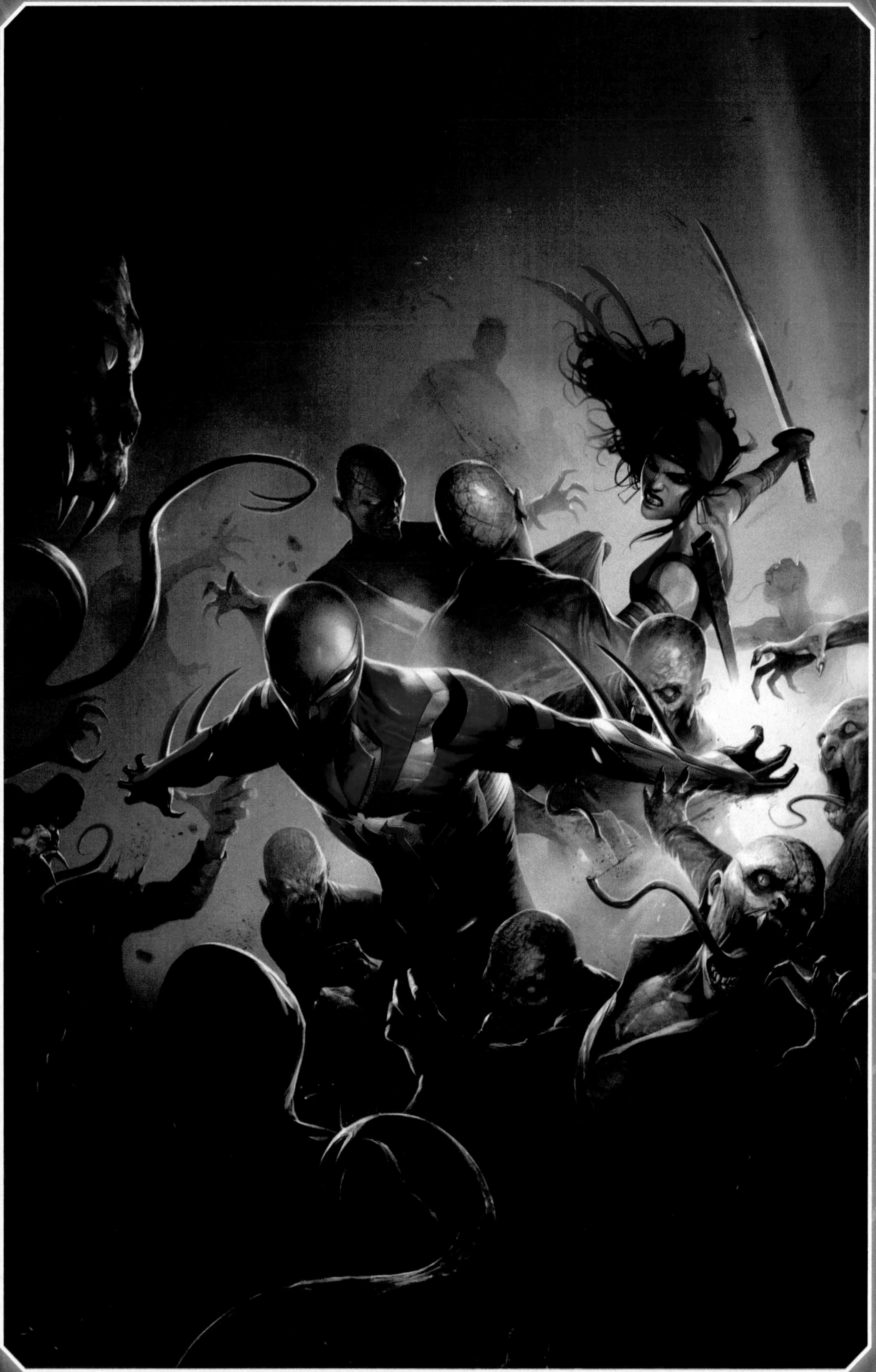

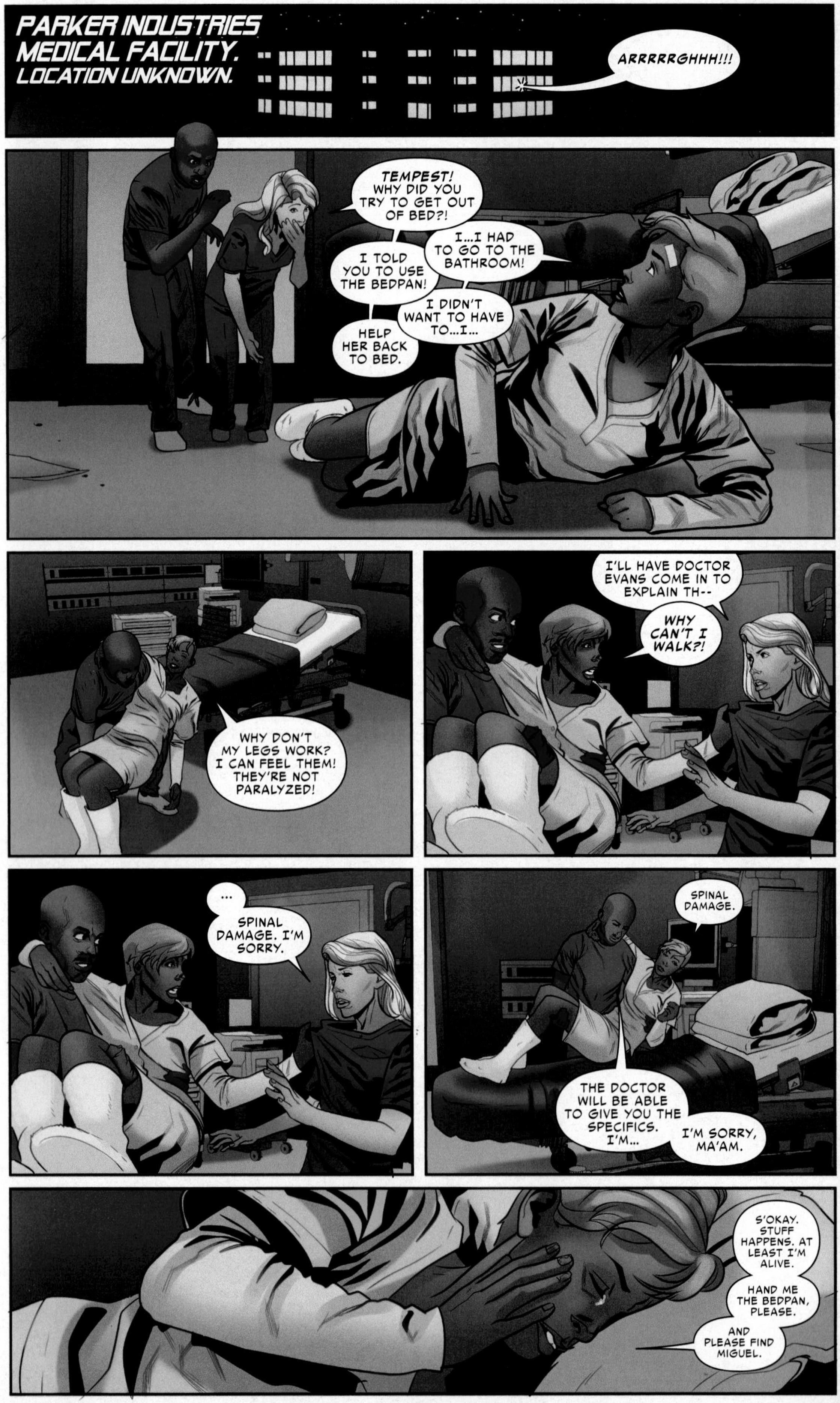

PARKER INDUSTRIES MEDICAL FACILITY. LOCATION UNKNOWN.
ARRRRRGHHH!!!
TEMPEST! WHY DID YOU TRY TO GET OUT OF BED?!
I TOLD YOU TO USE THE BEDPAN!
HELP HER BACK TO BED.
I...I HAD TO GO TO THE BATHROOM!
I DIDN'T WANT TO HAVE TO...I...
WHY DON'T MY LEGS WORK? I CAN FEEL THEM! THEY'RE NOT PARALYZED!
I'LL HAVE DOCTOR EVANS COME IN TO EXPLAIN TH--
WHY CAN'T I WALK?!
...
SPINAL DAMAGE. I'M SORRY.
SPINAL DAMAGE.
THE DOCTOR WILL BE ABLE TO GIVE YOU THE SPECIFICS. I'M...
I'M SORRY, MA'AM.
S'OKAY. STUFF HAPPENS. AT LEAST I'M ALIVE.
HAND ME THE BEDPAN, PLEASE.
AND PLEASE FIND MIGUEL.

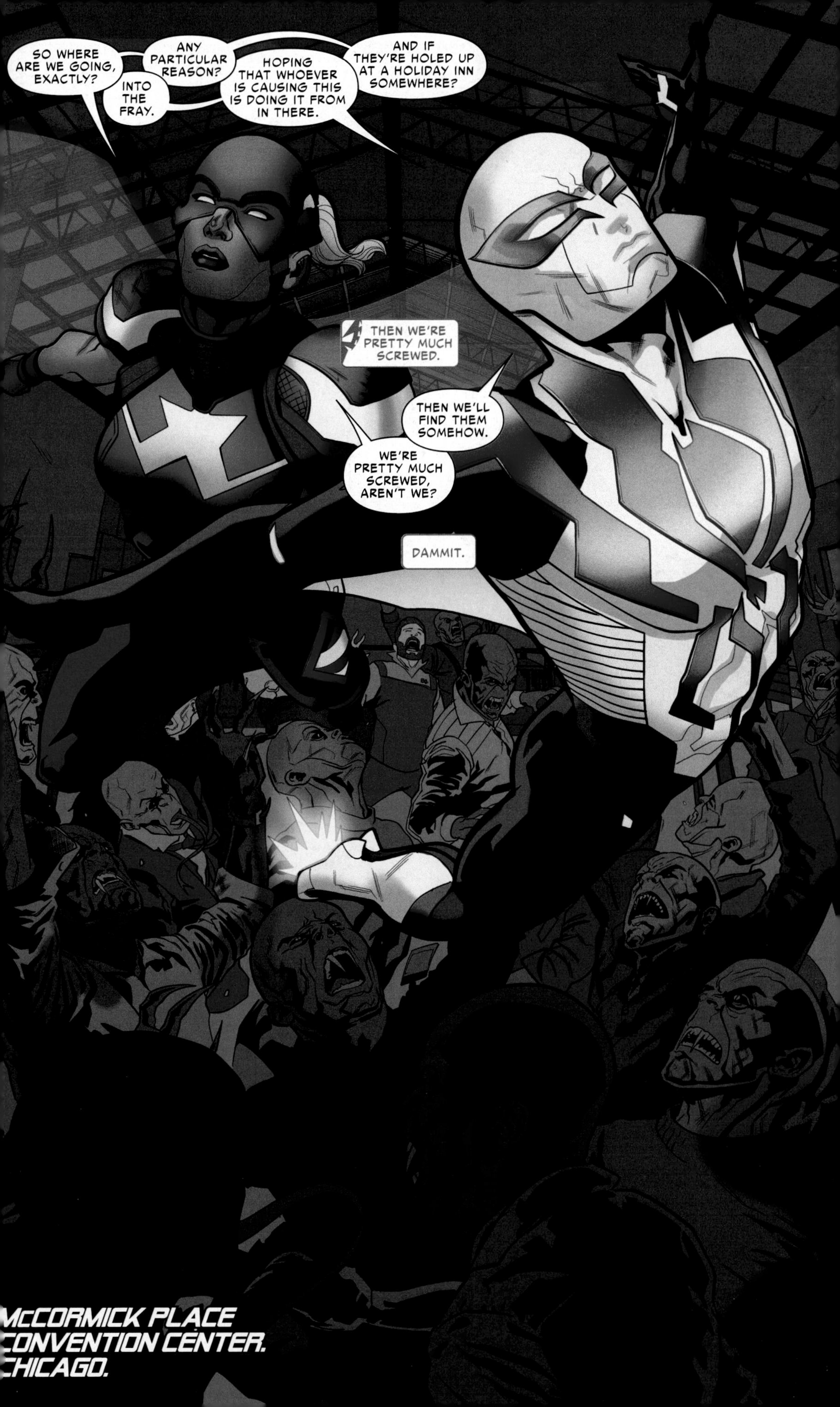
SO WHERE ARE WE GOING, EXACTLY?
INTO THE FRAY.
ANY PARTICULAR REASON?
HOPING THAT WHOEVER IS CAUSING THIS IS DOING IT FROM IN THERE.
AND IF THEY'RE HOLED UP AT A HOLIDAY INN SOMEWHERE?
THEN WE'RE PRETTY MUCH SCREWED.
THEN WE'LL FIND THEM SOMEHOW.
WE'RE PRETTY MUCH SCREWED, AREN'T WE?
DAMMIT.
McCORMICK PLACE CONVENTION CENTER. CHICAGO.

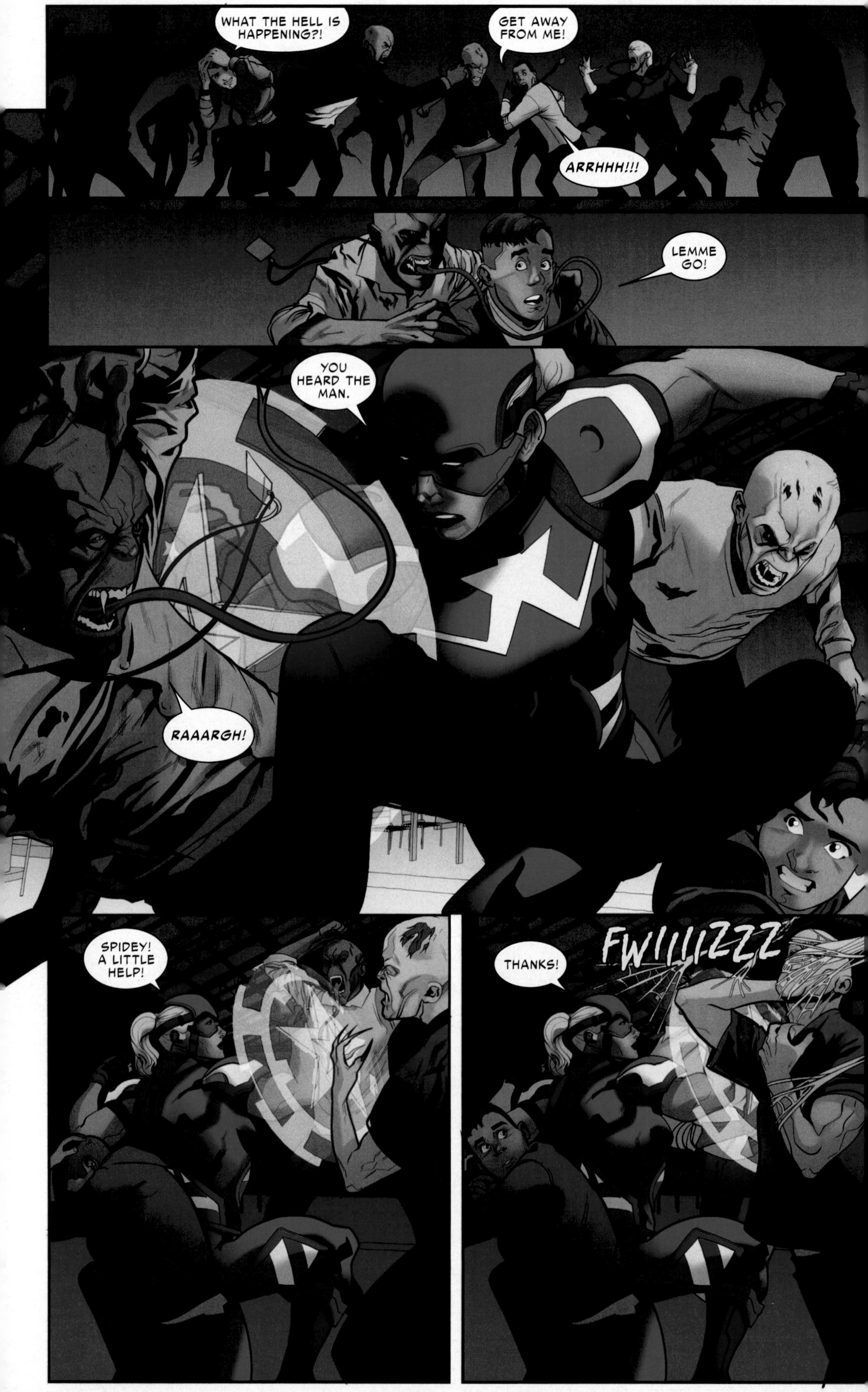
WHAT THE HELL IS HAPPENING?!
GET AWAY FROM ME!
ARRHHH!!!
LEMME GO!
YOU HEARD THE MAN.
RAAARGH!
SPIDEY! A LITTLE HELP!
THANKS!
FWIIIIZZZ

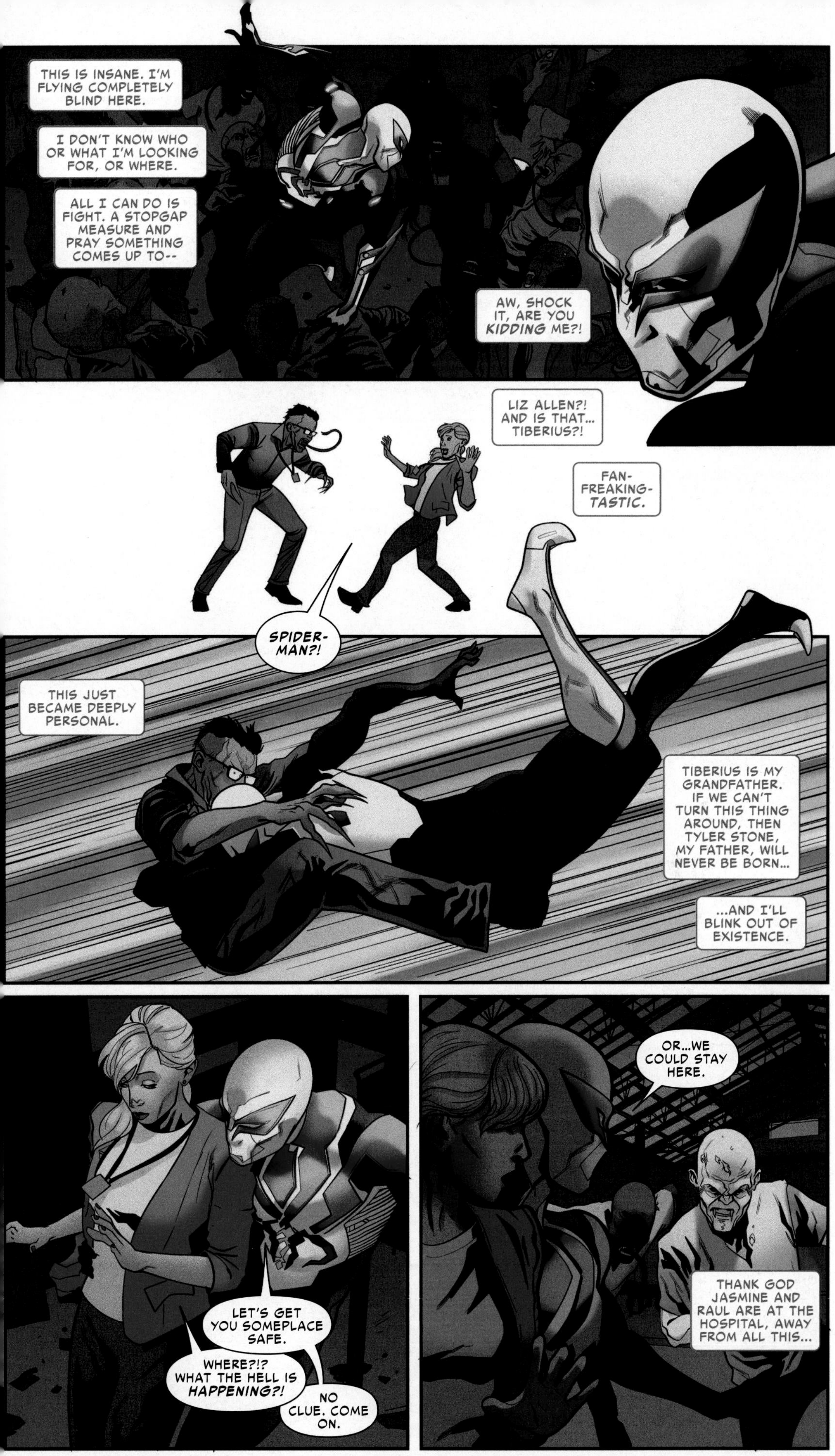
THIS IS INSANE. I'M FLYING COMPLETELY BLIND HERE.
I DON'T KNOW WHO OR WHAT I'M LOOKING FOR, OR WHERE.
ALL I CAN DO IS FIGHT. A STOPGAP MEASURE AND PRAY SOMETHING COMES UP TO--
AW, SHOCK IT, ARE YOU KIDDING ME?!
LIZ ALLEN?! AND IS THAT... TIBERIUS?!
FAN-FREAKING-TASTIC.
SPIDER-MAN?!
THIS JUST BECAME DEEPLY PERSONAL.
TIBERIUS IS MY GRANDFATHER. IF WE CAN'T TURN THIS THING AROUND, THEN TYLER STONE, MY FATHER, WILL NEVER BE BORN...
...AND I'LL BLINK OUT OF EXISTENCE.
LET'S GET YOU SOMEPLACE SAFE.
WHERE?!? WHAT THE HELL IS HAPPENING?!
NO CLUE. COME ON.
OR...WE COULD STAY HERE.
THANK GOD JASMINE AND RAUL ARE AT THE HOSPITAL, AWAY FROM ALL THIS...

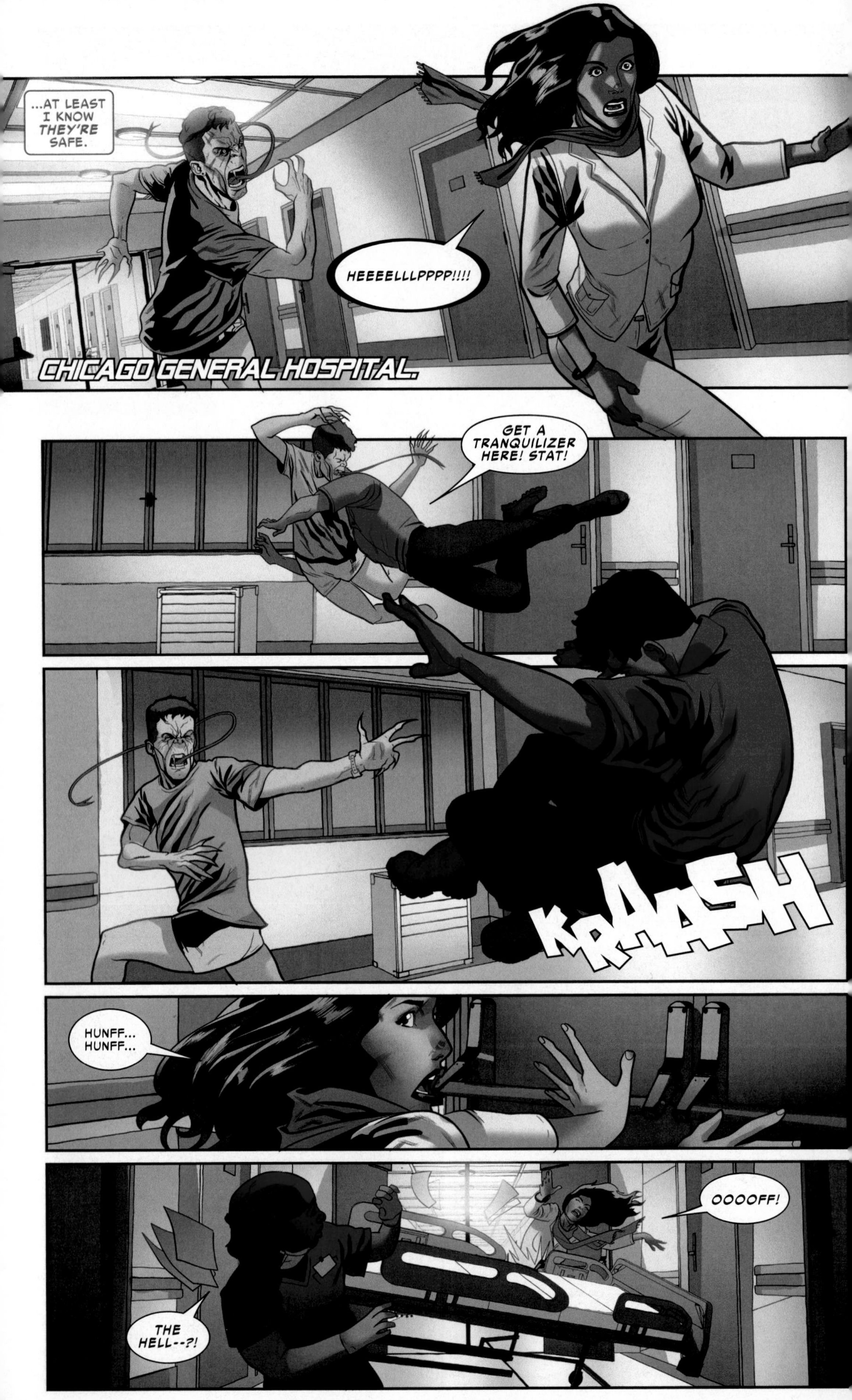
...AT LEAST I KNOW THEY'RE SAFE.
HEEEELLLPPPP!!!!
CHICAGO GENERAL HOSPITAL.
GET A TRANQUILIZER HERE! STAT!
KRAASH
HUNFF... HUNFF...
OOOOFF!
THE HELL--?!

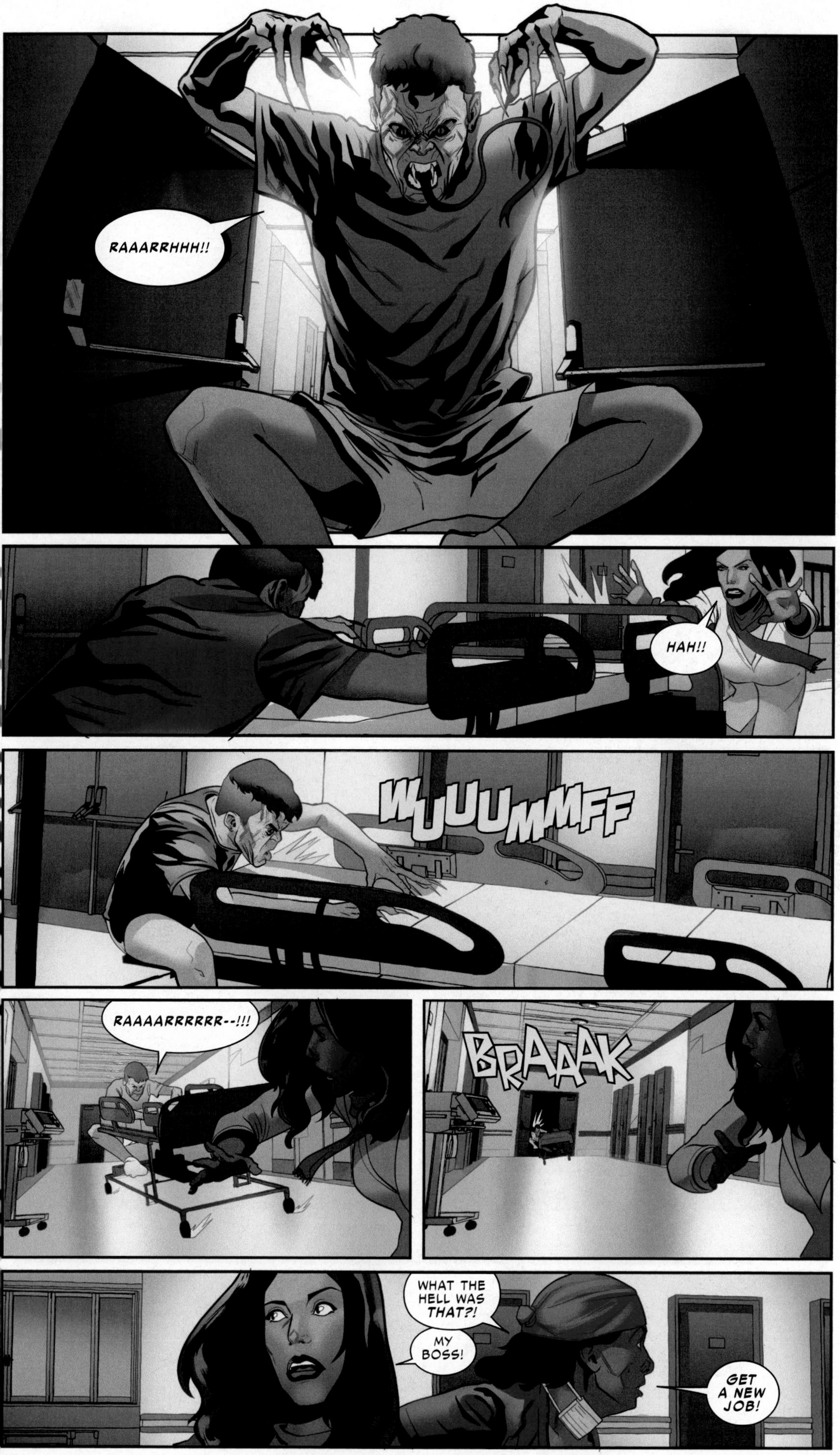
RAAARRHHH!!
HAH!!
WUUUMMFF
RAAAARRRRR--!!!
BRAAAK
WHAT THE HELL WAS THAT?!
MY BOSS!
GET A NEW JOB!

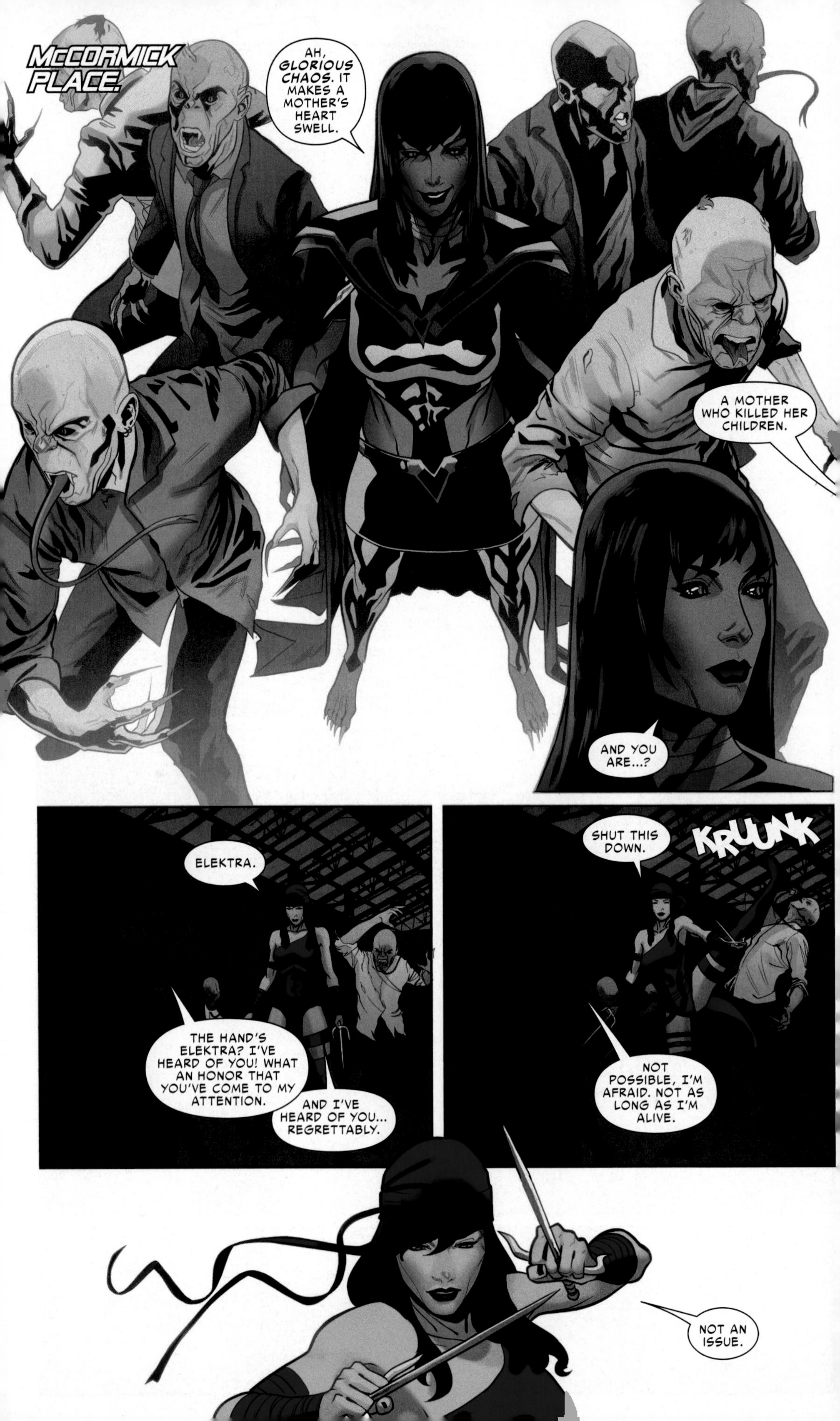
McCORMICK PLACE.
AH, GLORIOUS CHAOS. IT MAKES A MOTHER'S HEART SWELL.
A MOTHER WHO KILLED HER CHILDREN.
AND YOU ARE...?
ELEKTRA.
THE HAND'S ELEKTRA? I'VE HEARD OF YOU! WHAT AN HONOR THAT YOU'VE COME TO MY ATTENTION.
AND I'VE HEARD OF YOU... REGRETTABLY.
SHUT THIS DOWN.
KRUUNK
NOT POSSIBLE, I'M AFRAID. NOT AS LONG AS I'M ALIVE.
NOT AN ISSUE.

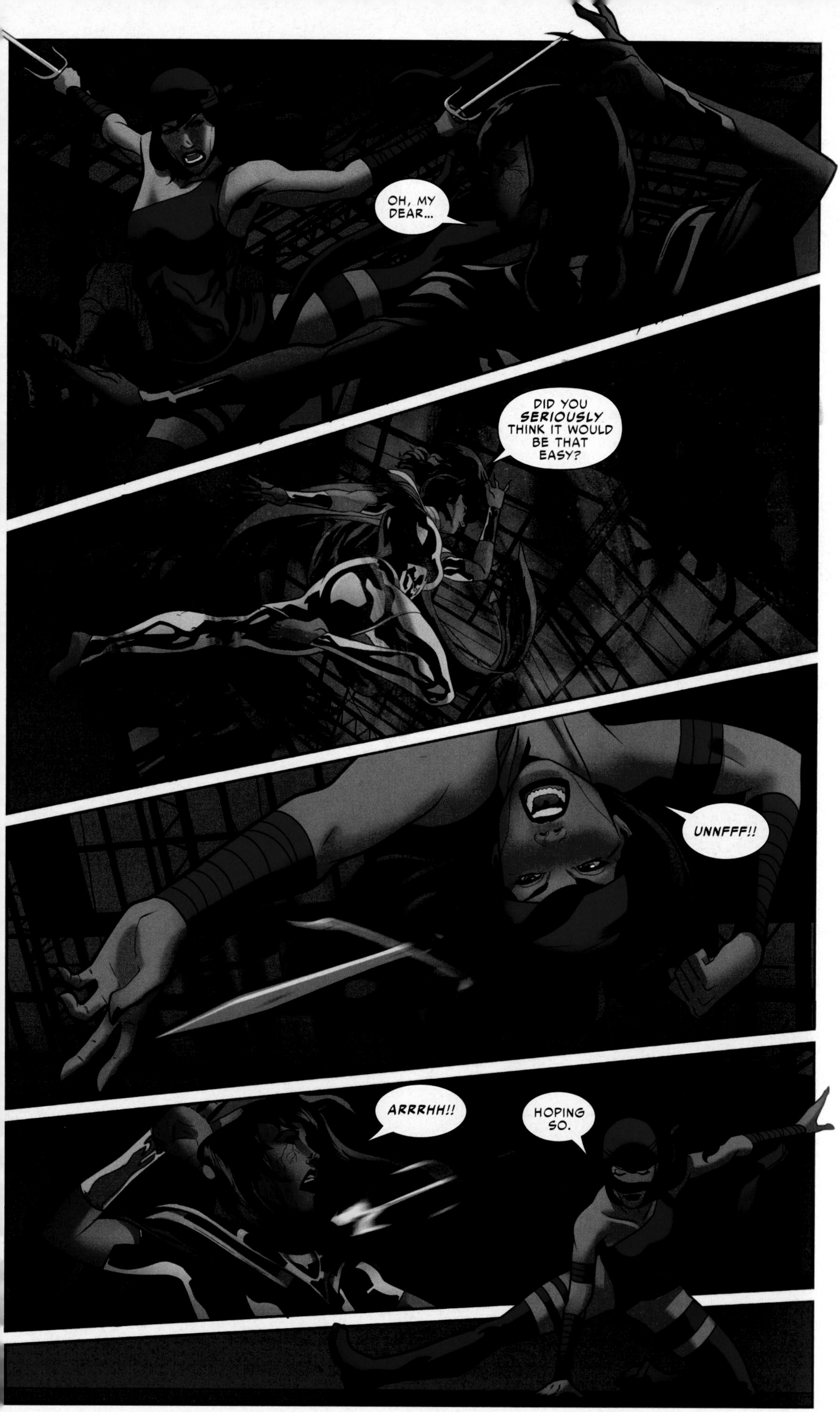

OH, MY DEAR...
DID YOU SERIOUSLY THINK IT WOULD BE THAT EASY?
UNNFFF!!
ARRRHH!!
HOPING SO.

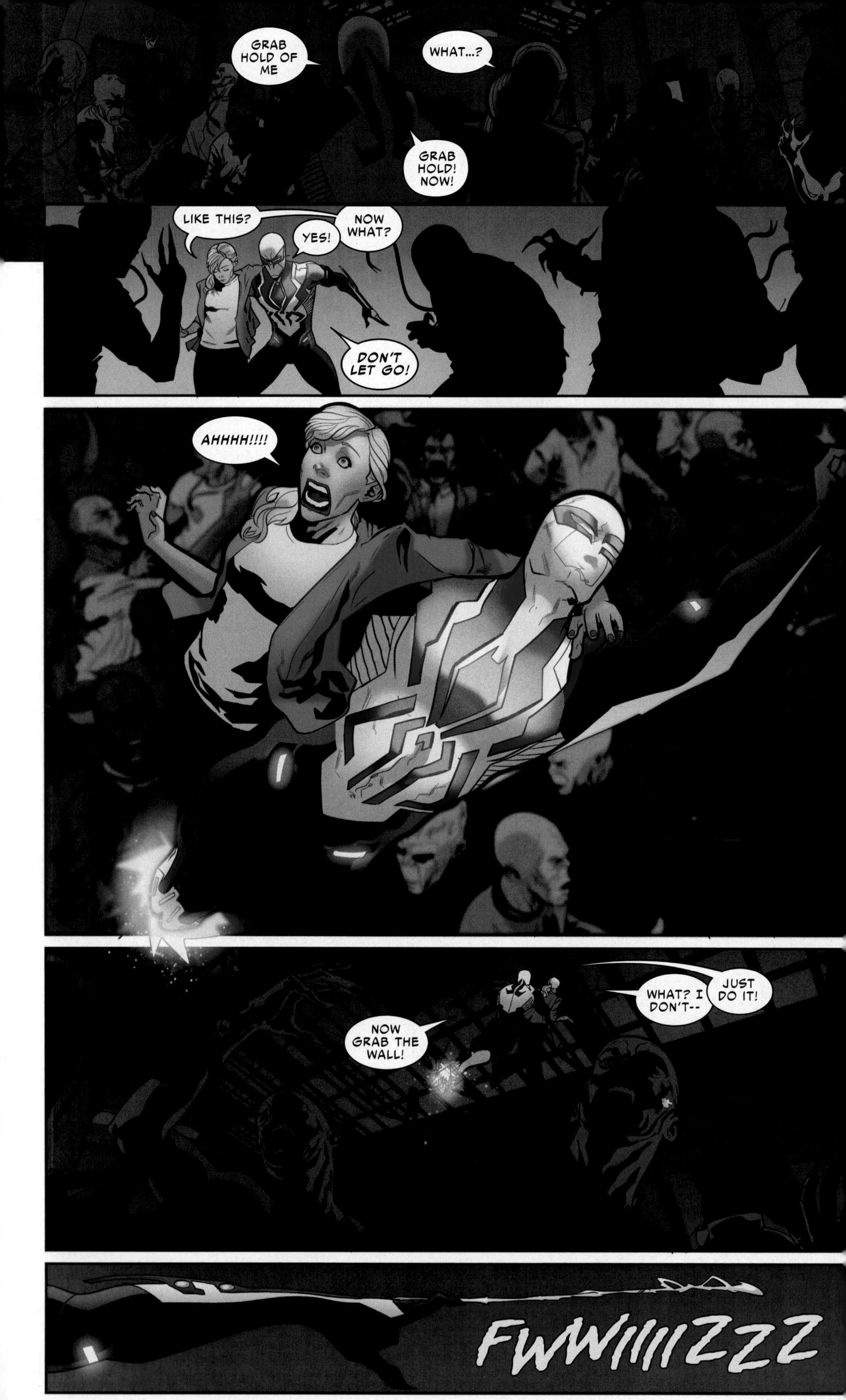
GRAB HOLD OF ME
WHAT...?
GRAB HOLD! NOW!
LIKE THIS?
NOW WHAT?
YES!
DON'T LET GO!
AHHHH!!!!
JUST DO IT!
WHAT? I DON'T--
NOW GRAB THE WALL!
FWWIIIIZZZ

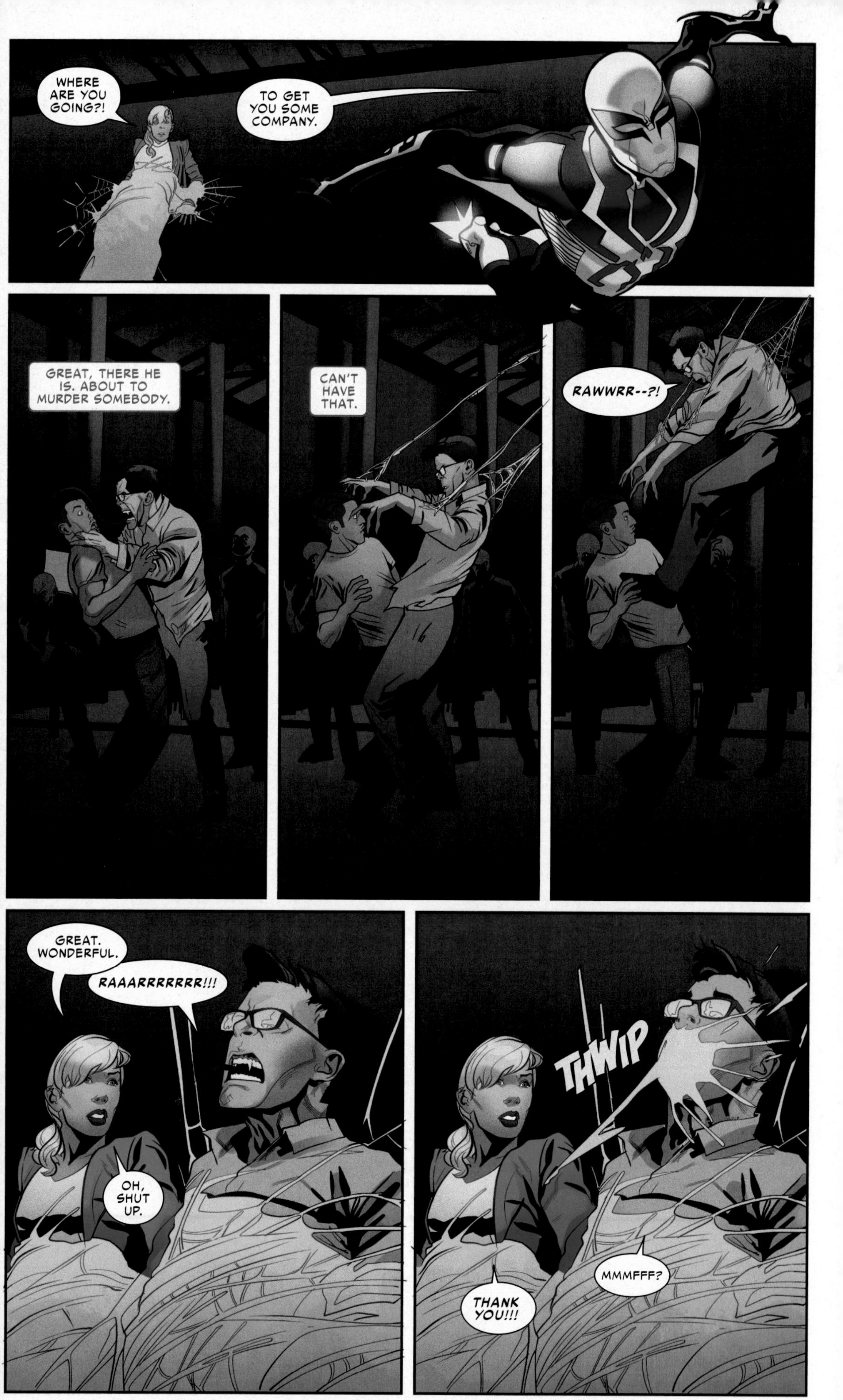
WHERE ARE YOU GOING?!
TO GET YOU SOME COMPANY.
GREAT, THERE HE IS. ABOUT TO MURDER SOMEBODY.
CAN'T HAVE THAT.
RAWWRR--?!
GREAT. WONDERFUL.
RAAARRRRRRR!!!
OH, SHUT UP.
THWIP
MMMFFF?
THANK YOU!!!

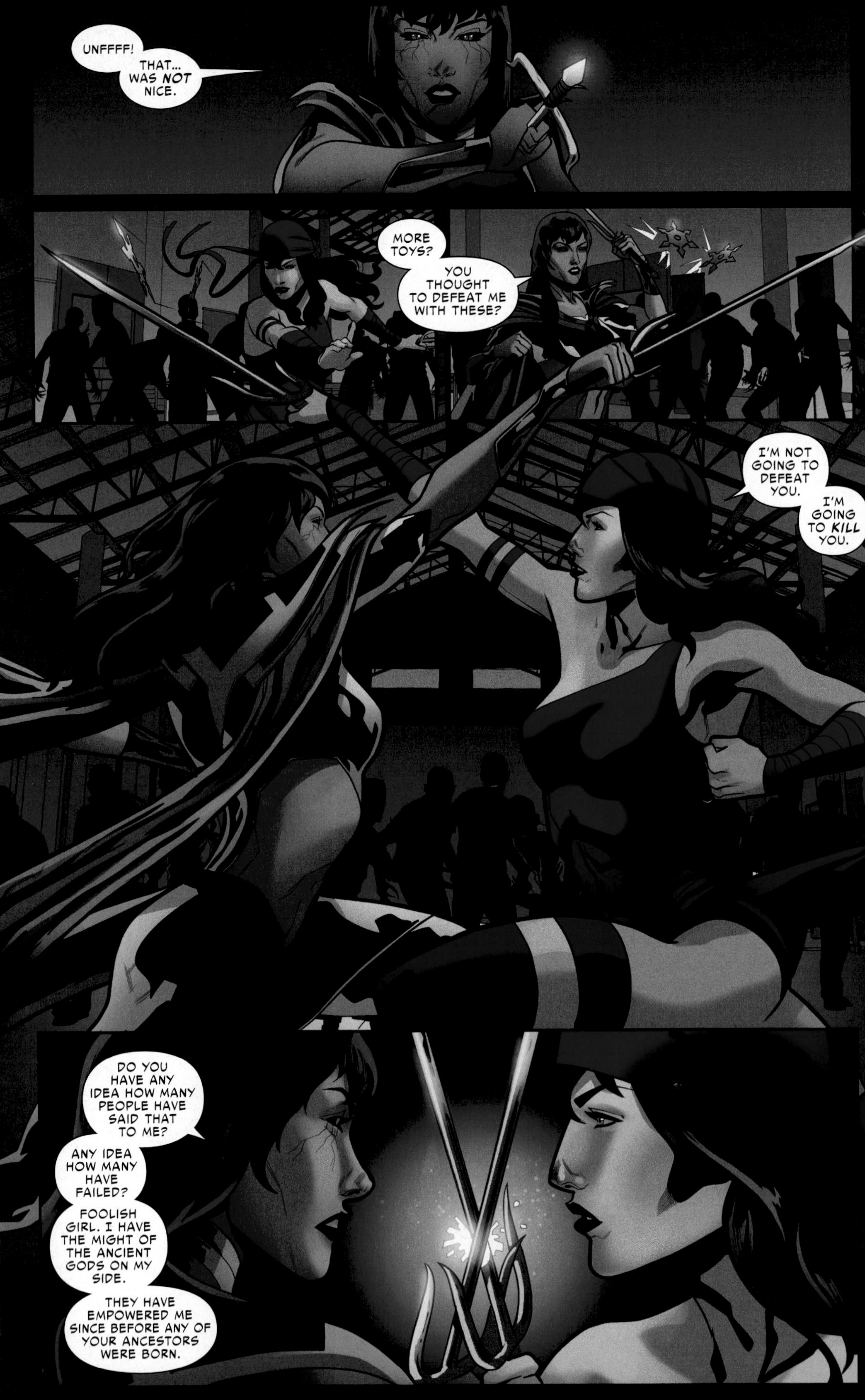

UNFFFF! THAT... WAS NOT NICE.
MORE TOYS?
YOU THOUGHT TO DEFEAT ME WITH THESE?
I'M NOT GOING TO DEFEAT YOU.
I'M GOING TO KILL YOU.
DO YOU HAVE ANY IDEA HOW MANY PEOPLE HAVE SAID THAT TO ME?
ANY IDEA HOW MANY HAVE FAILED?
FOOLISH GIRL. I HAVE THE MIGHT OF THE ANCIENT GODS ON MY SIDE.
THEY HAVE EMPOWERED ME SINCE BEFORE ANY OF YOUR ANCESTORS WERE BORN.

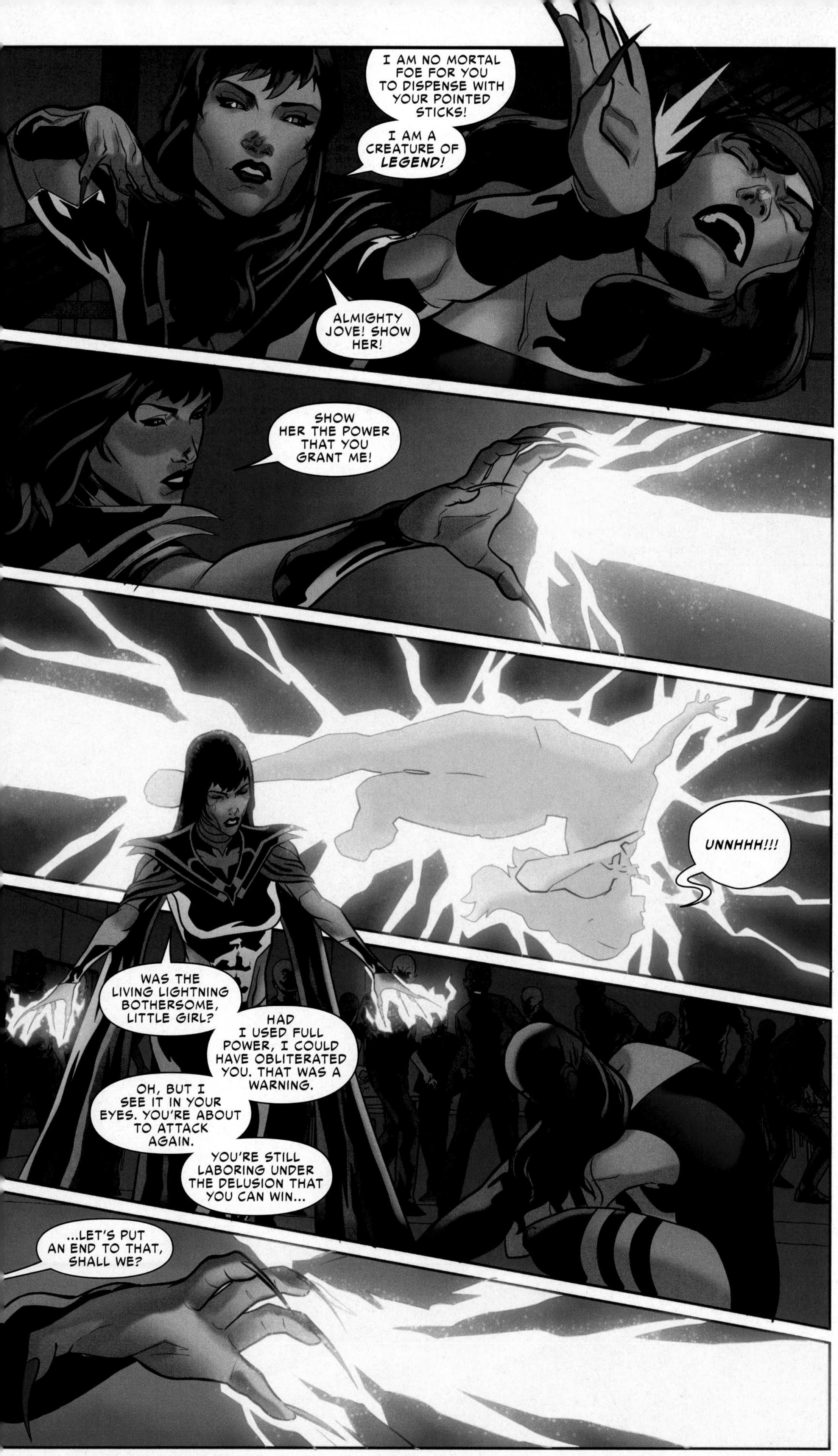
I AM NO MORTAL FOE FOR YOU TO DISPENSE WITH YOUR POINTED STICKS!
I AM A CREATURE OF LEGEND!
ALMIGHTY JOVE! SHOW HER!
SHOW HER THE POWER THAT YOU GRANT ME!
UNNHHH!!!
WAS THE LIVING LIGHTNING BOTHERSOME, LITTLE GIRL?
HAD I USED FULL POWER, I COULD HAVE OBLITERATED YOU. THAT WAS A WARNING.
OH, BUT I SEE IT IN YOUR EYES. YOU'RE ABOUT TO ATTACK AGAIN.
YOU'RE STILL LABORING UNDER THE DELUSION THAT YOU CAN WIN...
...LET'S PUT AN END TO THAT, SHALL WE?

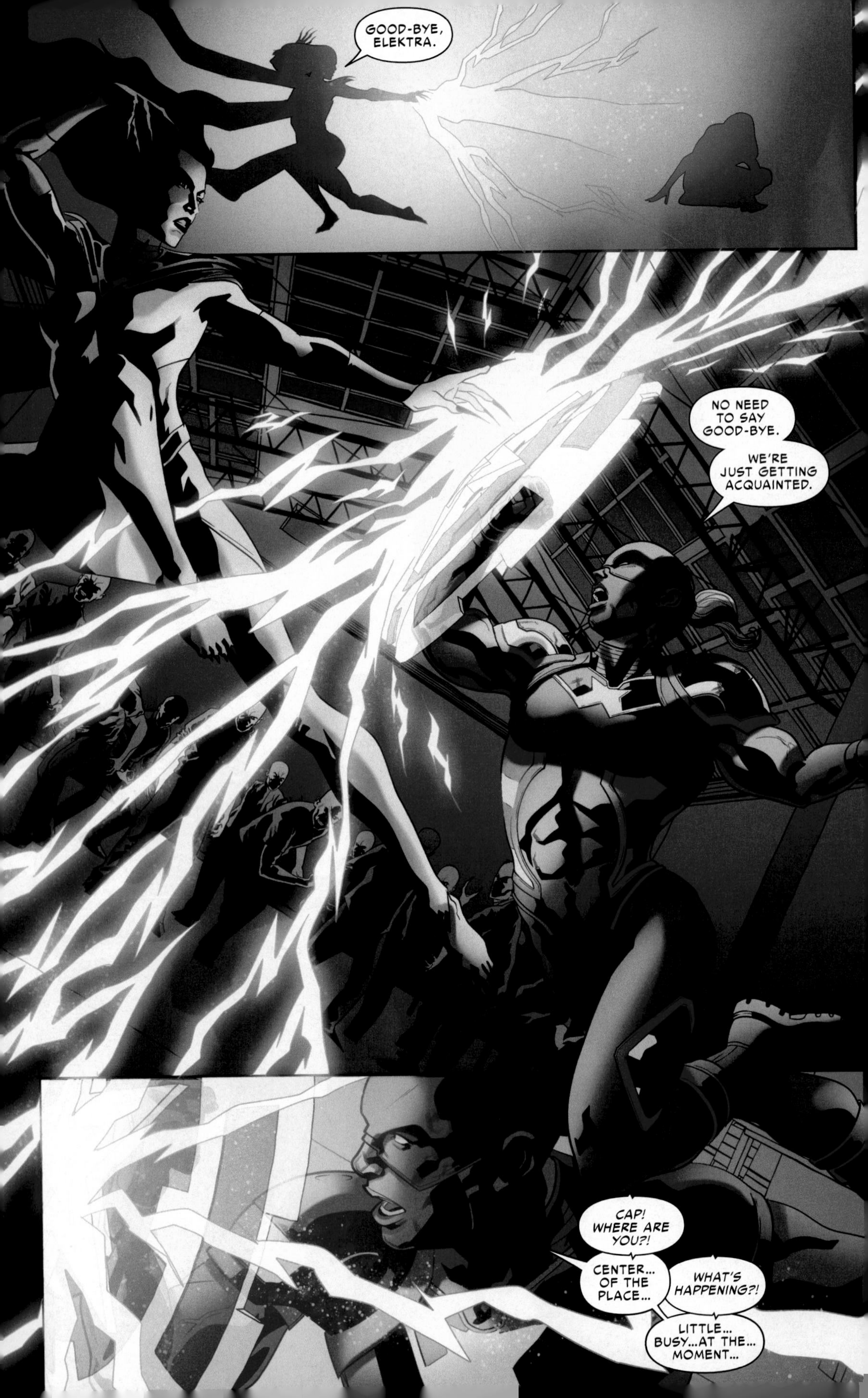
GOOD-BYE, ELEKTRA.
NO NEED TO SAY GOOD-BYE.
WE'RE JUST GETTING ACQUAINTED.
CAP! WHERE ARE YOU?!
CENTER... OF THE PLACE...
WHAT'S HAPPENING?!
LITTLE... BUSY...AT THE... MOMENT...

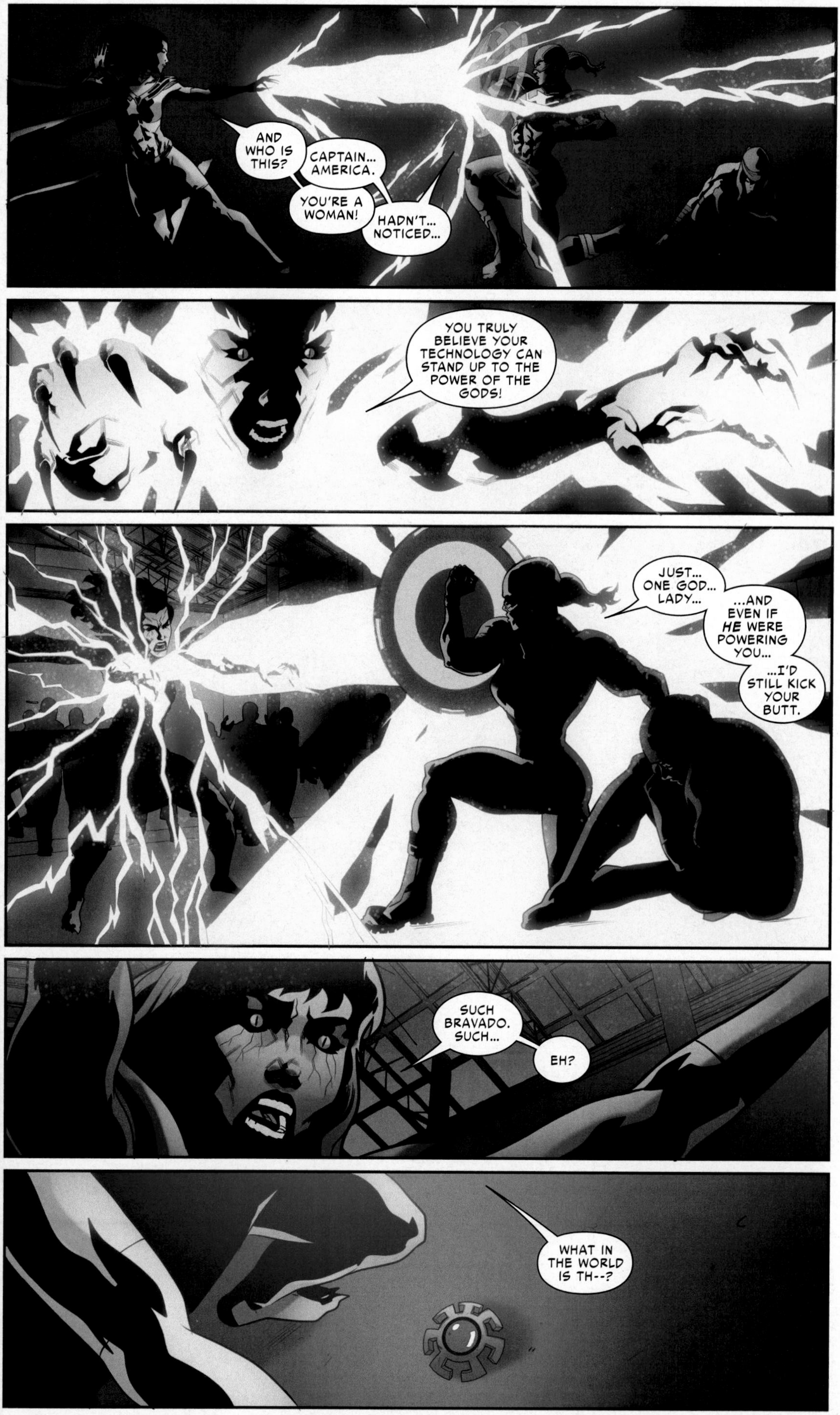
AND WHO IS THIS?
CAPTAIN... AMERICA.
YOU'RE A WOMAN!
HADN'T... NOTICED...
YOU TRULY BELIEVE YOUR TECHNOLOGY CAN STAND UP TO THE POWER OF THE GODS!
JUST... ONE GOD... LADY...
...AND EVEN IF HE WERE POWERING YOU...
...I'D STILL KICK YOUR BUTT.
SUCH BRAVADO. SUCH...
EH?
WHAT IN THE WORLD IS TH--?

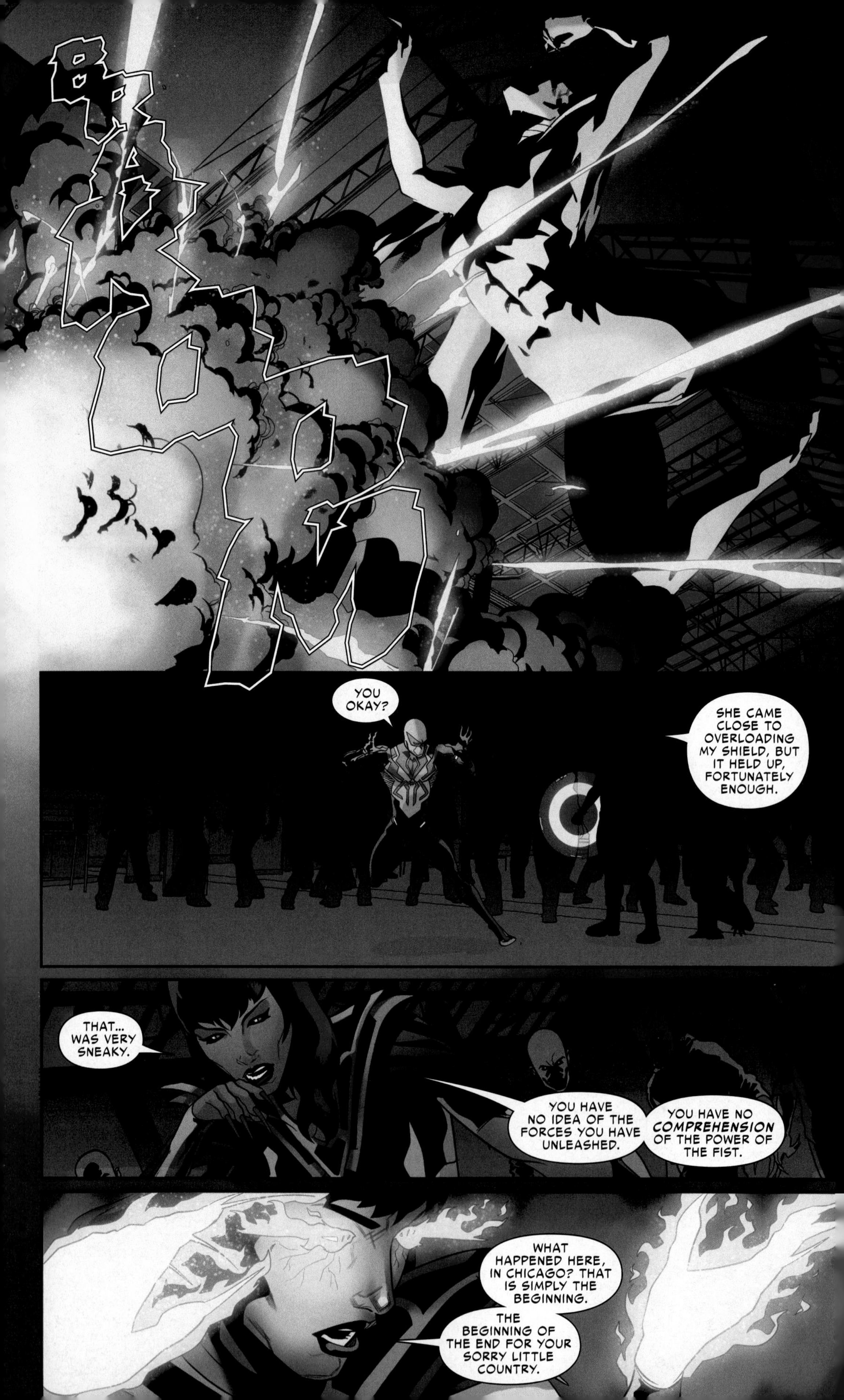
YOU OKAY?
SHE CAME CLOSE TO OVERLOADING MY SHIELD, BUT IT HELD UP, FORTUNATELY ENOUGH.
THAT... WAS VERY SNEAKY.
YOU HAVE NO IDEA OF THE FORCES YOU HAVE UNLEASHED.
YOU HAVE NO COMPREHENSION OF THE POWER OF THE FIST.
WHAT HAPPENED HERE, IN CHICAGO? THAT IS SIMPLY THE BEGINNING.
THE BEGINNING OF THE END FOR YOUR SORRY LITTLE COUNTRY.

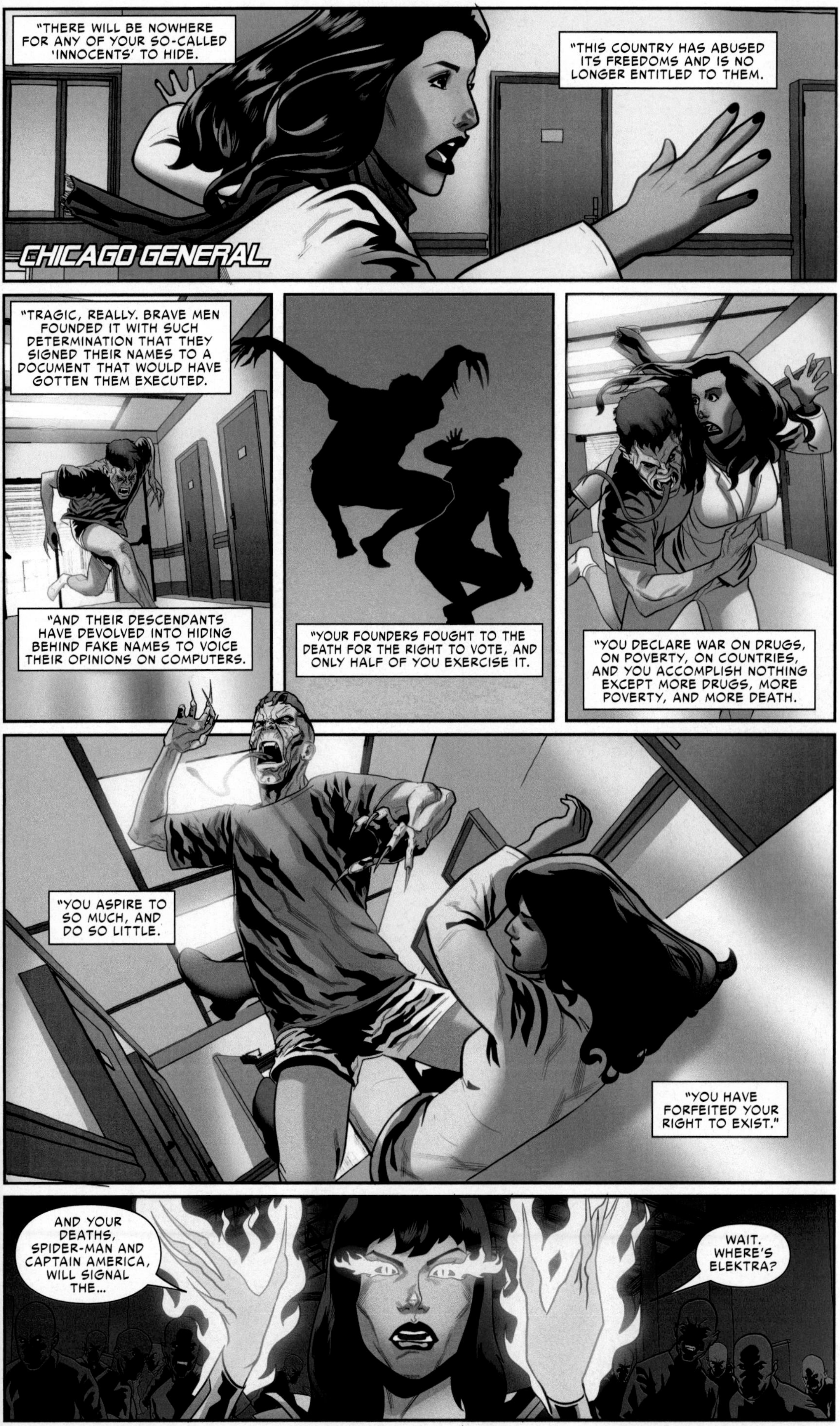
"THERE WILL BE NOWHERE FOR ANY OF YOUR SO-CALLED 'INNOCENTS' TO HIDE.
"THIS COUNTRY HAS ABUSED ITS FREEDOMS AND IS NO LONGER ENTITLED TO THEM.
CHICAGO GENERAL.
"TRAGIC, REALLY. BRAVE MEN FOUNDED IT WITH SUCH DETERMINATION THAT THEY SIGNED THEIR NAMES TO A DOCUMENT THAT WOULD HAVE GOTTEN THEM EXECUTED.
"AND THEIR DESCENDANTS HAVE DEVOLVED INTO HIDING BEHIND FAKE NAMES TO VOICE THEIR OPINIONS ON COMPUTERS.
"YOUR FOUNDERS FOUGHT TO THE DEATH FOR THE RIGHT TO VOTE, AND ONLY HALF OF YOU EXERCISE IT.
"YOU DECLARE WAR ON DRUGS, ON POVERTY, ON COUNTRIES, AND YOU ACCOMPLISH NOTHING EXCEPT MORE DRUGS, MORE POVERTY, AND MORE DEATH.
"YOU ASPIRE TO SO MUCH, AND DO SO LITTLE.
"YOU HAVE FORFEITED YOUR RIGHT TO EXIST."
AND YOUR DEATHS, SPIDER-MAN AND CAPTAIN AMERICA, WILL SIGNAL THE...
WAIT. WHERE'S ELEKTRA?

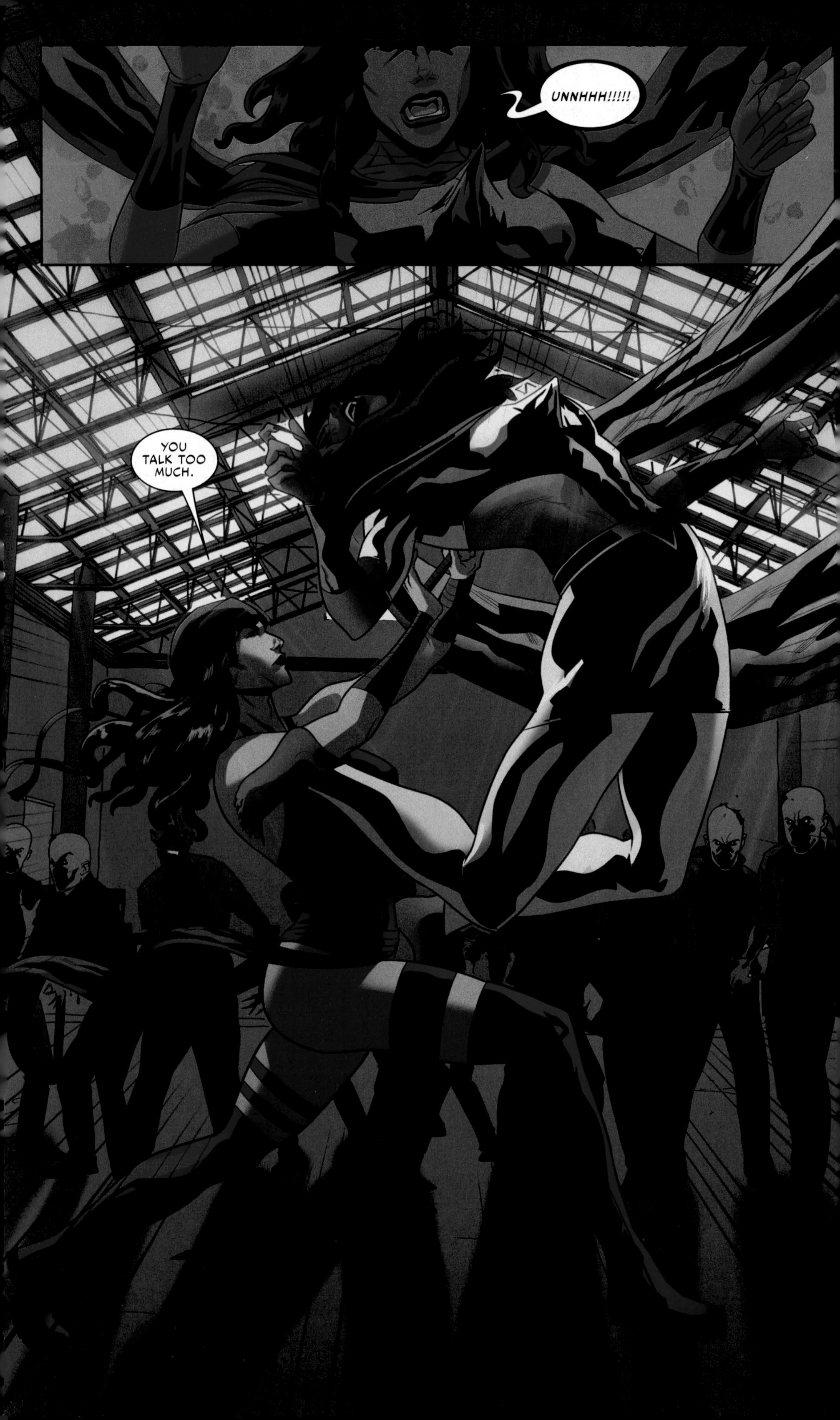
UNNHHH!!!!!
YOU TALK TOO MUCH.

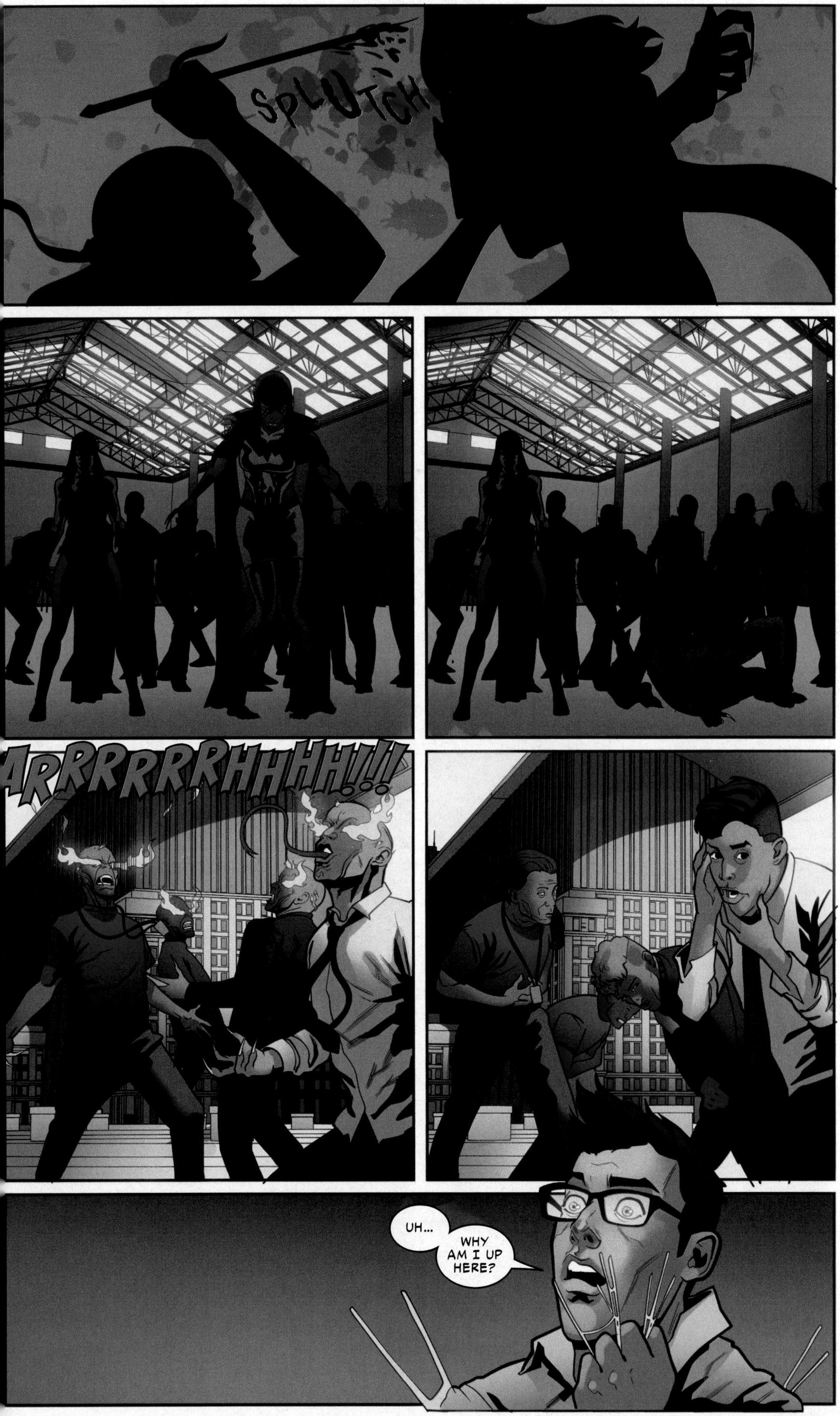
SPLUTCH
ARRRRRRHHHH!!!
UH...
WHY AM I UP HERE?

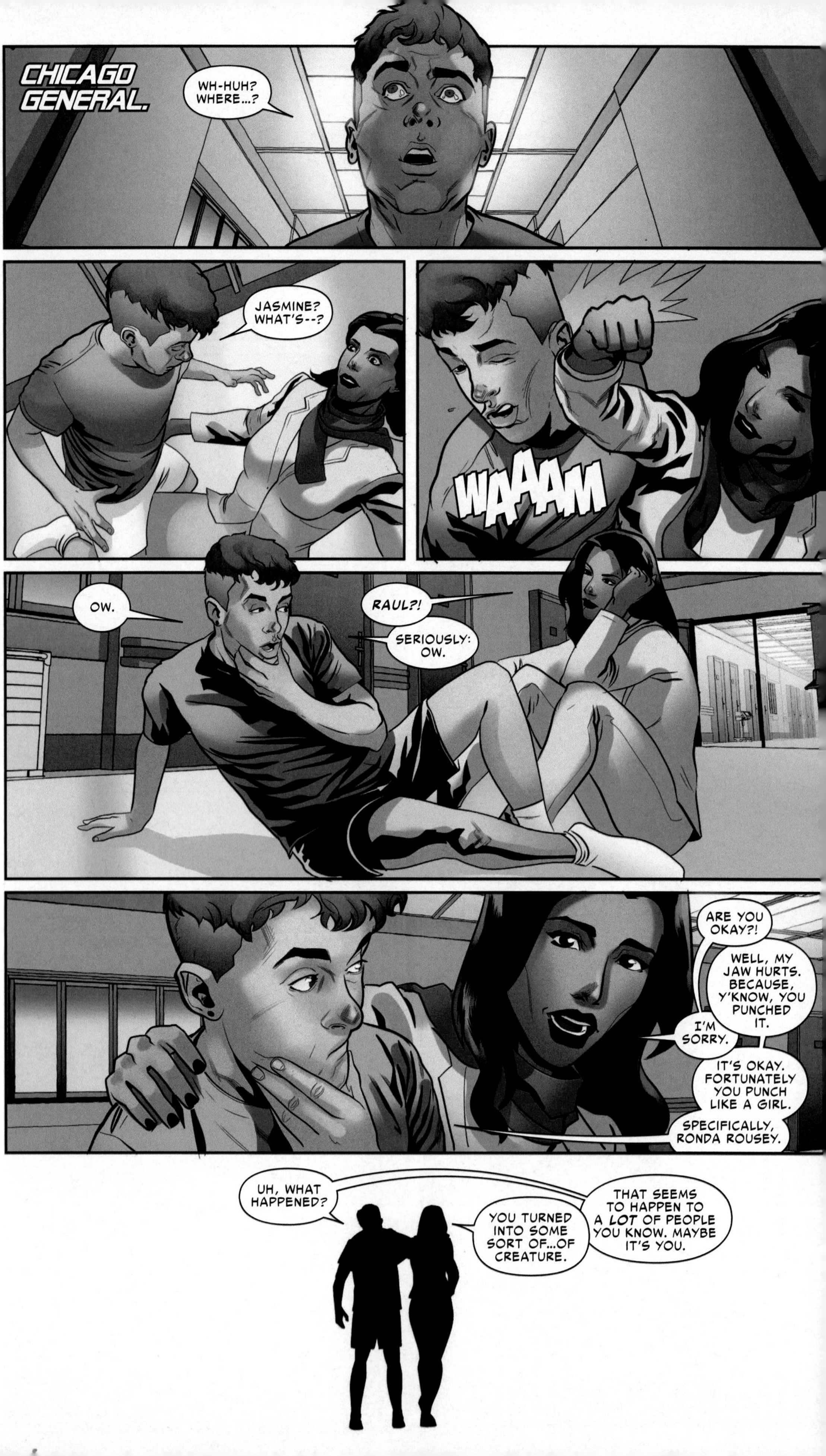
CHICAGO GENERAL.
WH-HUH? WHERE...?
JASMINE? WHAT'S--?
WAAAM
OW.
RAUL?!
SERIOUSLY: OW.
ARE YOU OKAY?!
WELL, MY JAW HURTS. BECAUSE, Y'KNOW, YOU PUNCHED IT.
I'M SORRY.
IT'S OKAY. FORTUNATELY YOU PUNCH LIKE A GIRL.
SPECIFICALLY, RONDA ROUSEY.
UH, WHAT HAPPENED?
YOU TURNED INTO SOME SORT OF...OF CREATURE.
THAT SEEMS TO HAPPEN TO A LOT OF PEOPLE YOU KNOW. MAYBE IT'S YOU.

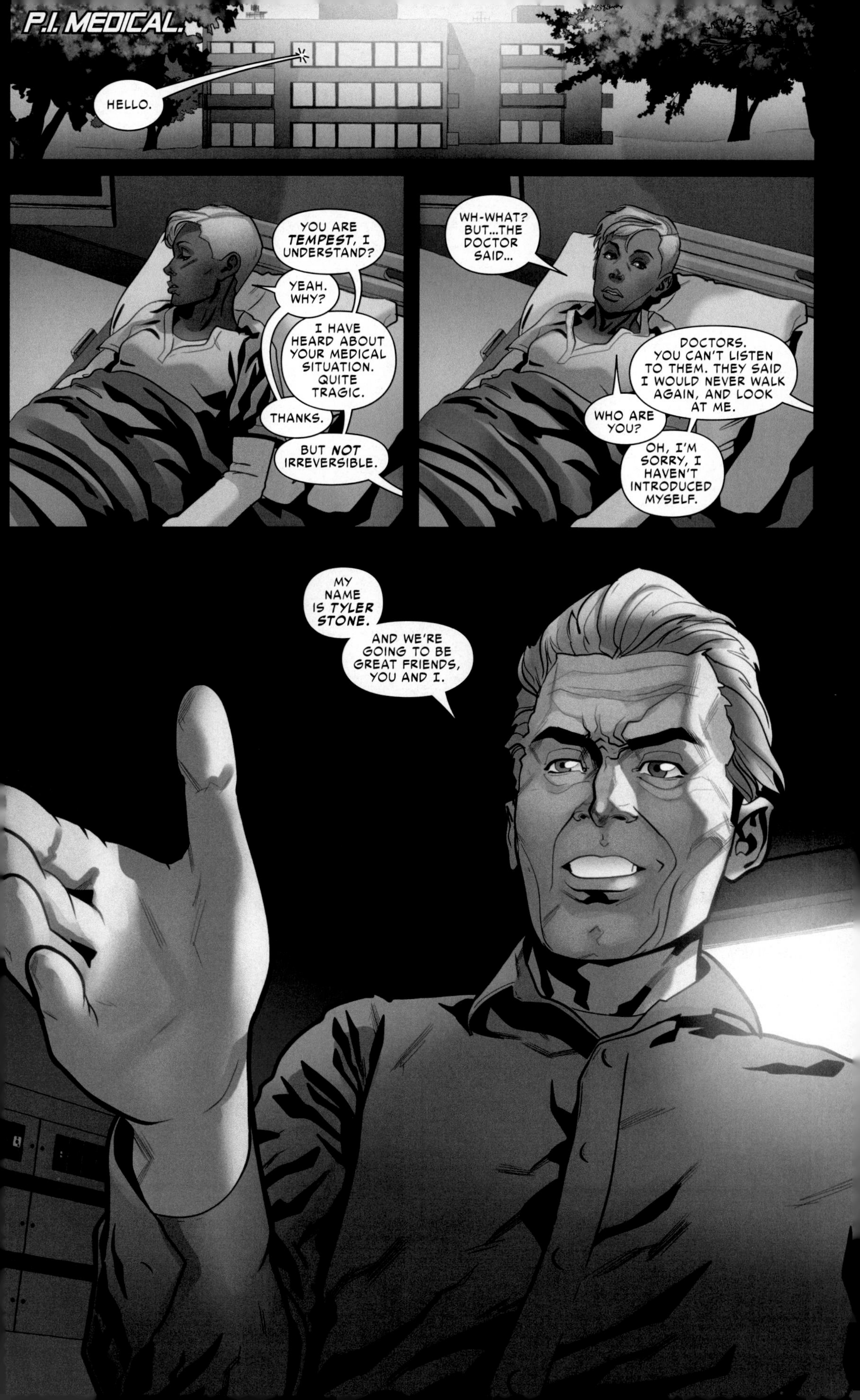
P.I. MEDICAL.
HELLO.
YOU ARE TEMPEST, I UNDERSTAND?
YEAH. WHY?
I HAVE HEARD ABOUT YOUR MEDICAL SITUATION. QUITE TRAGIC.
THANKS.
BUT NOT IRREVERSIBLE.
WH-WHAT? BUT...THE DOCTOR SAID...
DOCTORS. YOU CAN'T LISTEN TO THEM. THEY SAID I WOULD NEVER WALK AGAIN, AND LOOK AT ME.
WHO ARE YOU?
OH, I'M SORRY, I HAVEN'T INTRODUCED MYSELF.
MY NAME IS TYLER STONE.
AND WE'RE GOING TO BE GREAT FRIENDS, YOU AND I.

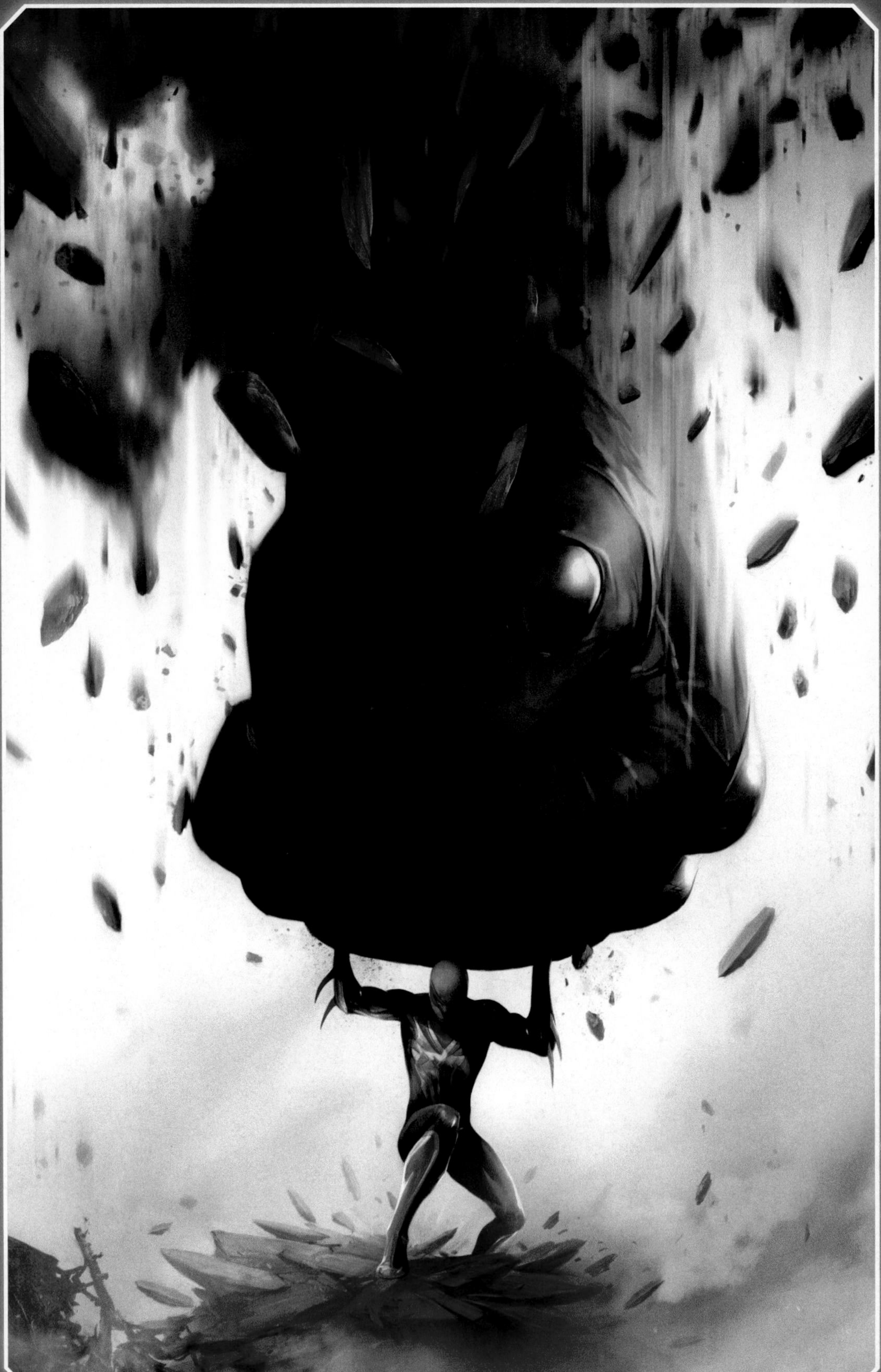

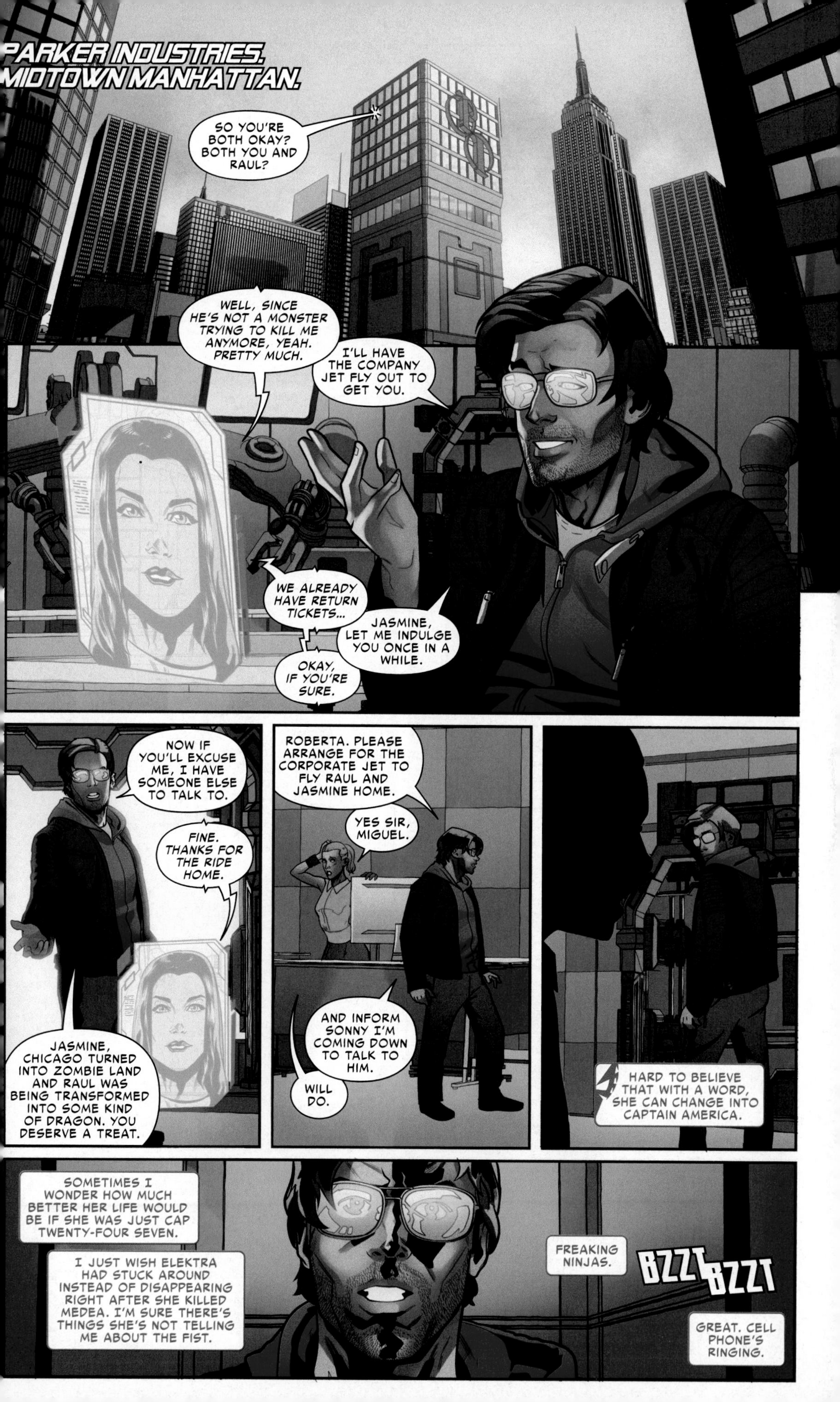
PARKER INDUSTRIES. MIDTOWN MANHATTAN.
SO YOU'RE BOTH OKAY? BOTH YOU AND RAUL?
WELL, SINCE HE'S NOT A MONSTER TRYING TO KILL ME ANYMORE, YEAH. PRETTY MUCH.
I'LL HAVE THE COMPANY JET FLY OUT TO GET YOU.
WE ALREADY HAVE RETURN TICKETS...
JASMINE, LET ME INDULGE YOU ONCE IN A WHILE.
OKAY, IF YOU'RE SURE.
NOW IF YOU'LL EXCUSE ME, I HAVE SOMEONE ELSE TO TALK TO.
FINE. THANKS FOR THE RIDE HOME.
JASMINE, CHICAGO TURNED INTO ZOMBIE LAND AND RAUL WAS BEING TRANSFORMED INTO SOME KIND OF DRAGON. YOU DESERVE A TREAT.
ROBERTA. PLEASE ARRANGE FOR THE CORPORATE JET TO FLY RAUL AND JASMINE HOME.
YES SIR, MIGUEL.
AND INFORM SONNY I'M COMING DOWN TO TALK TO HIM.
WILL DO.
HARD TO BELIEVE THAT WITH A WORD, SHE CAN CHANGE INTO CAPTAIN AMERICA.
SOMETIMES I WONDER HOW MUCH BETTER HER LIFE WOULD BE IF SHE WAS JUST CAP TWENTY-FOUR SEVEN.
I JUST WISH ELEKTRA HAD STUCK AROUND INSTEAD OF DISAPPEARING RIGHT AFTER SHE KILLED MEDEA. I'M SURE THERE'S THINGS SHE'S NOT TELLING ME ABOUT THE FIST.
FREAKING NINJAS.
BZZT BZZT
GREAT. CELL PHONE'S RINGING.

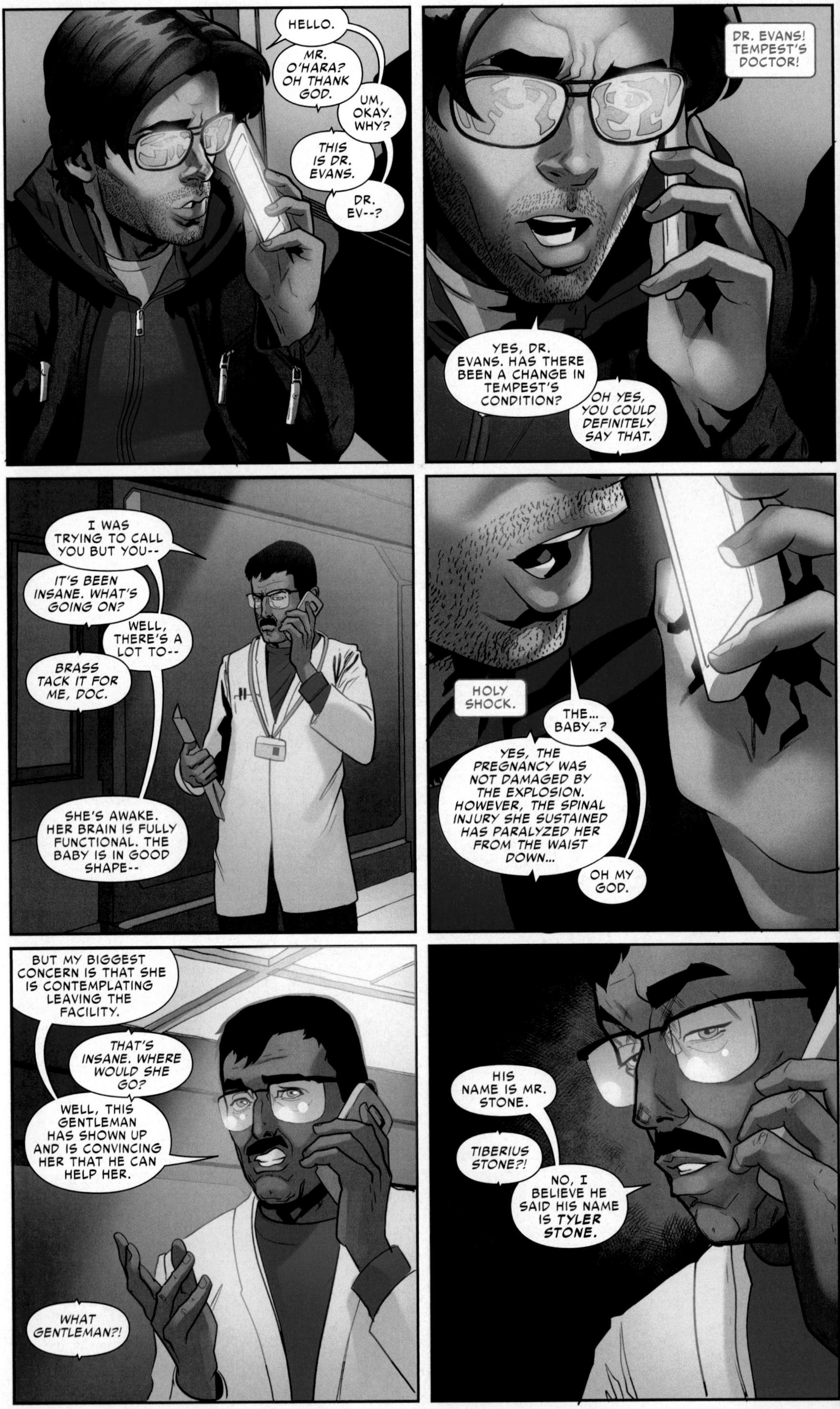
HELLO.
MR. O'HARA? OH THANK GOD.
UM, OKAY. WHY?
THIS IS DR. EVANS.
DR. EV--?
DR. EVANS! TEMPEST'S DOCTOR!
YES, DR. EVANS. HAS THERE BEEN A CHANGE IN TEMPEST'S CONDITION?
OH YES, YOU COULD DEFINITELY SAY THAT.
I WAS TRYING TO CALL YOU BUT YOU--
IT'S BEEN INSANE. WHAT'S GOING ON?
WELL, THERE'S A LOT TO--
BRASS TACK IT FOR ME, DOC.
SHE'S AWAKE. HER BRAIN IS FULLY FUNCTIONAL. THE BABY IS IN GOOD SHAPE--
HOLY SHOCK.
THE... BABY...?
YES, THE PREGNANCY WAS NOT DAMAGED BY THE EXPLOSION. HOWEVER, THE SPINAL INJURY SHE SUSTAINED HAS PARALYZED HER FROM THE WAIST DOWN...
OH MY GOD.
BUT MY BIGGEST CONCERN IS THAT SHE IS CONTEMPLATING LEAVING THE FACILITY.
THAT'S INSANE. WHERE WOULD SHE GO?
WELL, THIS GENTLEMAN HAS SHOWN UP AND IS CONVINCING HER THAT HE CAN HELP HER.
WHAT GENTLEMAN?!
HIS NAME IS MR. STONE.
TIBERIUS STONE?!
NO, I BELIEVE HE SAID HIS NAME IS TYLER STONE.

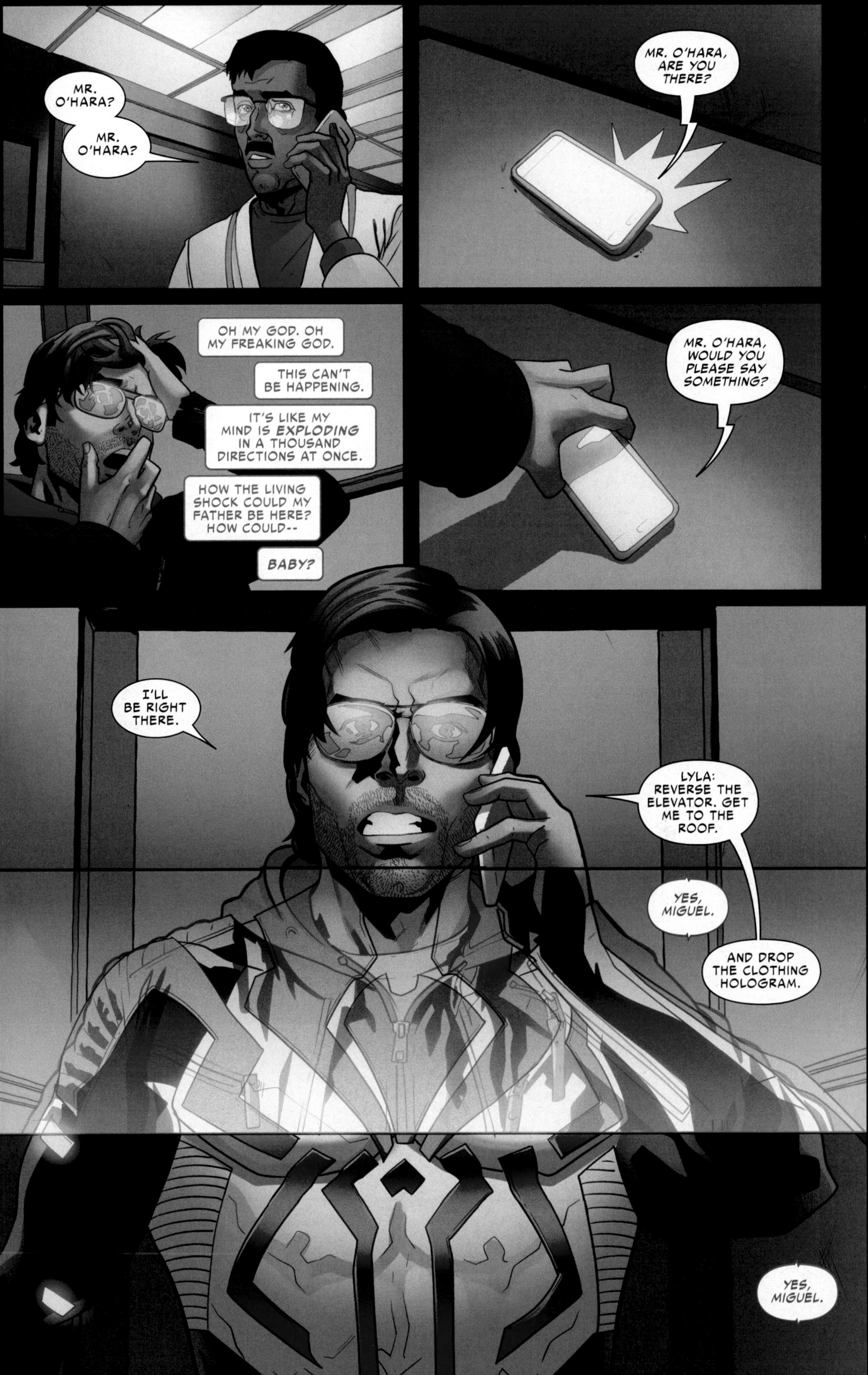
MR. O'HARA?
MR. O'HARA?
MR. O'HARA, ARE YOU THERE?
OH MY GOD. OH MY FREAKING GOD.
THIS CAN'T BE HAPPENING.
IT'S LIKE MY MIND IS EXPLODING IN A THOUSAND DIRECTIONS AT ONCE.
HOW THE LIVING SHOCK COULD MY FATHER BE HERE? HOW COULD--
BABY?
MR. O'HARA, WOULD YOU PLEASE SAY SOMETHING?
I'LL BE RIGHT THERE.
LYLA: REVERSE THE ELEVATOR. GET ME TO THE ROOF.
YES, MIGUEL.
AND DROP THE CLOTHING HOLOGRAM.
YES, MIGUEL.

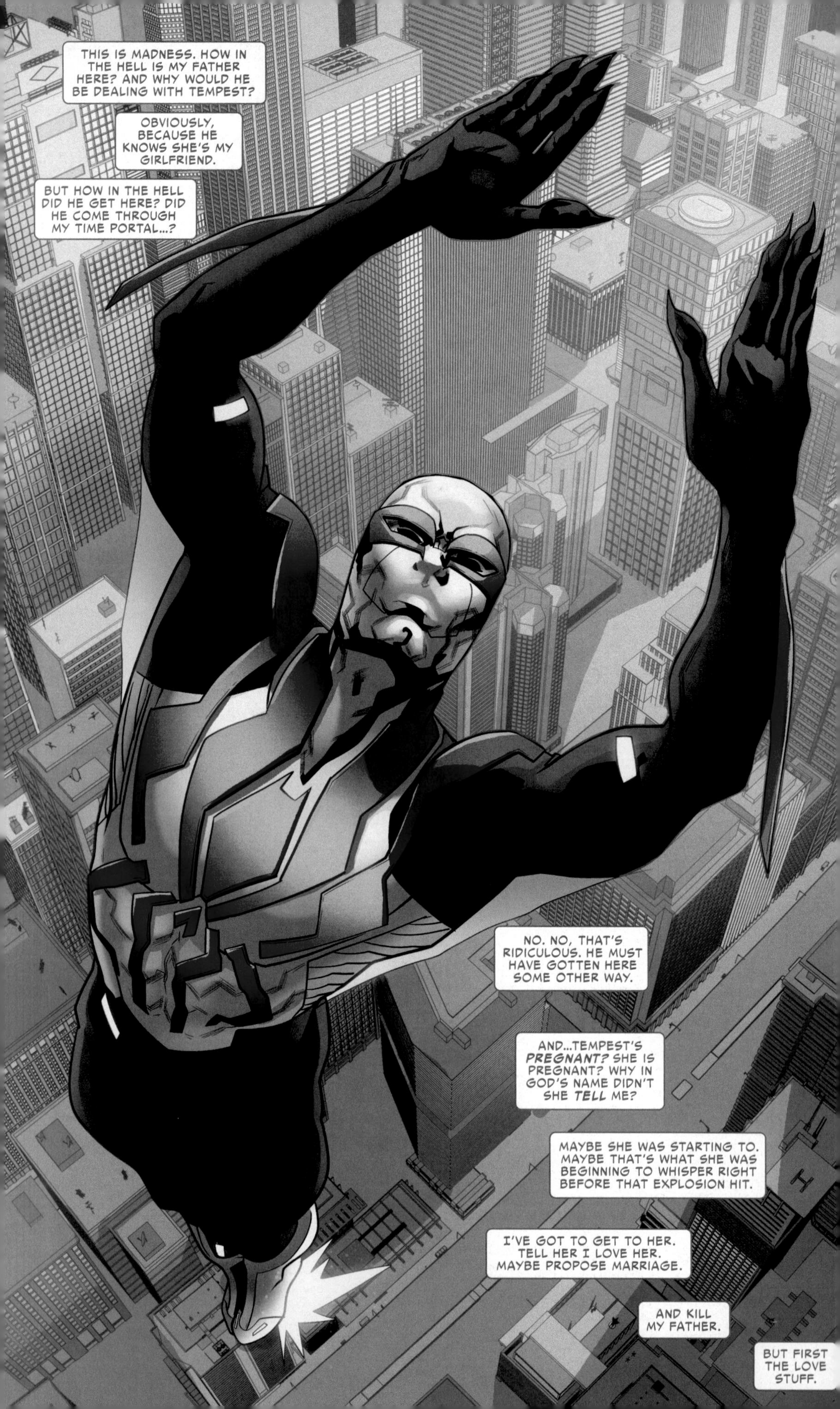

THIS IS MADNESS. HOW IN THE HELL IS MY FATHER HERE? AND WHY WOULD HE BE DEALING WITH TEMPEST?
OBVIOUSLY, BECAUSE HE KNOWS SHE'S MY GIRLFRIEND.
BUT HOW IN THE HELL DID HE GET HERE? DID HE COME THROUGH MY TIME PORTAL...?
NO. NO, THAT'S RIDICULOUS. HE MUST HAVE GOTTEN HERE SOME OTHER WAY.
AND...TEMPEST'S *PREGNANT?* SHE IS PREGNANT? WHY IN GOD'S NAME DIDN'T SHE *TELL* ME?
MAYBE SHE WAS STARTING TO. MAYBE THAT'S WHAT SHE WAS BEGINNING TO WHISPER RIGHT BEFORE THAT EXPLOSION HIT.
I'VE GOT TO GET TO HER. TELL HER I LOVE HER. MAYBE PROPOSE MARRIAGE.
AND KILL MY FATHER.
BUT FIRST THE LOVE STUFF.

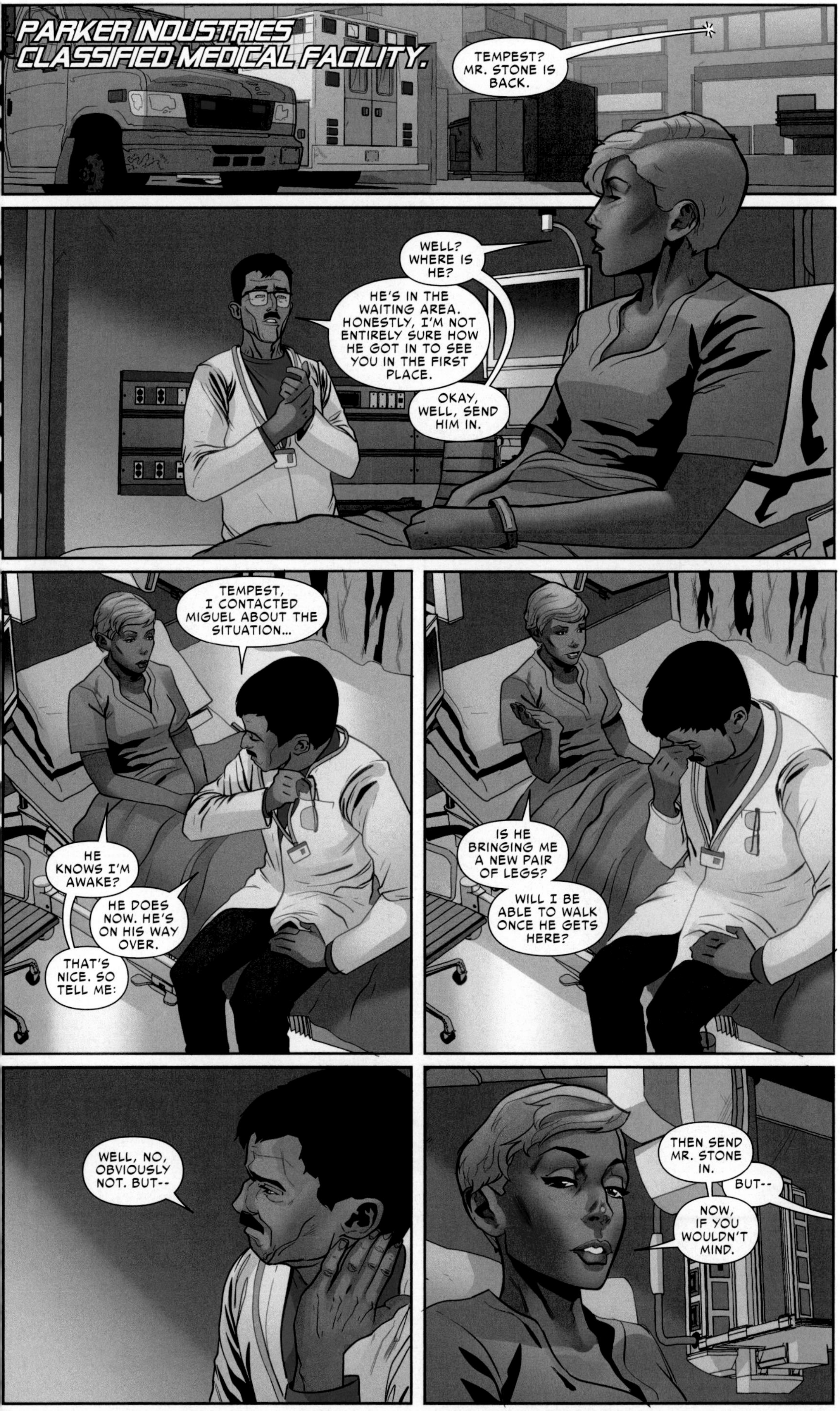
PARKER INDUSTRIES CLASSIFIED MEDICAL FACILITY.
TEMPEST? MR. STONE IS BACK.
WELL? WHERE IS HE?
HE'S IN THE WAITING AREA. HONESTLY, I'M NOT ENTIRELY SURE HOW HE GOT IN TO SEE YOU IN THE FIRST PLACE.
OKAY, WELL, SEND HIM IN.
TEMPEST, I CONTACTED MIGUEL ABOUT THE SITUATION...
HE KNOWS I'M AWAKE?
HE DOES NOW. HE'S ON HIS WAY OVER.
THAT'S NICE. SO TELL ME:
IS HE BRINGING ME A NEW PAIR OF LEGS?
WILL I BE ABLE TO WALK ONCE HE GETS HERE?
WELL, NO, OBVIOUSLY NOT. BUT--
THEN SEND MR. STONE IN.
BUT--
NOW, IF YOU WOULDN'T MIND.

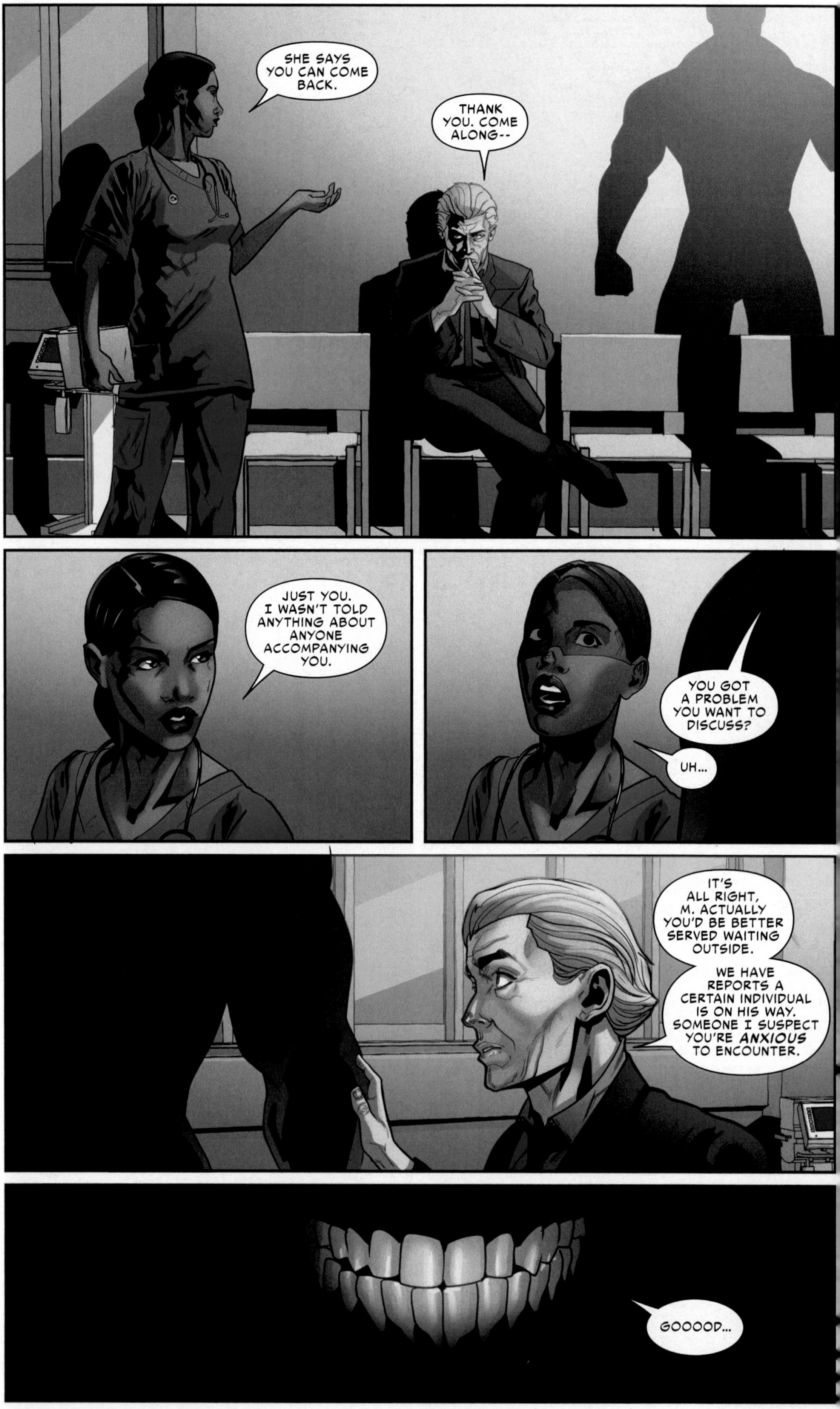
SHE SAYS YOU CAN COME BACK.
THANK YOU. COME ALONG--
JUST YOU. I WASN'T TOLD ANYTHING ABOUT ANYONE ACCOMPANYING YOU.
YOU GOT A PROBLEM YOU WANT TO DISCUSS?
UH...
IT'S ALL RIGHT, M. ACTUALLY YOU'D BE BETTER SERVED WAITING OUTSIDE.
WE HAVE REPORTS A CERTAIN INDIVIDUAL IS ON HIS WAY. SOMEONE I SUSPECT YOU'RE *ANXIOUS* TO ENCOUNTER.
GOOOOD...

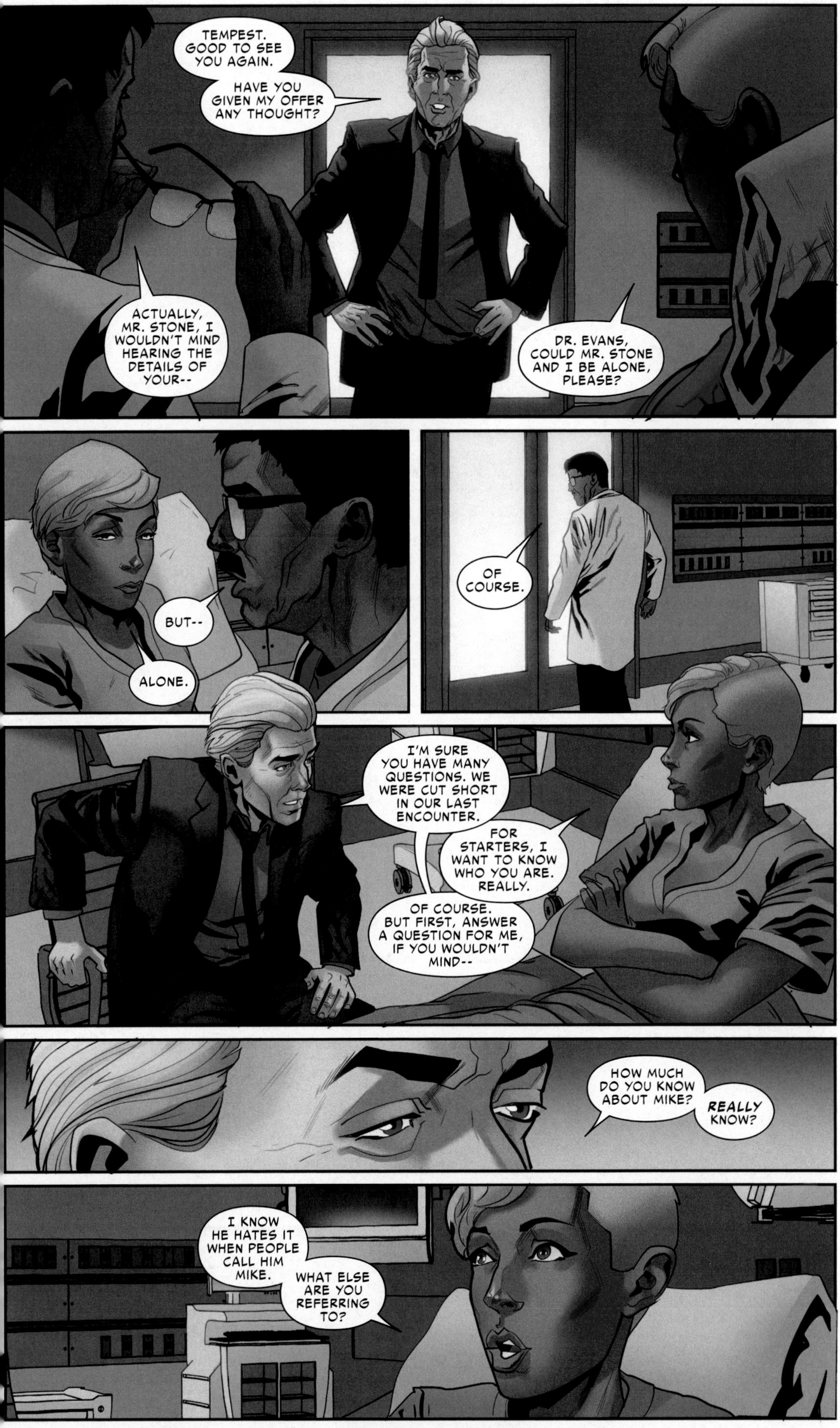
TEMPEST. GOOD TO SEE YOU AGAIN.
HAVE YOU GIVEN MY OFFER ANY THOUGHT?
ACTUALLY, MR. STONE, I WOULDN'T MIND HEARING THE DETAILS OF YOUR--
DR. EVANS, COULD MR. STONE AND I BE ALONE, PLEASE?
BUT--
ALONE.
OF COURSE.
I'M SURE YOU HAVE MANY QUESTIONS. WE WERE CUT SHORT IN OUR LAST ENCOUNTER.
FOR STARTERS, I WANT TO KNOW WHO YOU ARE. REALLY.
OF COURSE. BUT FIRST, ANSWER A QUESTION FOR ME, IF YOU WOULDN'T MIND--
HOW MUCH DO YOU KNOW ABOUT MIKE?
REALLY KNOW?
I KNOW HE HATES IT WHEN PEOPLE CALL HIM MIKE.
WHAT ELSE ARE YOU REFERRING TO?

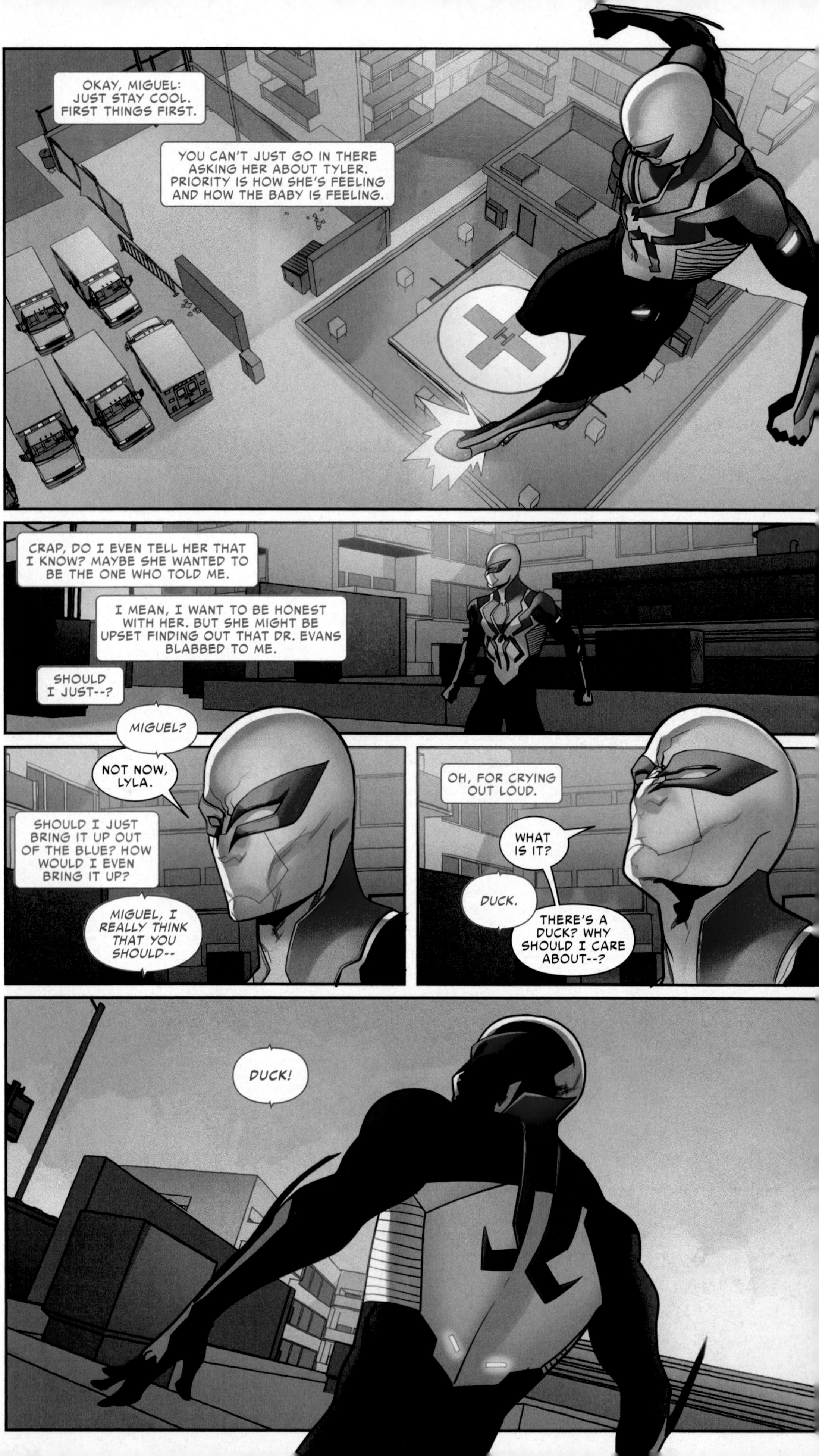
OKAY, MIGUEL: JUST STAY COOL. FIRST THINGS FIRST.
YOU CAN'T JUST GO IN THERE ASKING HER ABOUT TYLER. PRIORITY IS HOW SHE'S FEELING AND HOW THE BABY IS FEELING.
CRAP, DO I EVEN TELL HER THAT I KNOW? MAYBE SHE WANTED TO BE THE ONE WHO TOLD ME.
I MEAN, I WANT TO BE HONEST WITH HER. BUT SHE MIGHT BE UPSET FINDING OUT THAT DR. EVANS BLABBED TO ME.
SHOULD I JUST--?
MIGUEL?
NOT NOW, LYLA.
SHOULD I JUST BRING IT UP OUT OF THE BLUE? HOW WOULD I EVEN BRING IT UP?
MIGUEL, I REALLY THINK THAT YOU SHOULD--
OH, FOR CRYING OUT LOUD.
WHAT IS IT?
DUCK.
THERE'S A DUCK? WHY SHOULD I CARE ABOUT--?
DUCK!

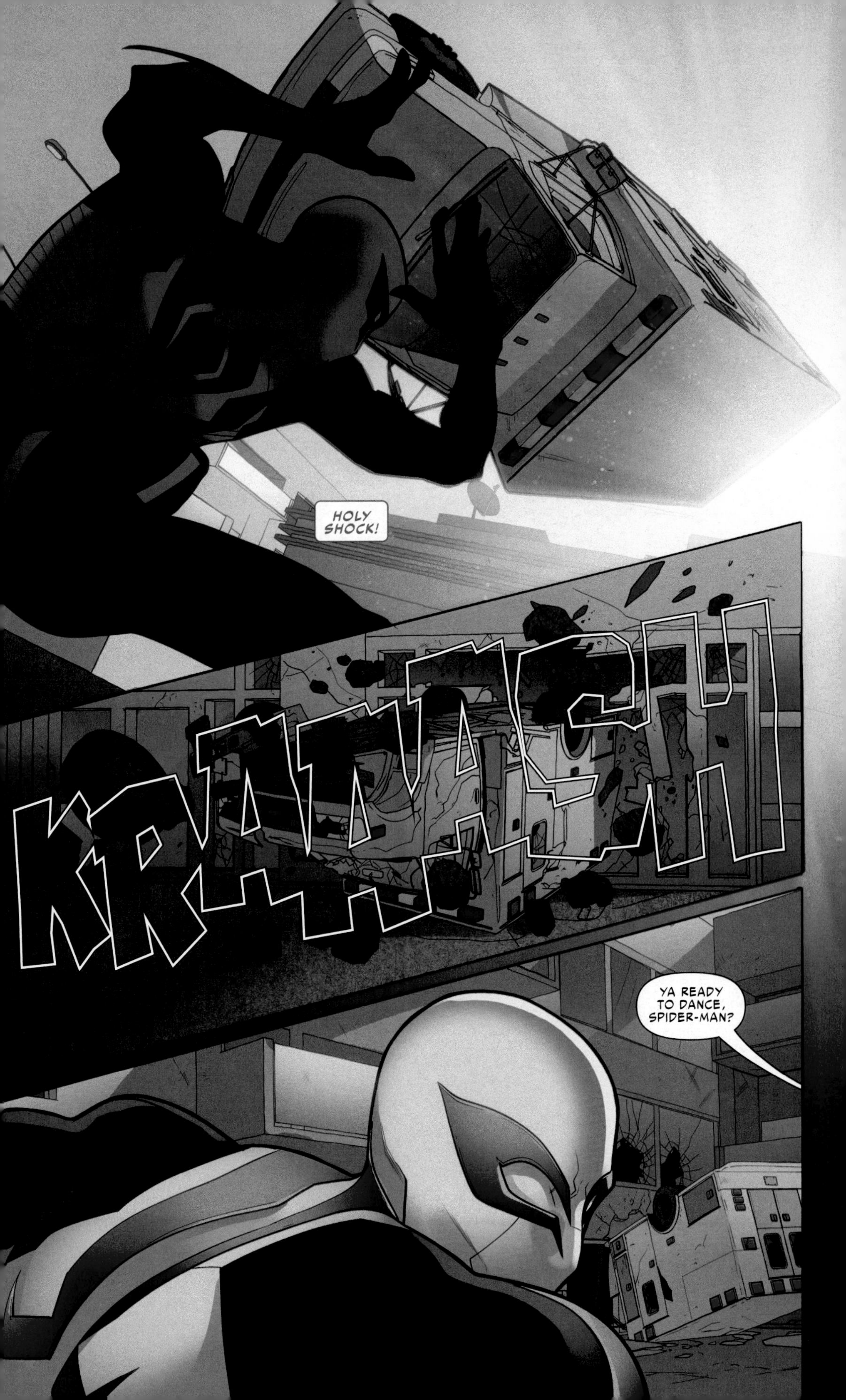
HOLY SHOCK!
KRAAASH
YA READY TO DANCE, SPIDER-MAN?

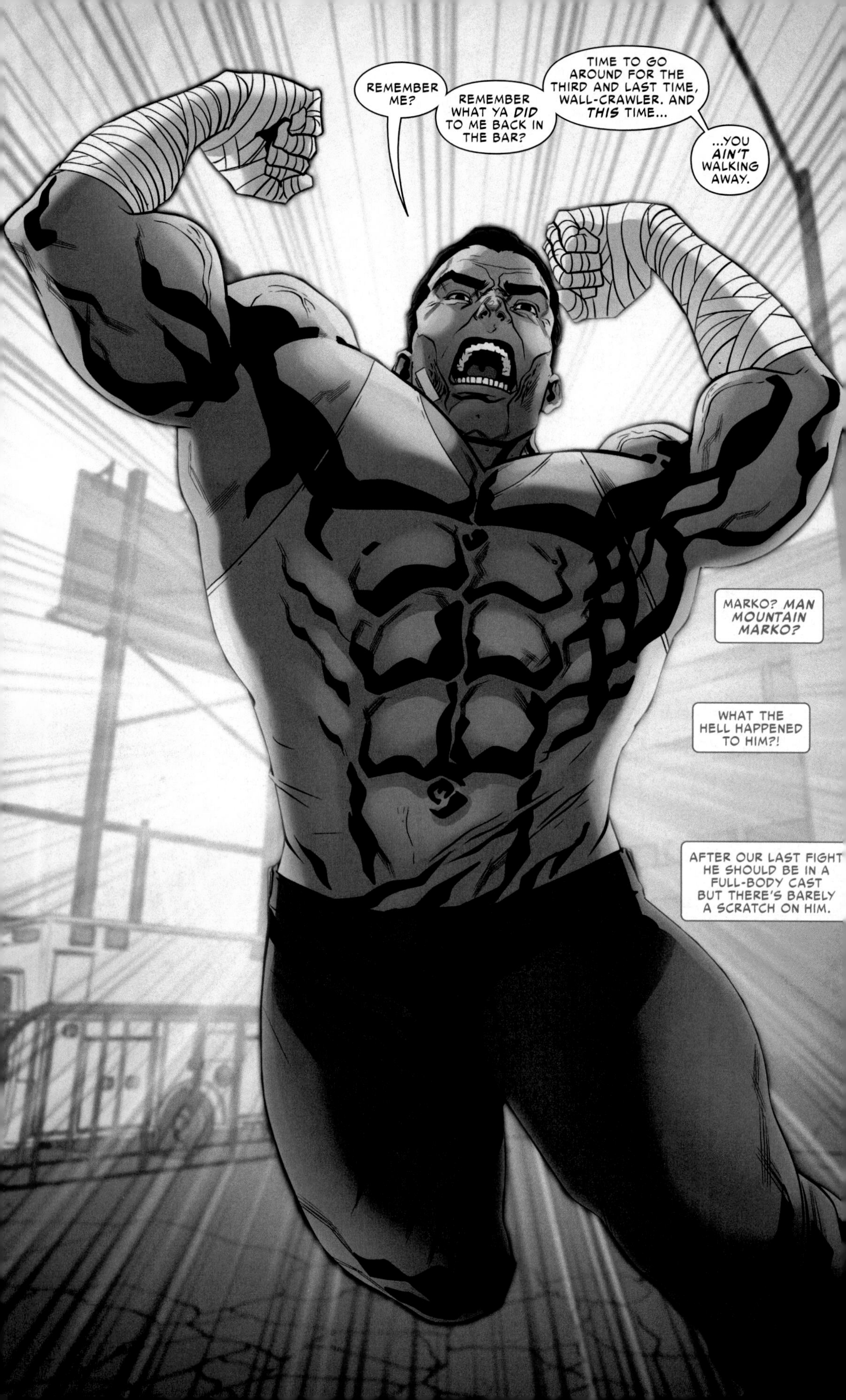

REMEMBER ME?
REMEMBER WHAT YA *DID* TO ME BACK IN THE BAR?
TIME TO GO AROUND FOR THE THIRD AND LAST TIME, WALL-CRAWLER. AND *THIS* TIME...
...YOU *AIN'T* WALKING AWAY.
MARKO? *MAN MOUNTAIN MARKO?*
WHAT THE HELL HAPPENED TO HIM?!
AFTER OUR LAST FIGHT HE SHOULD BE IN A FULL-BODY CAST BUT THERE'S BARELY A SCRATCH ON HIM.

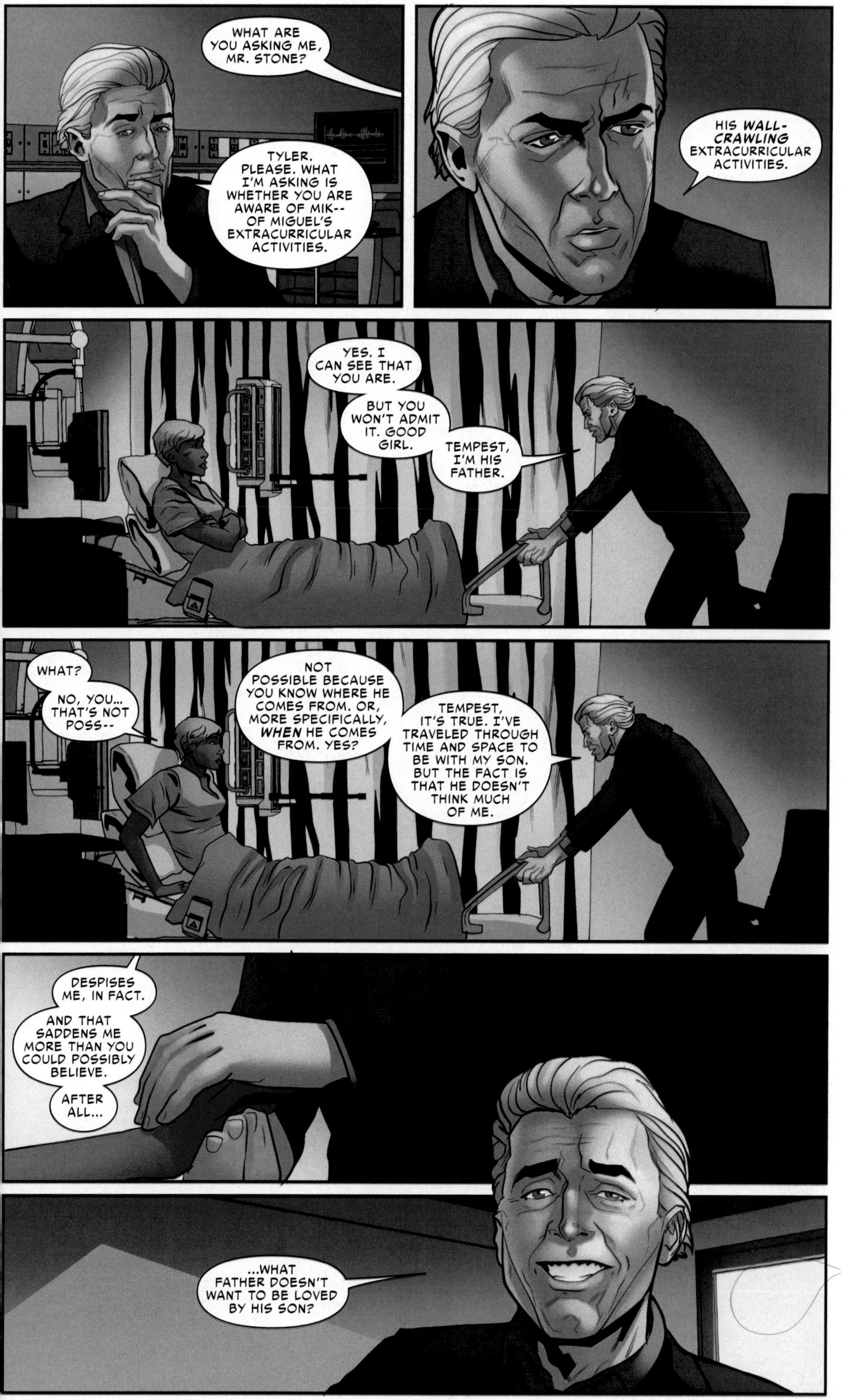
WHAT ARE YOU ASKING ME, MR. STONE?
TYLER. PLEASE. WHAT I'M ASKING IS WHETHER YOU ARE AWARE OF MIK-- OF MIGUEL'S EXTRACURRICULAR ACTIVITIES.
HIS WALL-CRAWLING EXTRACURRICULAR ACTIVITIES.
YES. I CAN SEE THAT YOU ARE.
BUT YOU WON'T ADMIT IT. GOOD GIRL.
TEMPEST, I'M HIS FATHER.
WHAT?
NO, YOU... THAT'S NOT POSS--
NOT POSSIBLE BECAUSE YOU KNOW WHERE HE COMES FROM. OR, MORE SPECIFICALLY, WHEN HE COMES FROM. YES?
TEMPEST, IT'S TRUE. I'VE TRAVELED THROUGH TIME AND SPACE TO BE WITH MY SON. BUT THE FACT IS THAT HE DOESN'T THINK MUCH OF ME.
DESPISES ME, IN FACT.
AND THAT SADDENS ME MORE THAN YOU COULD POSSIBLY BELIEVE.
AFTER ALL...
...WHAT FATHER DOESN'T WANT TO BE LOVED BY HIS SON?

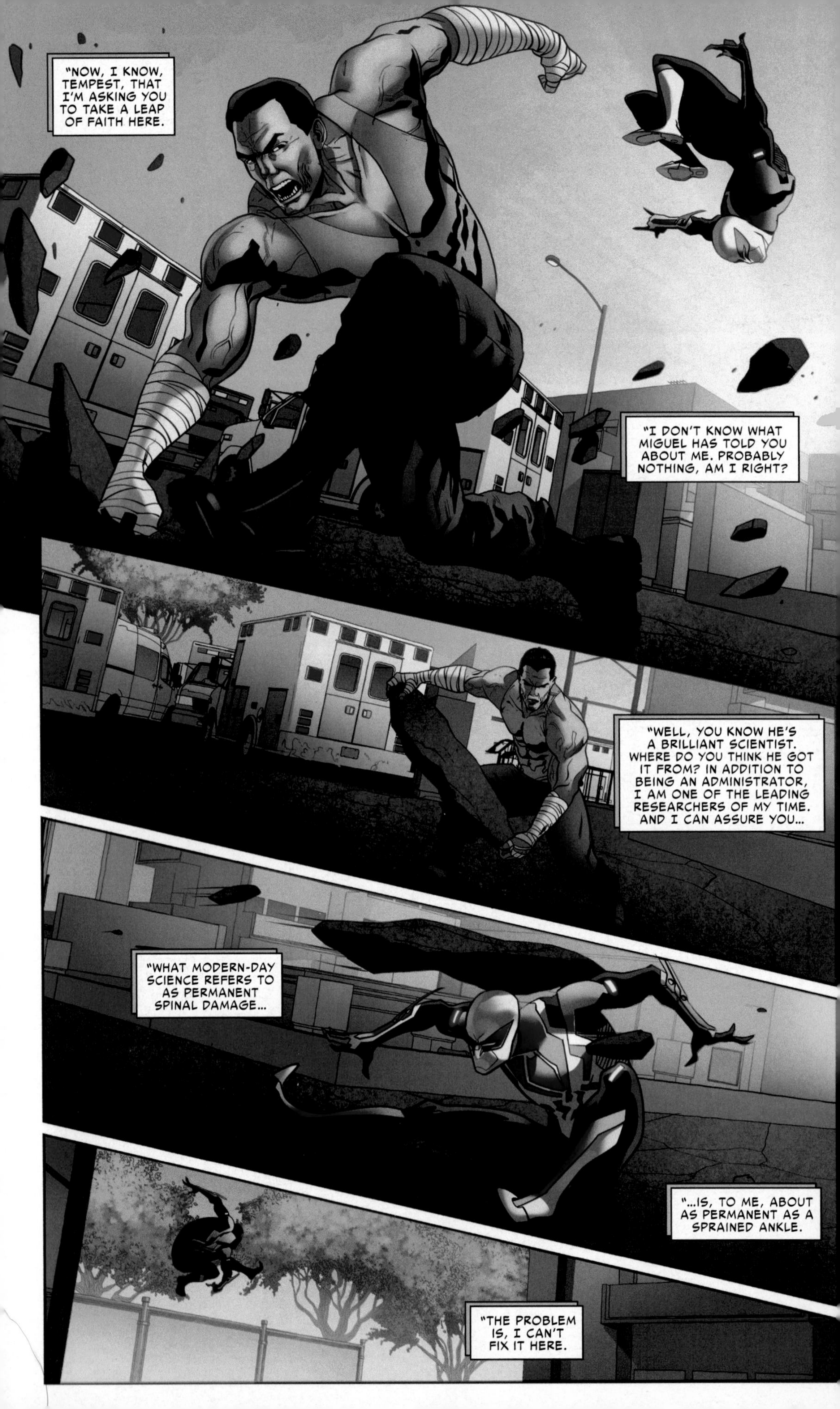
"NOW, I KNOW, TEMPEST, THAT I'M ASKING YOU TO TAKE A LEAP OF FAITH HERE.
"I DON'T KNOW WHAT MIGUEL HAS TOLD YOU ABOUT ME. PROBABLY NOTHING, AM I RIGHT?
"WELL, YOU KNOW HE'S A BRILLIANT SCIENTIST. WHERE DO YOU THINK HE GOT IT FROM? IN ADDITION TO BEING AN ADMINISTRATOR, I AM ONE OF THE LEADING RESEARCHERS OF MY TIME. AND I CAN ASSURE YOU...
"WHAT MODERN-DAY SCIENCE REFERS TO AS PERMANENT SPINAL DAMAGE...
"...IS, TO ME, ABOUT AS PERMANENT AS A SPRAINED ANKLE.
"THE PROBLEM IS, I CAN'T FIX IT HERE.

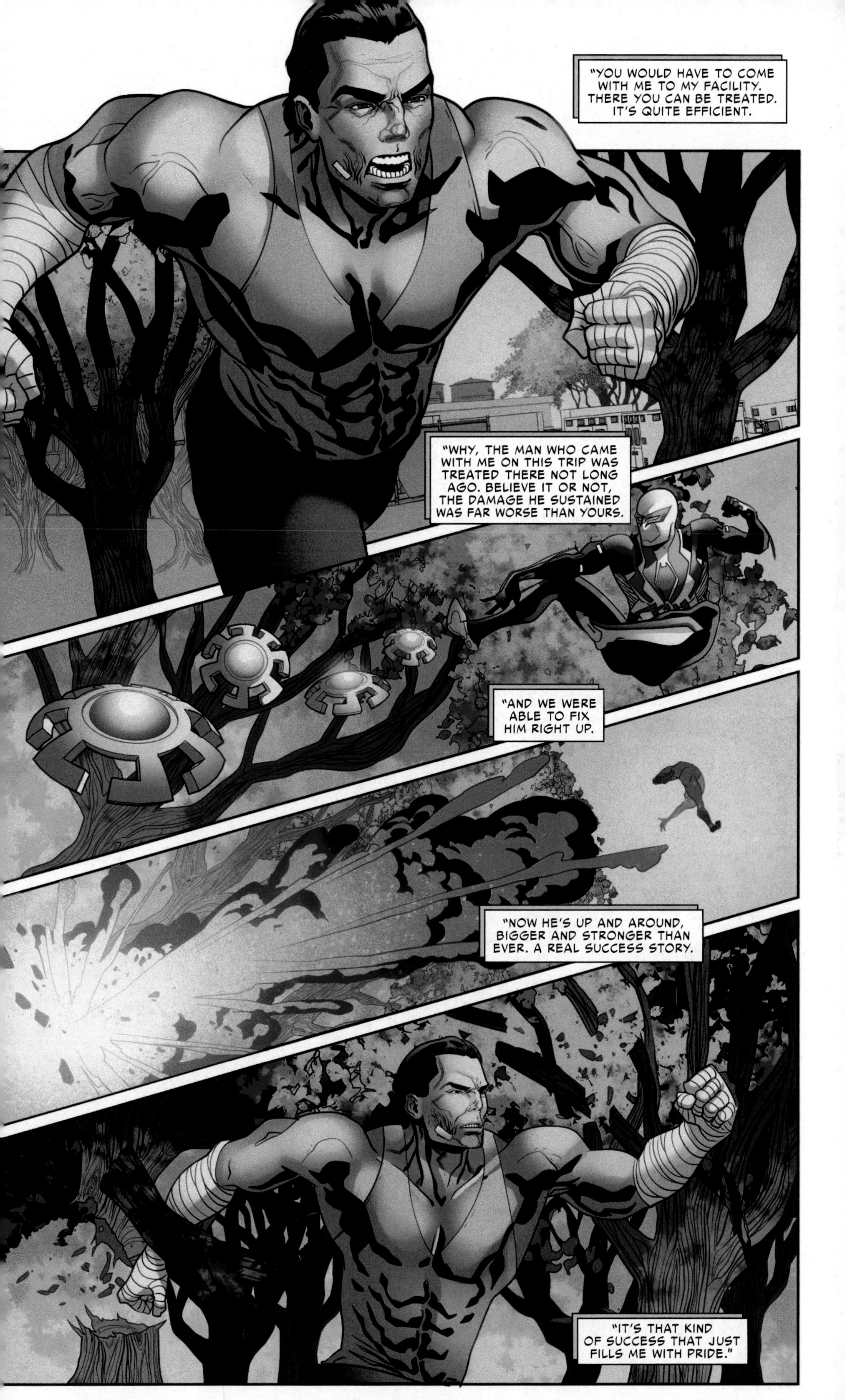
"YOU WOULD HAVE TO COME
WITH ME TO MY FACILITY.
THERE YOU CAN BE TREATED.
IT'S QUITE EFFICIENT.
"WHY, THE MAN WHO CAME
WITH ME ON THIS TRIP WAS
TREATED THERE NOT LONG
AGO. BELIEVE IT OR NOT,
THE DAMAGE HE SUSTAINED
WAS FAR WORSE THAN YOURS.
"AND WE WERE
ABLE TO FIX
HIM RIGHT UP.
"NOW HE'S UP AND AROUND,
BIGGER AND STRONGER THAN
EVER. A REAL SUCCESS STORY.
"IT'S THAT KIND
OF SUCCESS THAT JUST
FILLS ME WITH PRIDE."

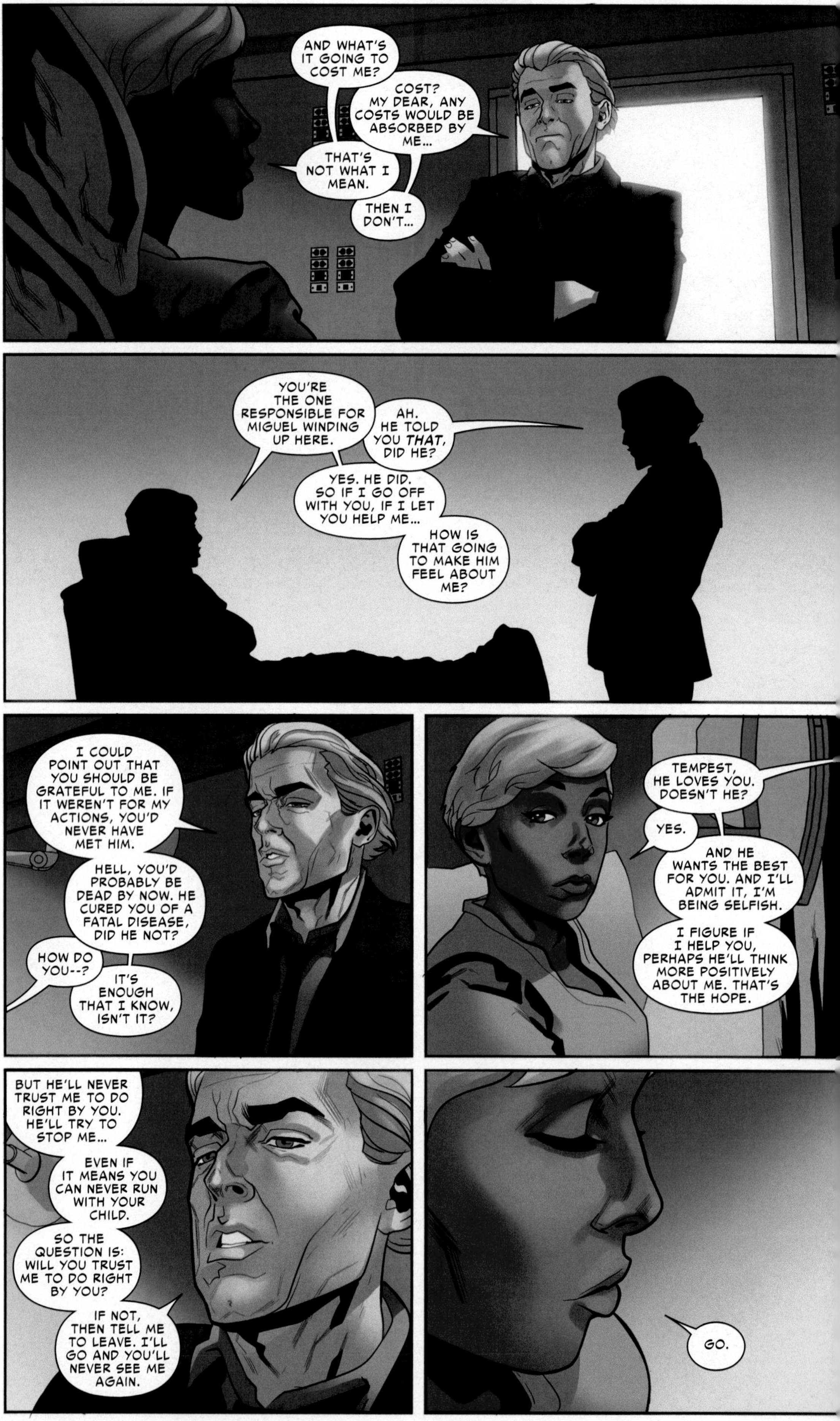
AND WHAT'S IT GOING TO COST ME?
COST? MY DEAR, ANY COSTS WOULD BE ABSORBED BY ME...
THAT'S NOT WHAT I MEAN.
THEN I DON'T...
YOU'RE THE ONE RESPONSIBLE FOR MIGUEL WINDING UP HERE.
AH. HE TOLD YOU *THAT*, DID HE?
YES. HE DID. SO IF I GO OFF WITH YOU, IF I LET YOU HELP ME...
HOW IS THAT GOING TO MAKE HIM FEEL ABOUT ME?
I COULD POINT OUT THAT YOU SHOULD BE GRATEFUL TO ME. IF IT WEREN'T FOR MY ACTIONS, YOU'D NEVER HAVE MET HIM.
HELL, YOU'D PROBABLY BE DEAD BY NOW. HE CURED YOU OF A FATAL DISEASE, DID HE NOT?
HOW DO YOU--?
IT'S ENOUGH THAT I KNOW, ISN'T IT?
TEMPEST, HE LOVES YOU. DOESN'T HE?
YES.
AND HE WANTS THE BEST FOR YOU. AND I'LL ADMIT IT, I'M BEING SELFISH.
I FIGURE IF I HELP YOU, PERHAPS HE'LL THINK MORE POSITIVELY ABOUT ME. THAT'S THE HOPE.
BUT HE'LL NEVER TRUST ME TO DO RIGHT BY YOU. HE'LL TRY TO STOP ME...
EVEN IF IT MEANS YOU CAN NEVER RUN WITH YOUR CHILD.
SO THE QUESTION IS: WILL YOU TRUST ME TO DO RIGHT BY YOU?
IF NOT, THEN TELL ME TO LEAVE. I'LL GO AND YOU'LL NEVER SEE ME AGAIN.
GO.

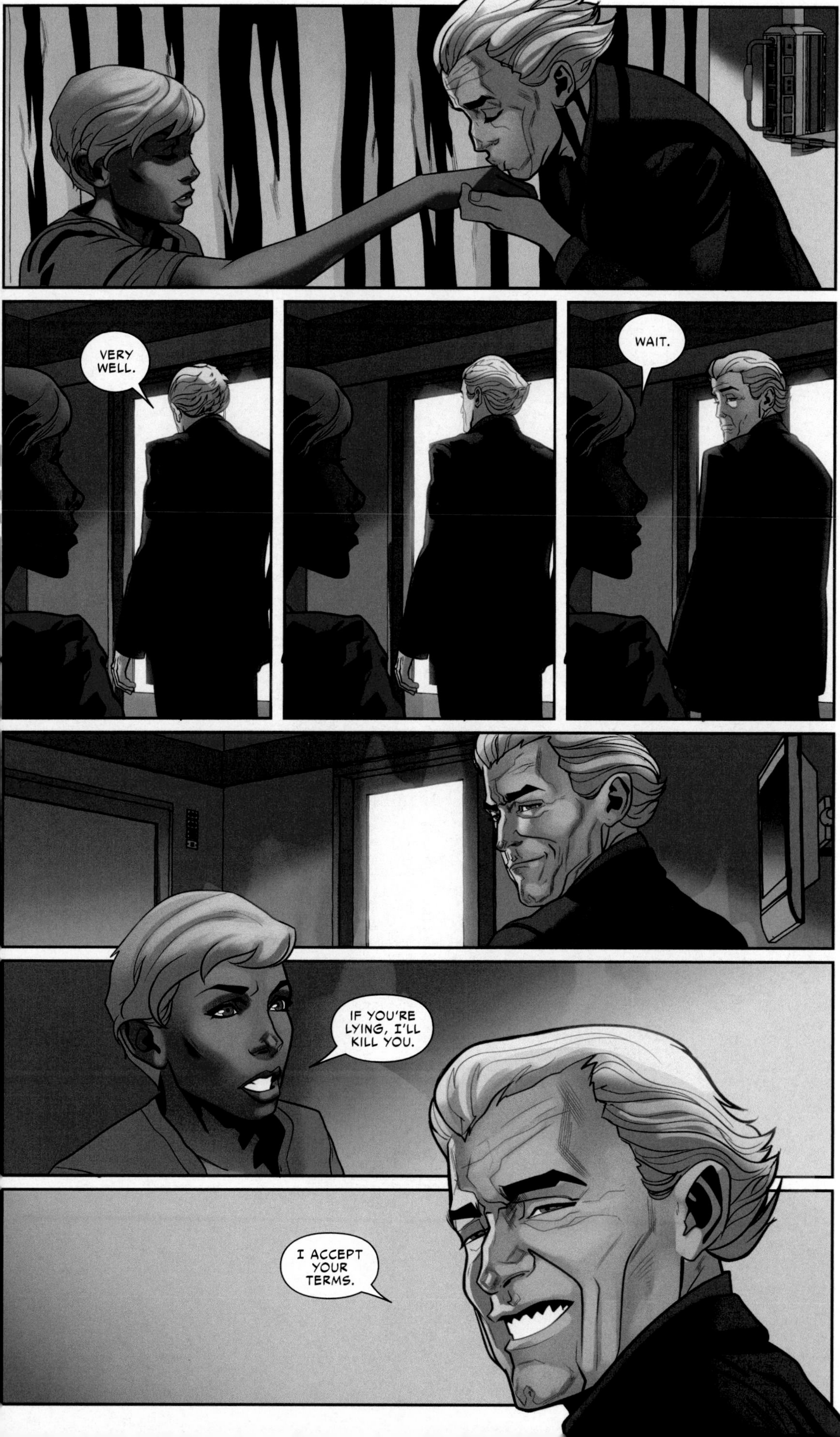
VERY WELL.
WAIT.
IF YOU'RE LYING, I'LL KILL YOU.
I ACCEPT YOUR TERMS.

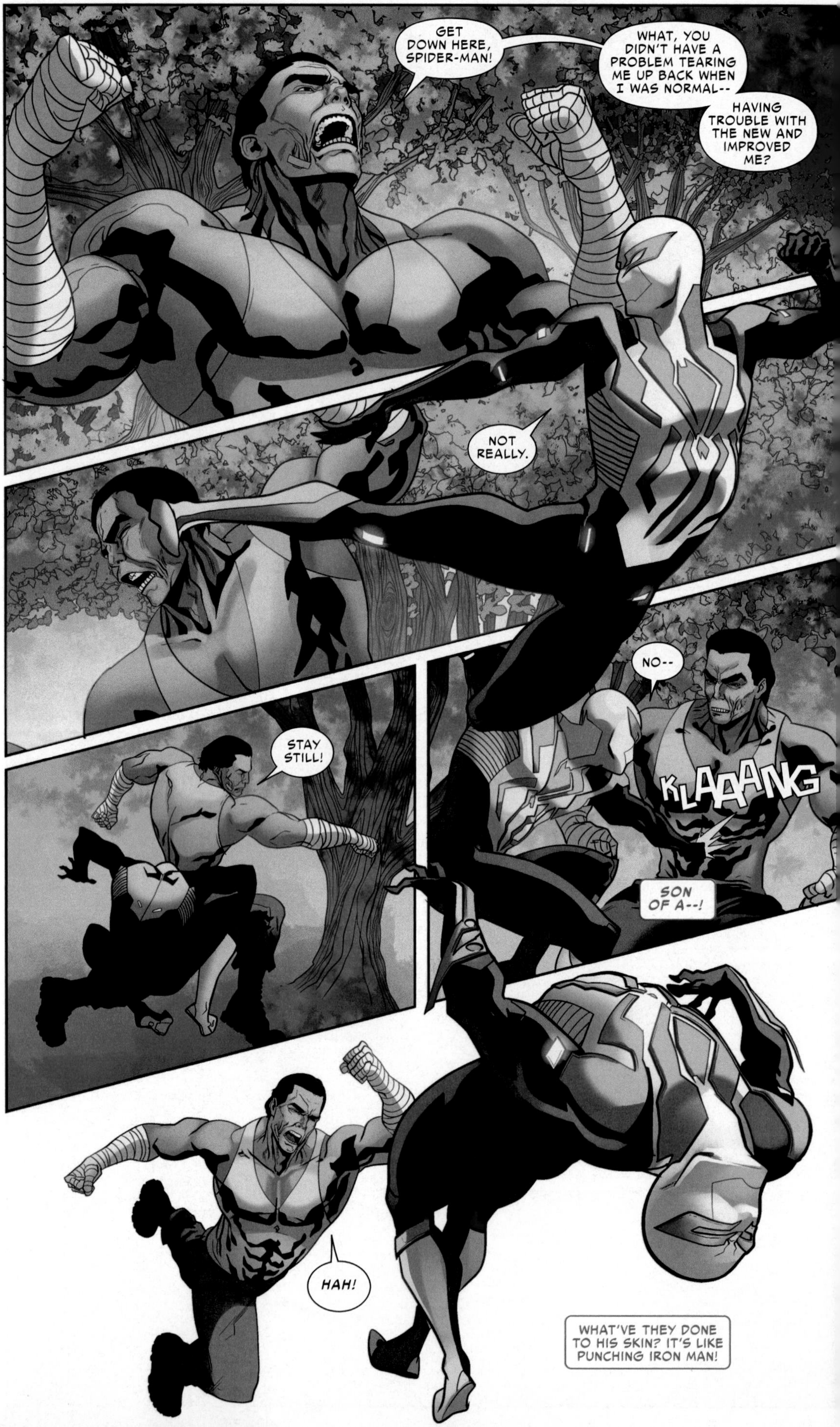
GET DOWN HERE, SPIDER-MAN!
WHAT, YOU DIDN'T HAVE A PROBLEM TEARING ME UP BACK WHEN I WAS NORMAL--
HAVING TROUBLE WITH THE NEW AND IMPROVED ME?
NOT REALLY.
STAY STILL!
NO--
KLAAAANG
SON OF A--!
HAH!
WHAT'VE THEY DONE TO HIS SKIN? IT'S LIKE PUNCHING IRON MAN!

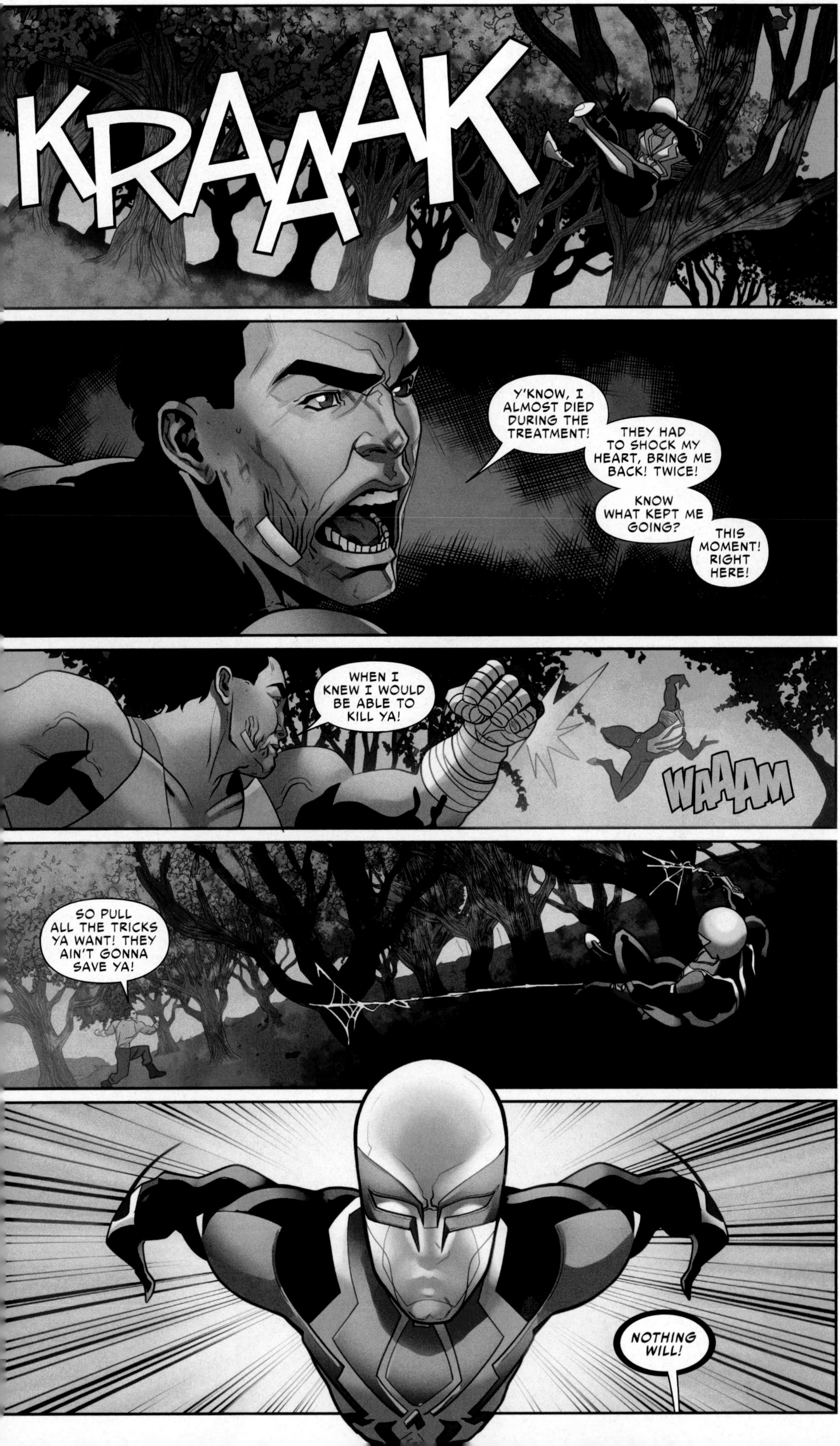
KRAAAK
Y'KNOW, I ALMOST DIED DURING THE TREATMENT!
THEY HAD TO SHOCK MY HEART, BRING ME BACK! TWICE!
KNOW WHAT KEPT ME GOING?
THIS MOMENT! RIGHT HERE!
WHEN I KNEW I WOULD BE ABLE TO KILL YA!
WAAAM
SO PULL ALL THE TRICKS YA WANT! THEY AIN'T GONNA SAVE YA!
NOTHING WILL!

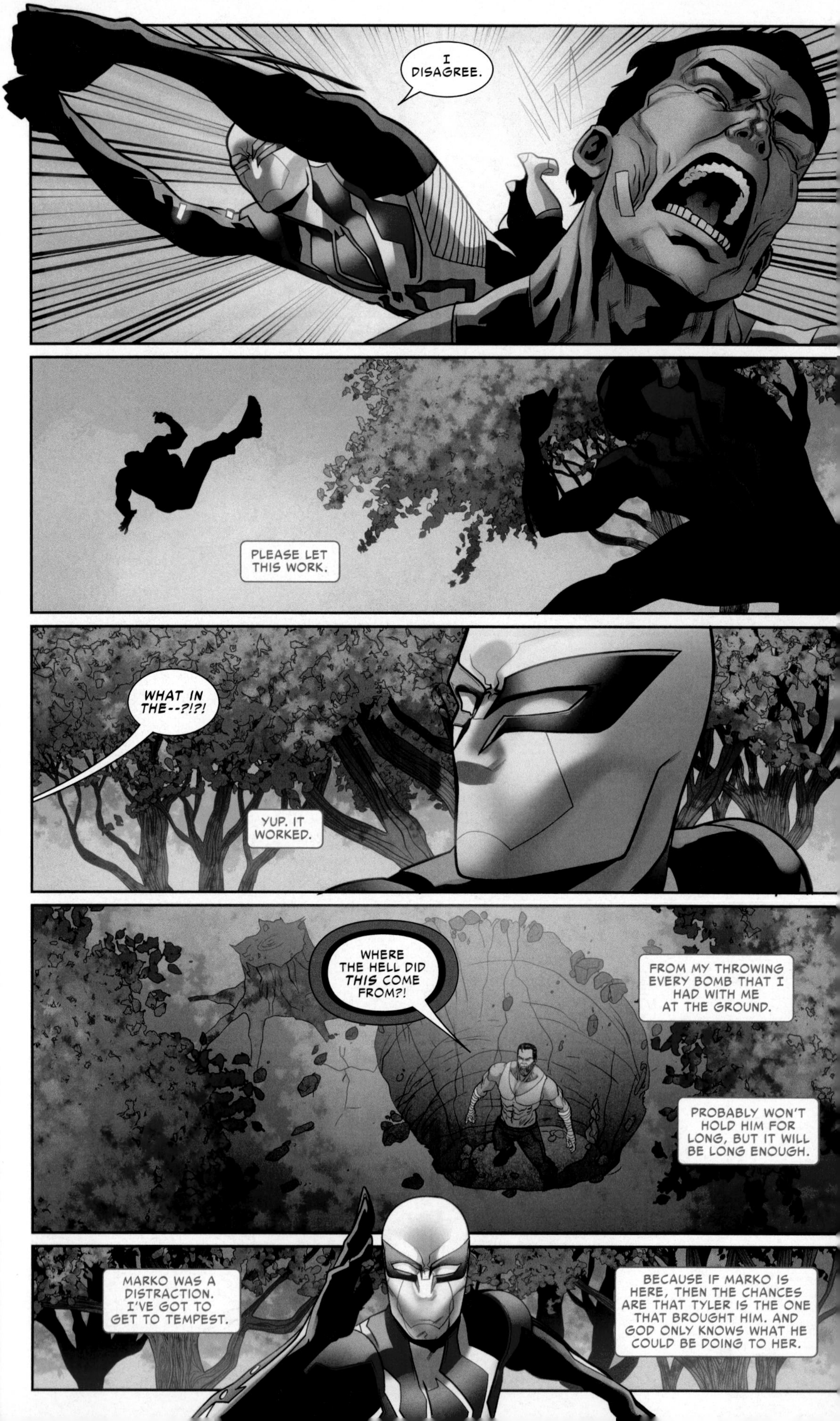
I DISAGREE.
PLEASE LET THIS WORK.
WHAT IN THE--?!?!
YUP. IT WORKED.
WHERE THE HELL DID *THIS* COME FROM?!
FROM MY THROWING EVERY BOMB THAT I HAD WITH ME AT THE GROUND.
PROBABLY WON'T HOLD HIM FOR LONG, BUT IT WILL BE LONG ENOUGH.
MARKO WAS A DISTRACTION. I'VE GOT TO GET TO TEMPEST.
BECAUSE IF MARKO IS HERE, THEN THE CHANCES ARE THAT TYLER IS THE ONE THAT BROUGHT HIM. AND GOD ONLY KNOWS WHAT HE COULD BE DOING TO HER.

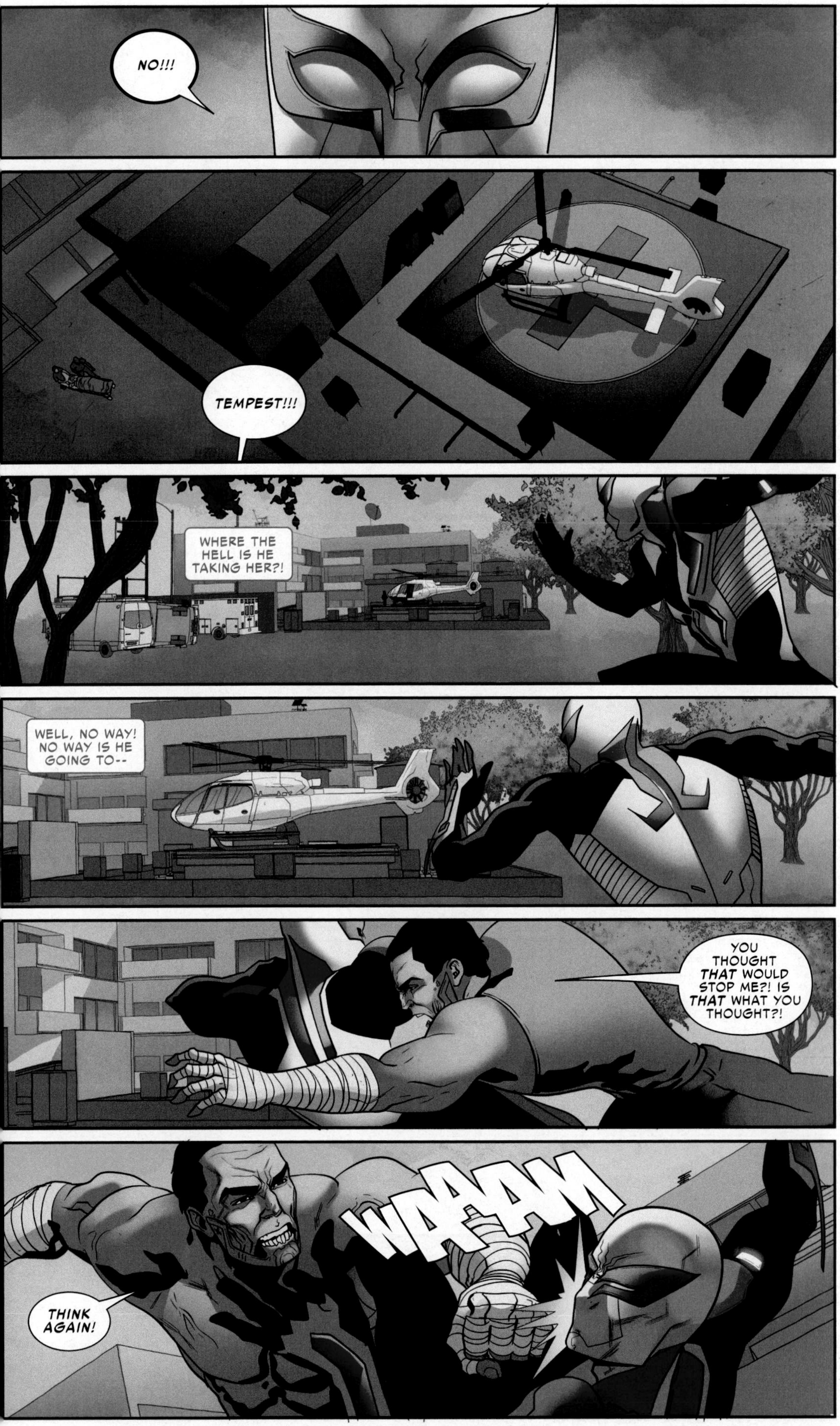
NO!!!
TEMPEST!!!
WHERE THE HELL IS HE TAKING HER?!
WELL, NO WAY! NO WAY IS HE GOING TO--
YOU THOUGHT THAT WOULD STOP ME?! IS THAT WHAT YOU THOUGHT?!
WAAAM
THINK AGAIN!

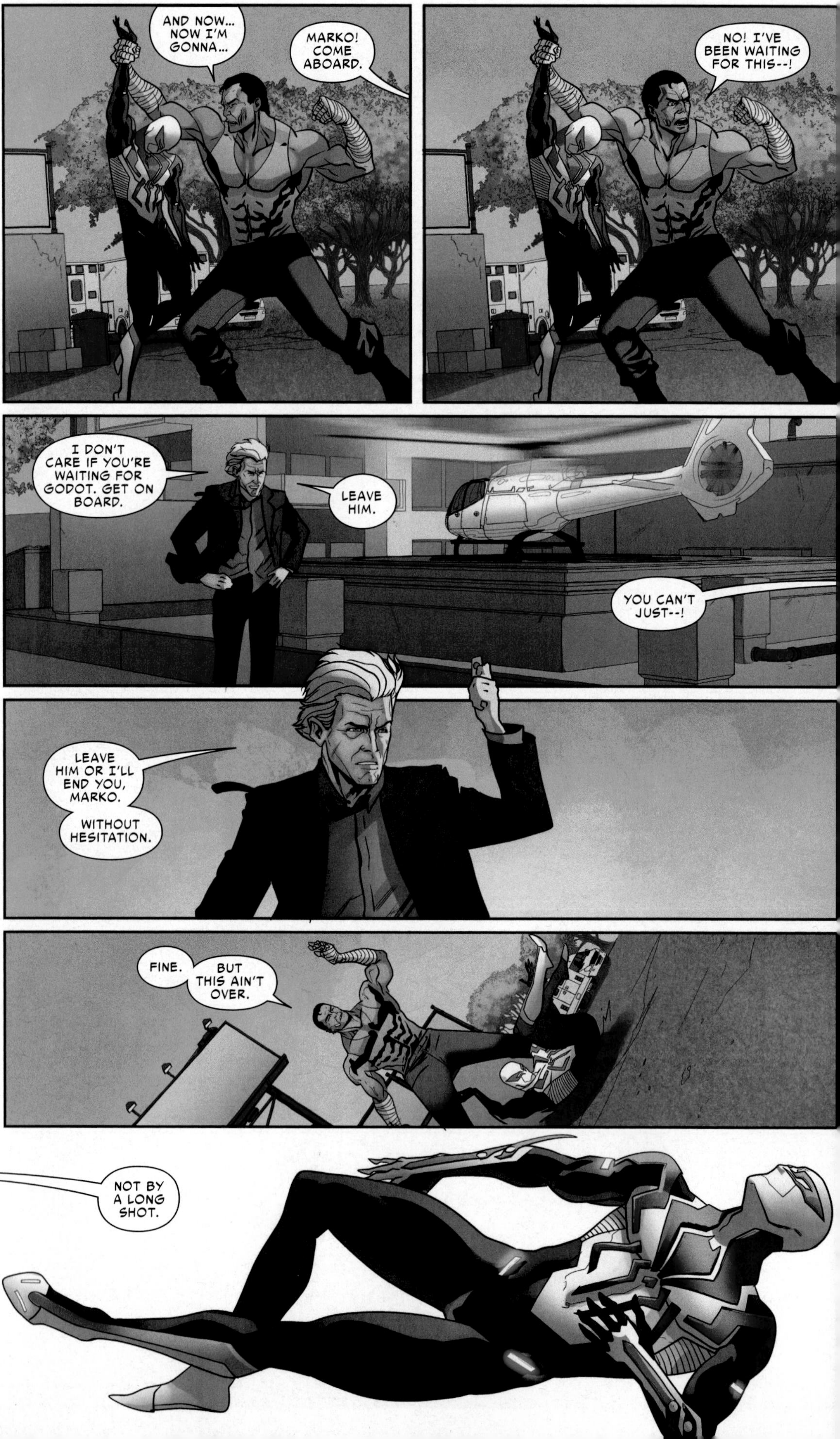

AND NOW... NOW I'M GONNA...
MARKO! COME ABOARD.
NO! I'VE BEEN WAITING FOR THIS--!
I DON'T CARE IF YOU'RE WAITING FOR GODOT. GET ON BOARD.
LEAVE HIM.
YOU CAN'T JUST--!
LEAVE HIM OR I'LL END YOU, MARKO.
WITHOUT HESITATION.
FINE.
BUT THIS AIN'T OVER.
NOT BY A LONG SHOT.

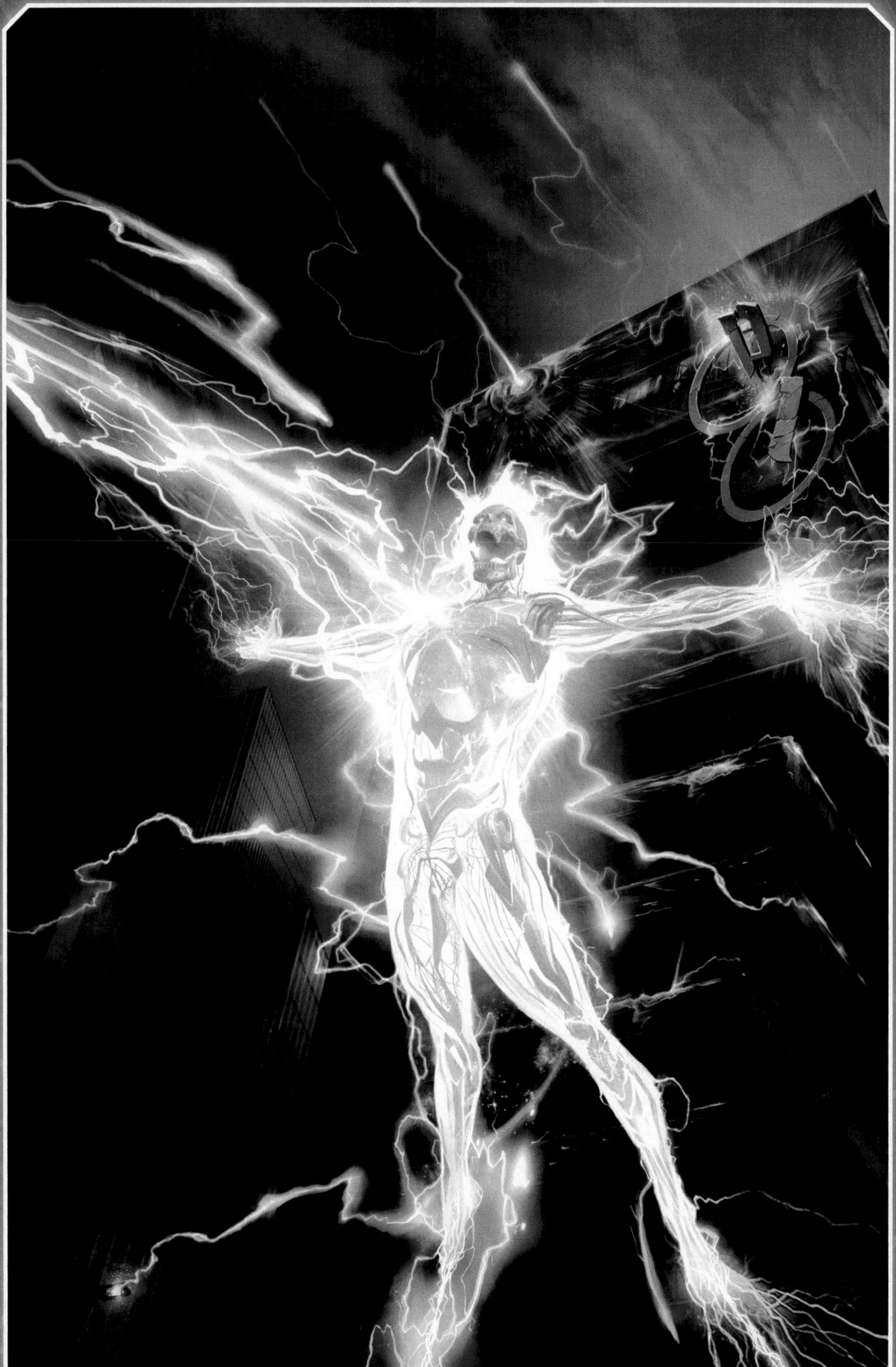

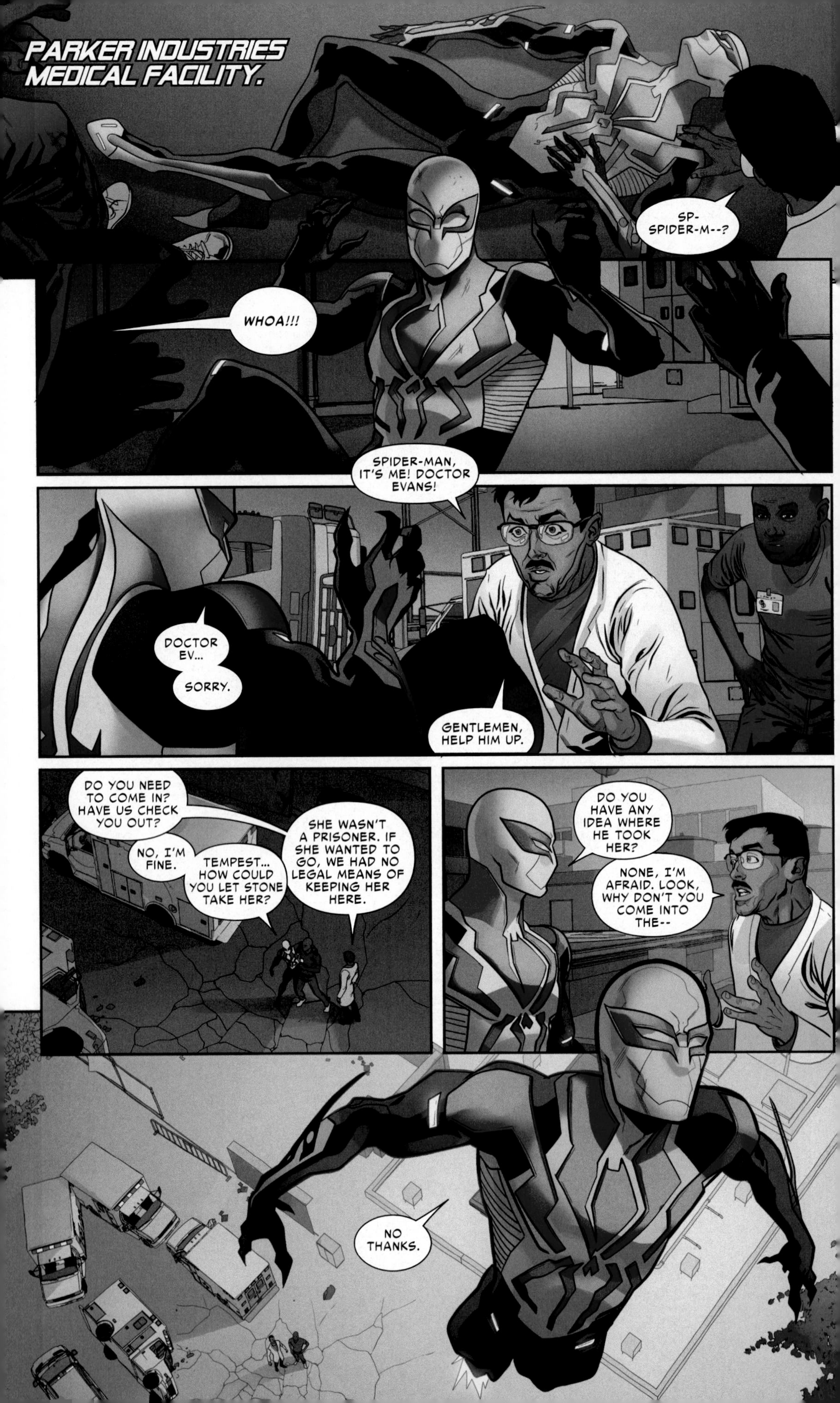

PARKER INDUSTRIES MEDICAL FACILITY.
SP- SPIDER-M--?
WHOA!!!
SPIDER-MAN, IT'S ME! DOCTOR EVANS!
DOCTOR EV...
SORRY.
GENTLEMEN, HELP HIM UP.
DO YOU NEED TO COME IN? HAVE US CHECK YOU OUT?
NO, I'M FINE.
TEMPEST... HOW COULD YOU LET STONE TAKE HER?
SHE WASN'T A PRISONER. IF SHE WANTED TO GO, WE HAD NO LEGAL MEANS OF KEEPING HER HERE.
DO YOU HAVE ANY IDEA WHERE HE TOOK HER?
NONE, I'M AFRAID. LOOK, WHY DON'T YOU COME INTO THE--
NO THANKS.

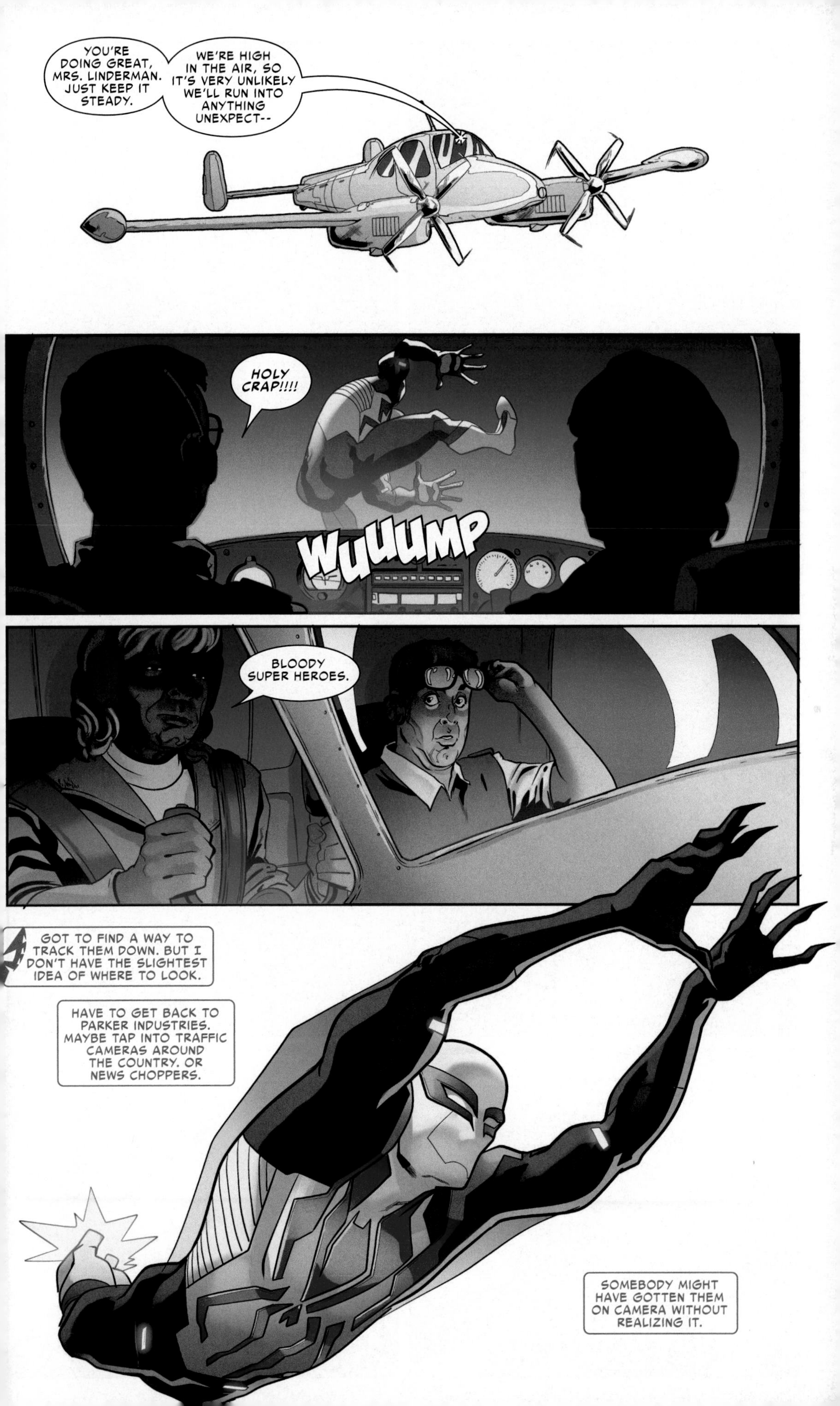
YOU'RE DOING GREAT, MRS. LINDERMAN. JUST KEEP IT STEADY.
WE'RE HIGH IN THE AIR, SO IT'S VERY UNLIKELY WE'LL RUN INTO ANYTHING UNEXPECT--
HOLY CRAP!!!!
WUUUMP
BLOODY SUPER HEROES.
GOT TO FIND A WAY TO TRACK THEM DOWN. BUT I DON'T HAVE THE SLIGHTEST IDEA OF WHERE TO LOOK.
HAVE TO GET BACK TO PARKER INDUSTRIES. MAYBE TAP INTO TRAFFIC CAMERAS AROUND THE COUNTRY. OR NEWS CHOPPERS.
SOMEBODY MIGHT HAVE GOTTEN THEM ON CAMERA WITHOUT REALIZING IT.

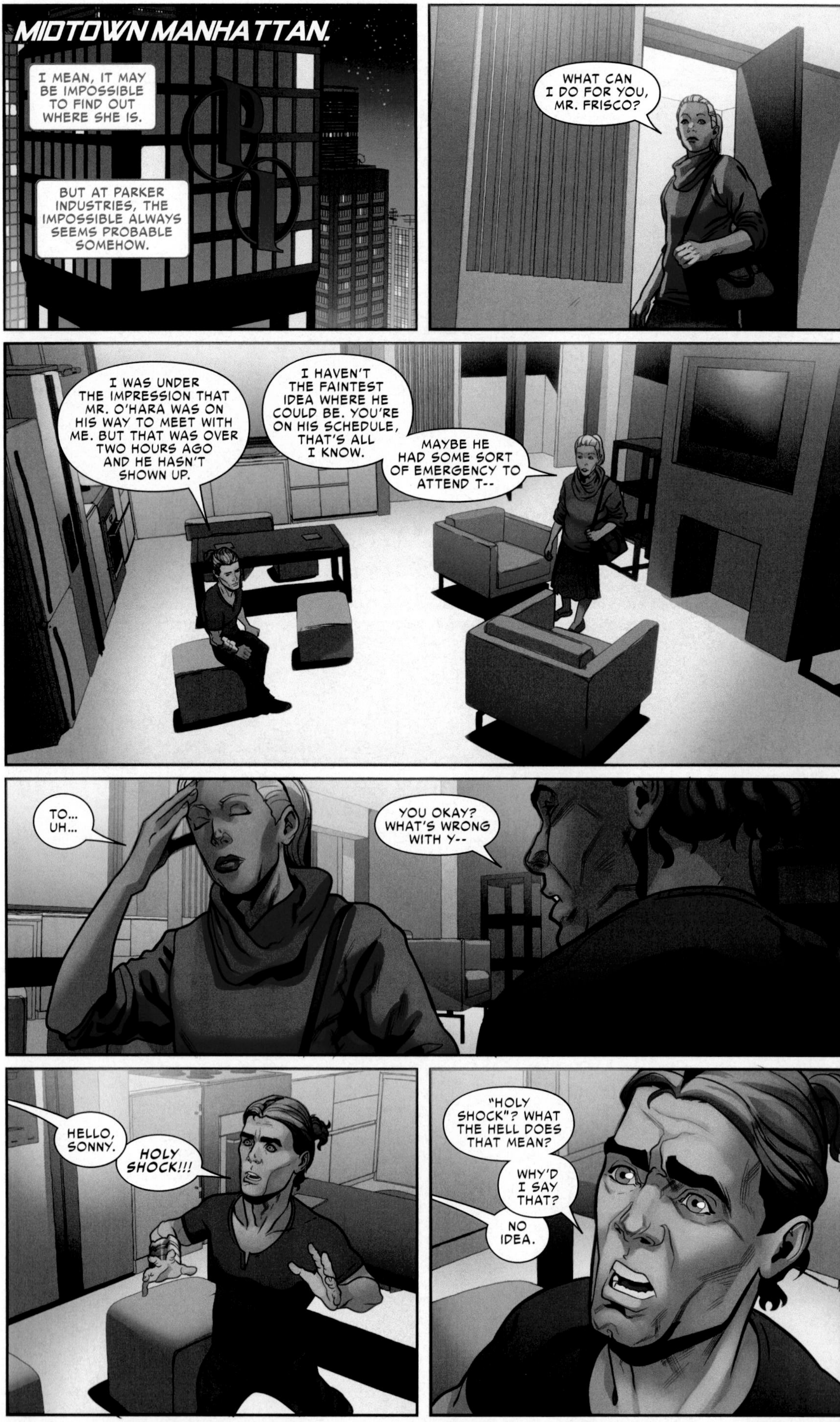
MIDTOWN MANHATTAN.
I MEAN, IT MAY BE IMPOSSIBLE TO FIND OUT WHERE SHE IS.
BUT AT PARKER INDUSTRIES, THE IMPOSSIBLE ALWAYS SEEMS PROBABLE SOMEHOW.
WHAT CAN I DO FOR YOU, MR. FRISCO?
I WAS UNDER THE IMPRESSION THAT MR. O'HARA WAS ON HIS WAY TO MEET WITH ME. BUT THAT WAS OVER TWO HOURS AGO AND HE HASN'T SHOWN UP.
I HAVEN'T THE FAINTEST IDEA WHERE HE COULD BE. YOU'RE ON HIS SCHEDULE, THAT'S ALL I KNOW.
MAYBE HE HAD SOME SORT OF EMERGENCY TO ATTEND T--
TO... UH...
YOU OKAY? WHAT'S WRONG WITH Y--
HELLO, SONNY.
HOLY SHOCK!!!
"HOLY SHOCK"? WHAT THE HELL DOES THAT MEAN?
WHY'D I SAY THAT?
NO IDEA.

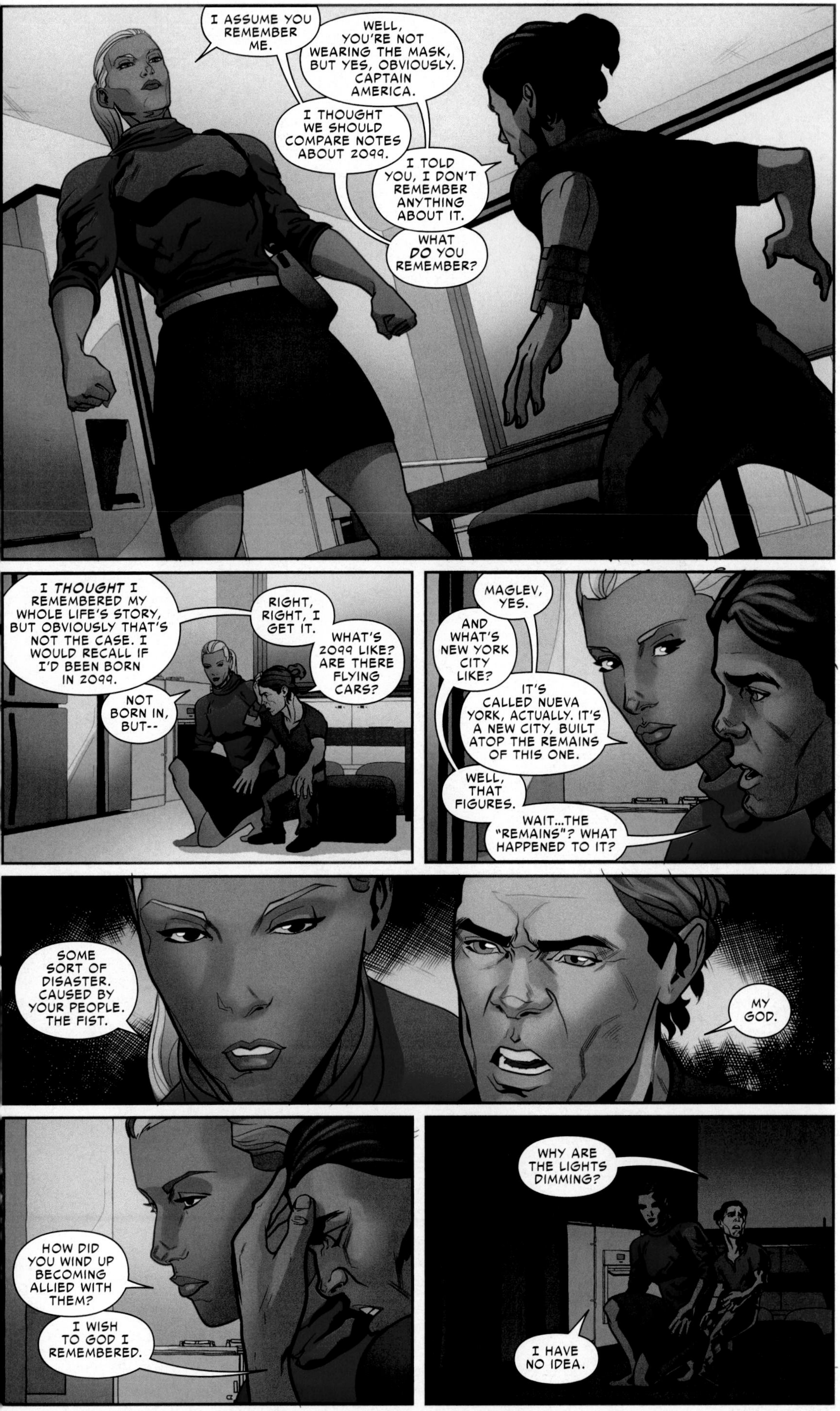

I ASSUME YOU REMEMBER ME.
WELL, YOU'RE NOT WEARING THE MASK, BUT YES, OBVIOUSLY. CAPTAIN AMERICA.
I THOUGHT WE SHOULD COMPARE NOTES ABOUT 2099.
I TOLD YOU, I DON'T REMEMBER ANYTHING ABOUT IT.
WHAT DO YOU REMEMBER?
I THOUGHT I REMEMBERED MY WHOLE LIFE'S STORY, BUT OBVIOUSLY THAT'S NOT THE CASE. I WOULD RECALL IF I'D BEEN BORN IN 2099.
NOT BORN IN, BUT--
RIGHT, RIGHT, I GET IT.
WHAT'S 2099 LIKE? ARE THERE FLYING CARS?
MAGLEV, YES.
AND WHAT'S NEW YORK CITY LIKE?
IT'S CALLED NUEVA YORK, ACTUALLY. IT'S A NEW CITY, BUILT ATOP THE REMAINS OF THIS ONE.
WELL, THAT FIGURES.
WAIT...THE "REMAINS"? WHAT HAPPENED TO IT?
SOME SORT OF DISASTER. CAUSED BY YOUR PEOPLE. THE FIST.
MY GOD.
HOW DID YOU WIND UP BECOMING ALLIED WITH THEM?
I WISH TO GOD I REMEMBERED.
WHY ARE THE LIGHTS DIMMING?
I HAVE NO IDEA.

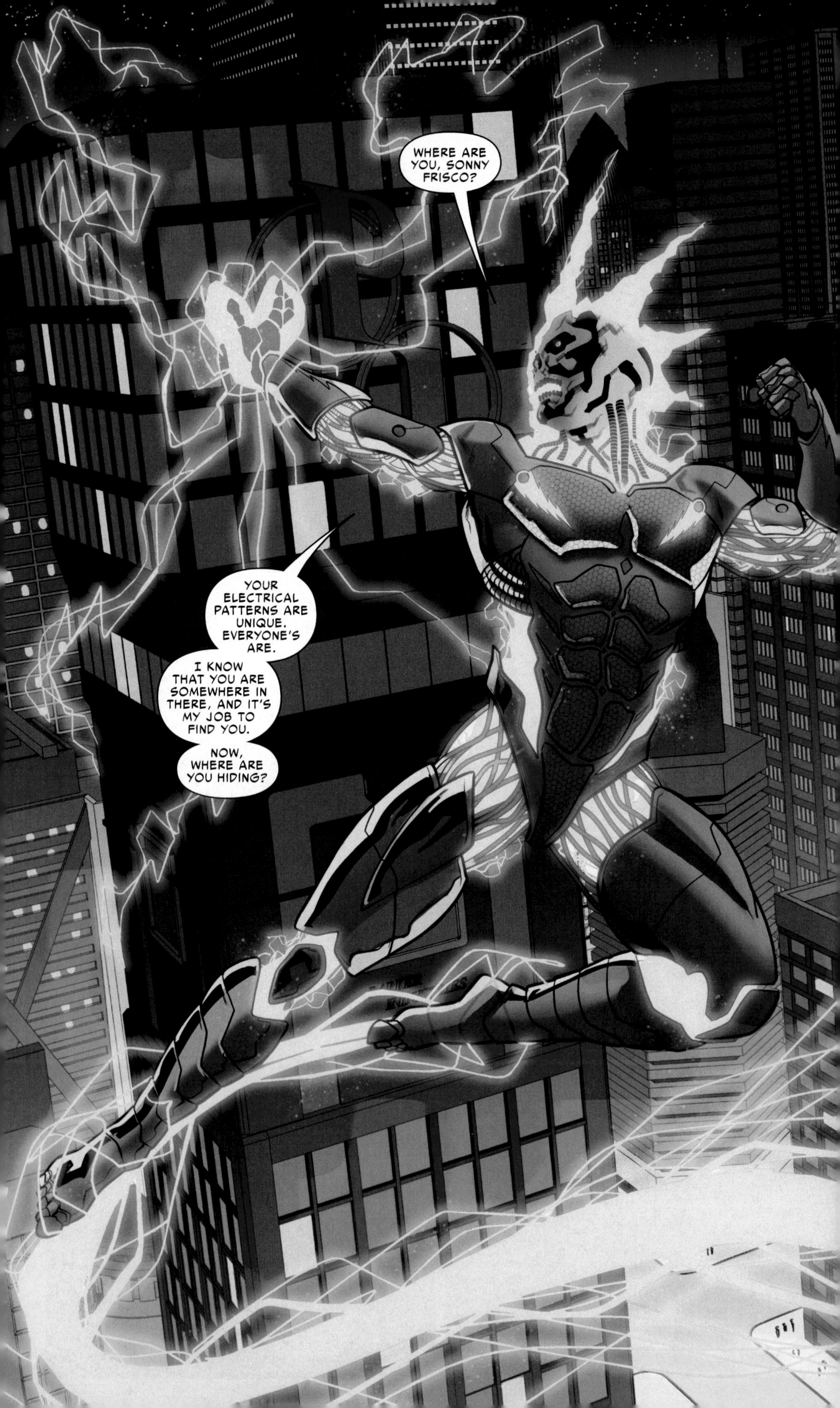
WHERE ARE YOU, SONNY FRISCO?
YOUR ELECTRICAL PATTERNS ARE UNIQUE. EVERYONE'S ARE.
I KNOW THAT YOU ARE SOMEWHERE IN THERE, AND IT'S MY JOB TO FIND YOU.
NOW, WHERE ARE YOU HIDING?

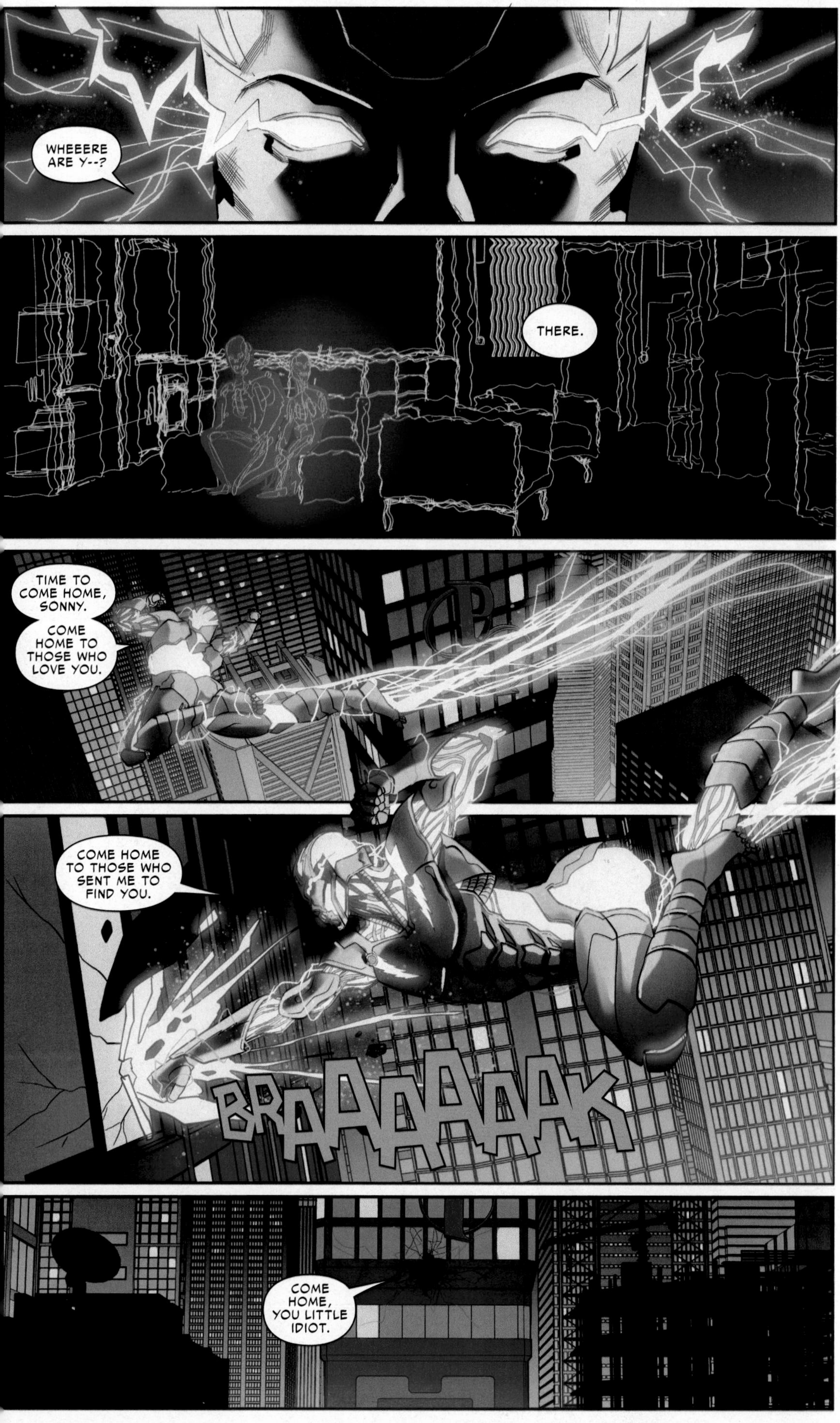
WHEEERE ARE Y--?
THERE.
TIME TO COME HOME, SONNY.
COME HOME TO THOSE WHO LOVE YOU.
COME HOME TO THOSE WHO SENT ME TO FIND YOU.
BRAAAAAK
COME HOME, YOU LITTLE IDIOT.

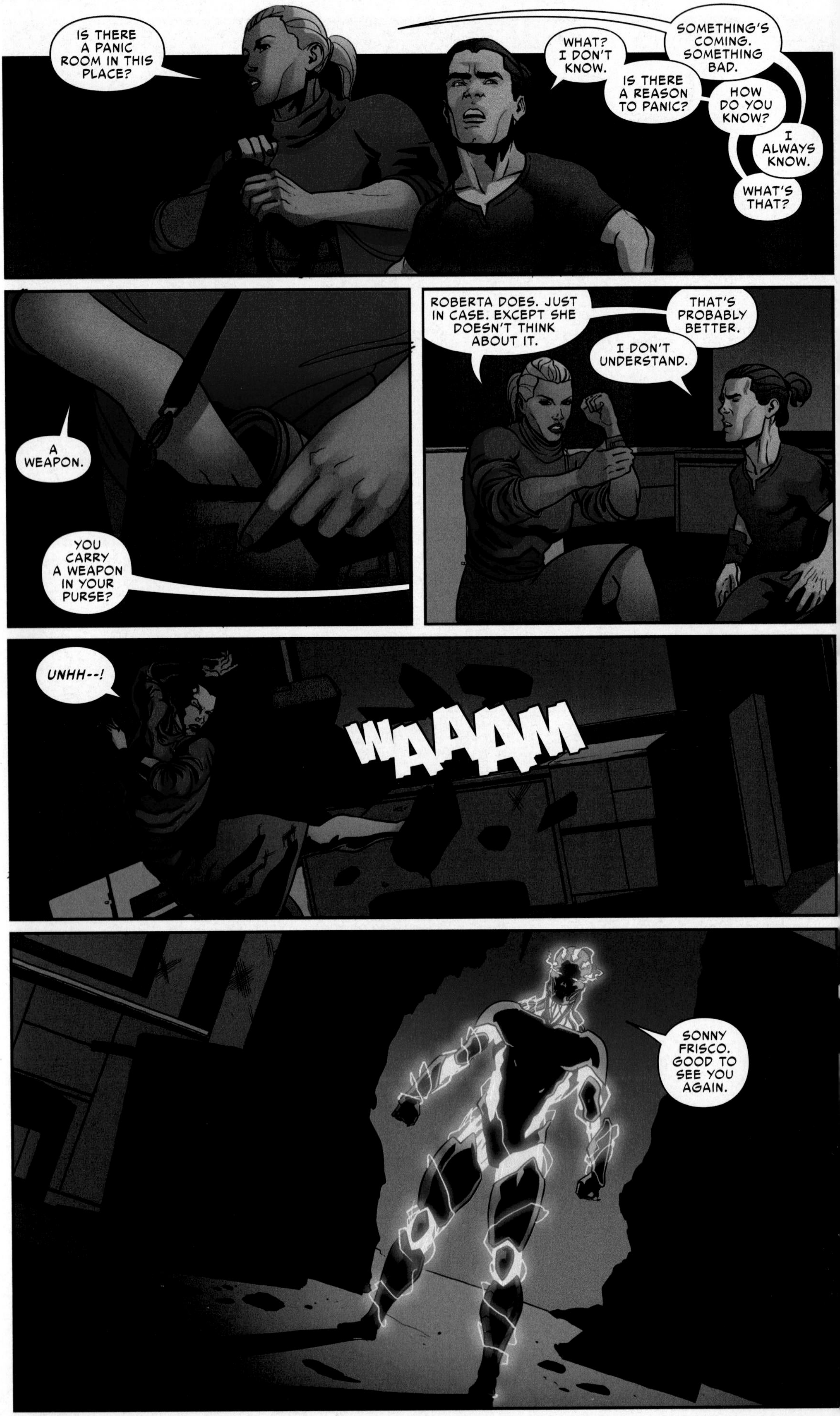
IS THERE A PANIC ROOM IN THIS PLACE?
WHAT? I DON'T KNOW.
IS THERE A REASON TO PANIC?
SOMETHING'S COMING. SOMETHING BAD.
HOW DO YOU KNOW?
I ALWAYS KNOW.
WHAT'S THAT?
A WEAPON.
YOU CARRY A WEAPON IN YOUR PURSE?
ROBERTA DOES. JUST IN CASE. EXCEPT SHE DOESN'T THINK ABOUT IT.
THAT'S PROBABLY BETTER.
I DON'T UNDERSTAND.
UNHH--!
WAAAM
SONNY FRISCO. GOOD TO SEE YOU AGAIN.

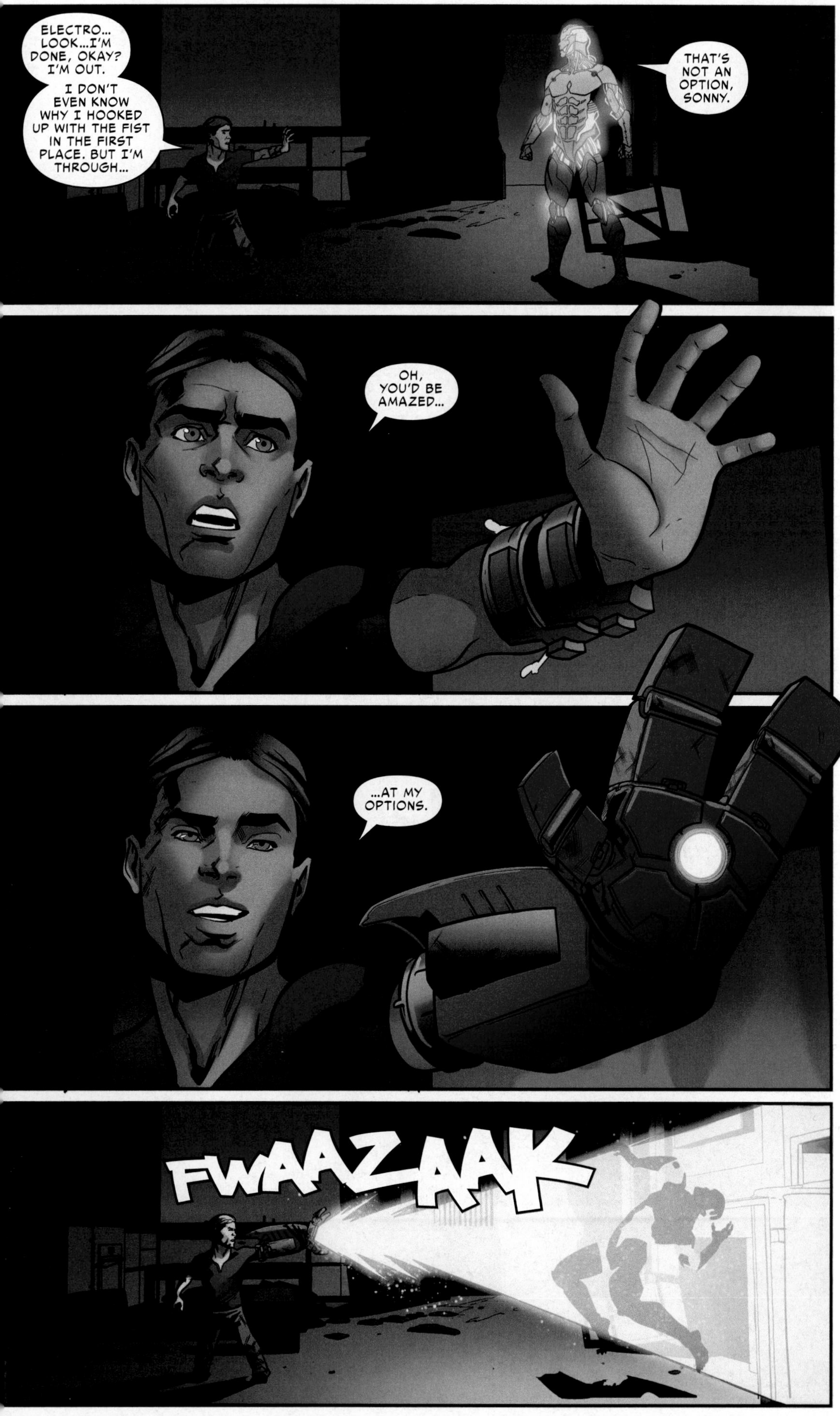

ELECTRO... LOOK...I'M DONE, OKAY? I'M OUT.
I DON'T EVEN KNOW WHY I HOOKED UP WITH THE FIST IN THE FIRST PLACE. BUT I'M THROUGH...
THAT'S NOT AN OPTION, SONNY.
OH, YOU'D BE AMAZED...
...AT MY OPTIONS.
FWAAZAAK

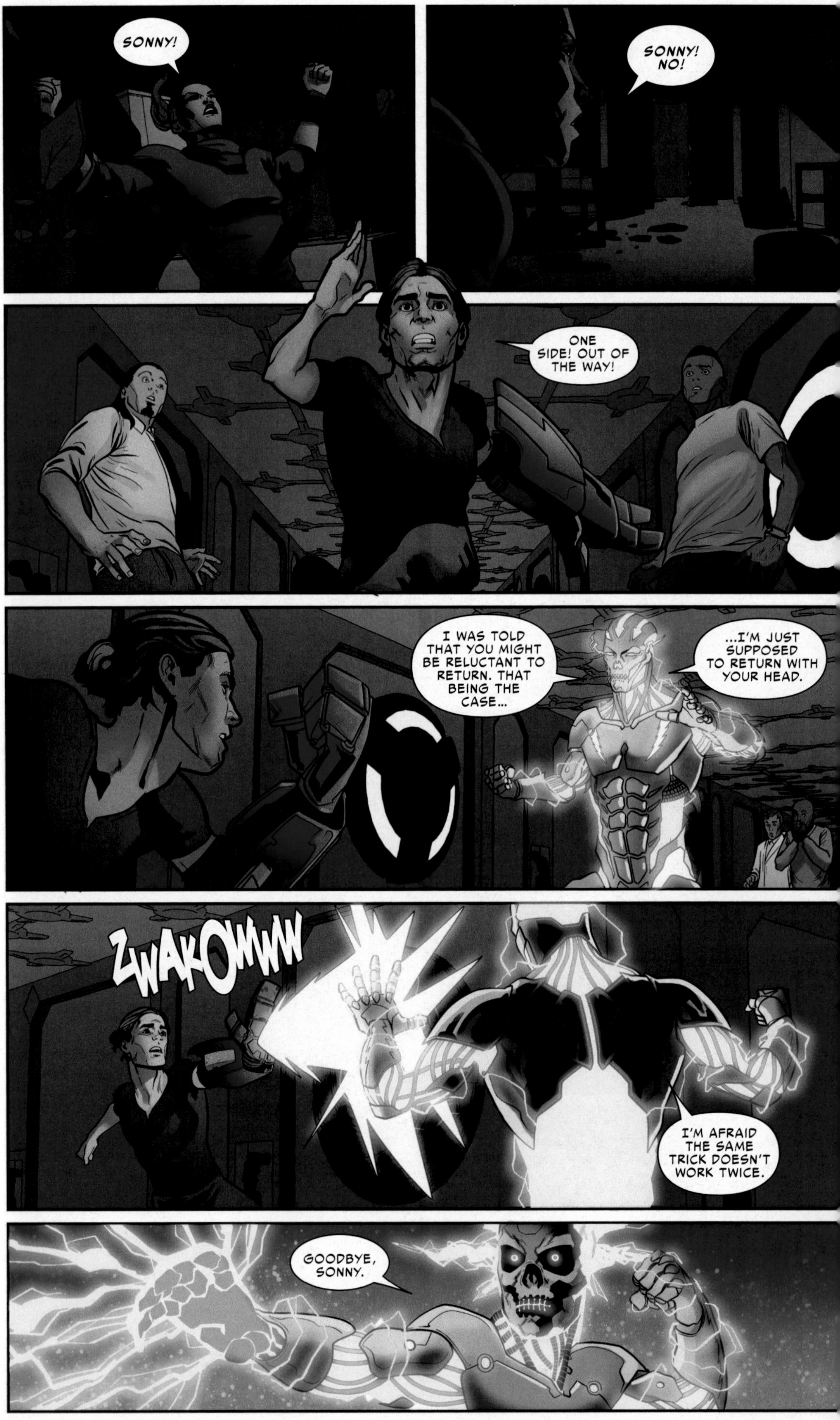
SONNY!
SONNY! NO!
ONE SIDE! OUT OF THE WAY!
I WAS TOLD THAT YOU MIGHT BE RELUCTANT TO RETURN. THAT BEING THE CASE...
...I'M JUST SUPPOSED TO RETURN WITH YOUR HEAD.
ZWAKOMWW
I'M AFRAID THE SAME TRICK DOESN'T WORK TWICE.
GOODBYE, SONNY.

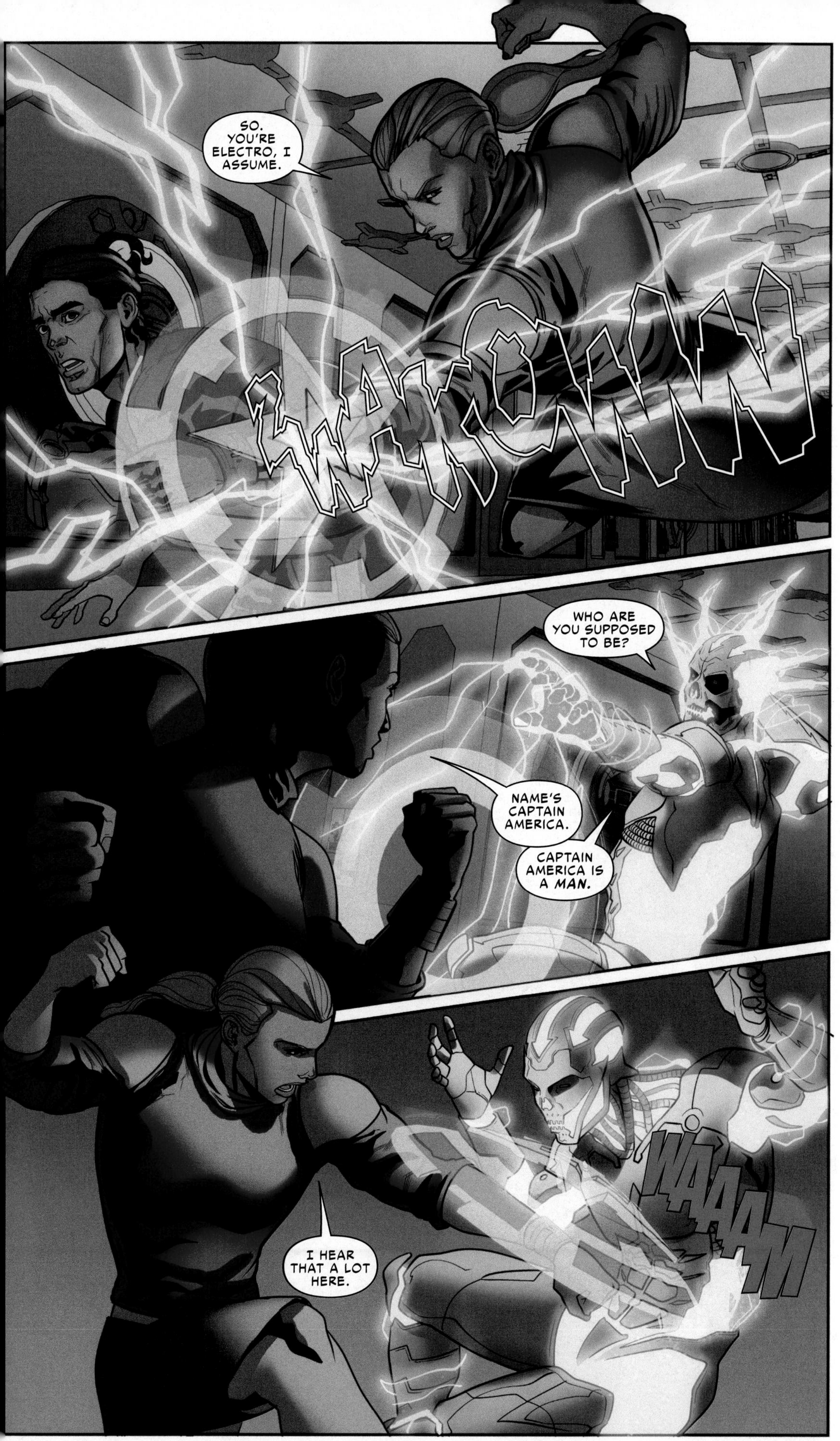
SO. YOU'RE ELECTRO, I ASSUME.
WAKOWW
WHO ARE YOU SUPPOSED TO BE?
NAME'S CAPTAIN AMERICA.
CAPTAIN AMERICA IS A MAN.
I HEAR THAT A LOT HERE.
WAAAM

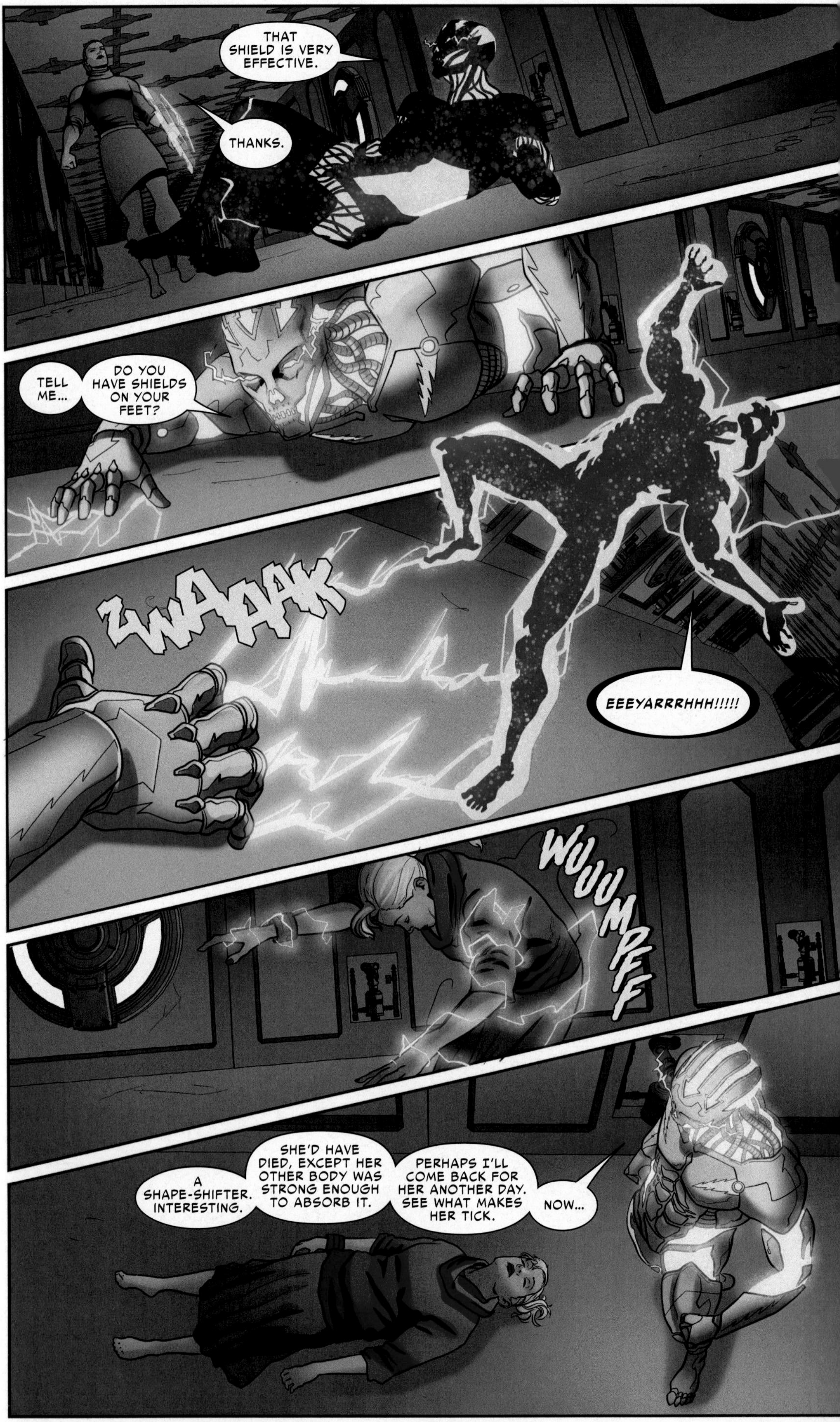

THAT SHIELD IS VERY EFFECTIVE.
THANKS.
TELL ME...
DO YOU HAVE SHIELDS ON YOUR FEET?
ZWAAAK
EEEYARRRHHH!!!!!
WUUUMPFF
A SHAPE-SHIFTER. INTERESTING.
SHE'D HAVE DIED, EXCEPT HER OTHER BODY WAS STRONG ENOUGH TO ABSORB IT.
PERHAPS I'LL COME BACK FOR HER ANOTHER DAY. SEE WHAT MAKES HER TICK.
NOW...

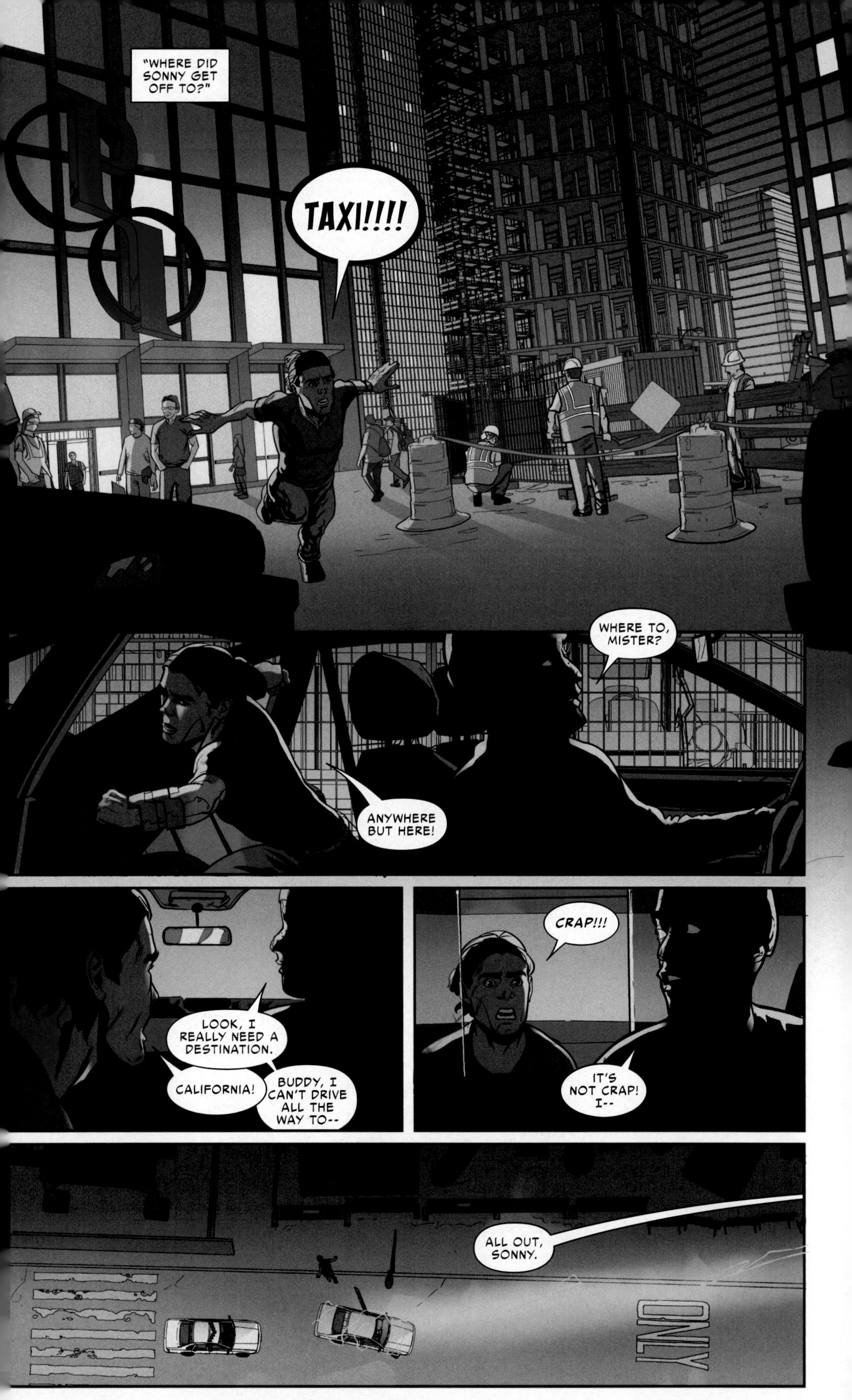
"WHERE DID SONNY GET OFF TO?"
TAXI!!!!!
WHERE TO, MISTER?
ANYWHERE BUT HERE!
LOOK, I REALLY NEED A DESTINATION.
CALIFORNIA!
BUDDY, I CAN'T DRIVE ALL THE WAY TO--
CRAP!!!
IT'S NOT CRAP! I--
ALL OUT, SONNY.
ONLY

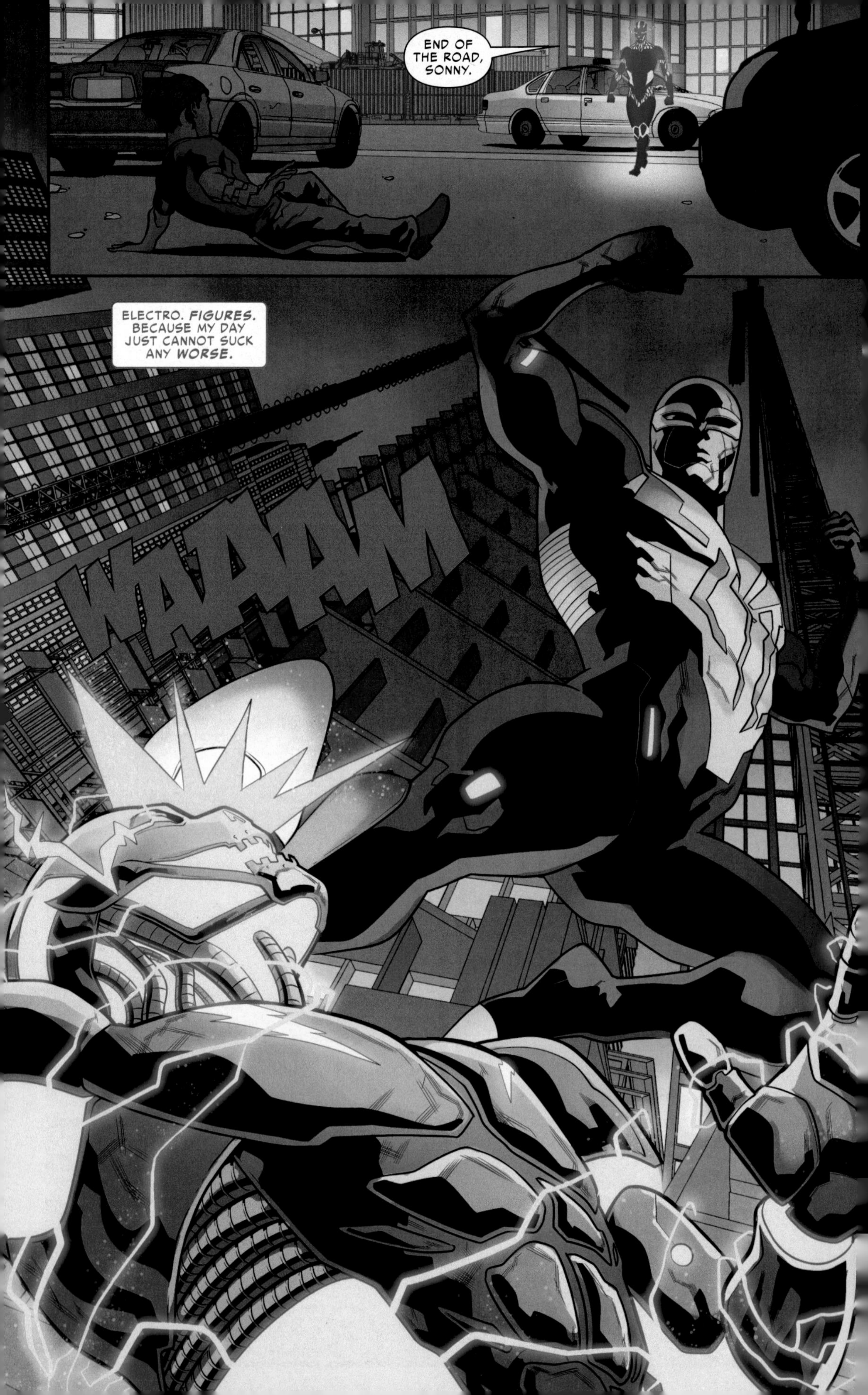
END OF THE ROAD, SONNY.
ELECTRO. *FIGURES.* BECAUSE MY DAY JUST CANNOT SUCK ANY *WORSE.*
WAAAM

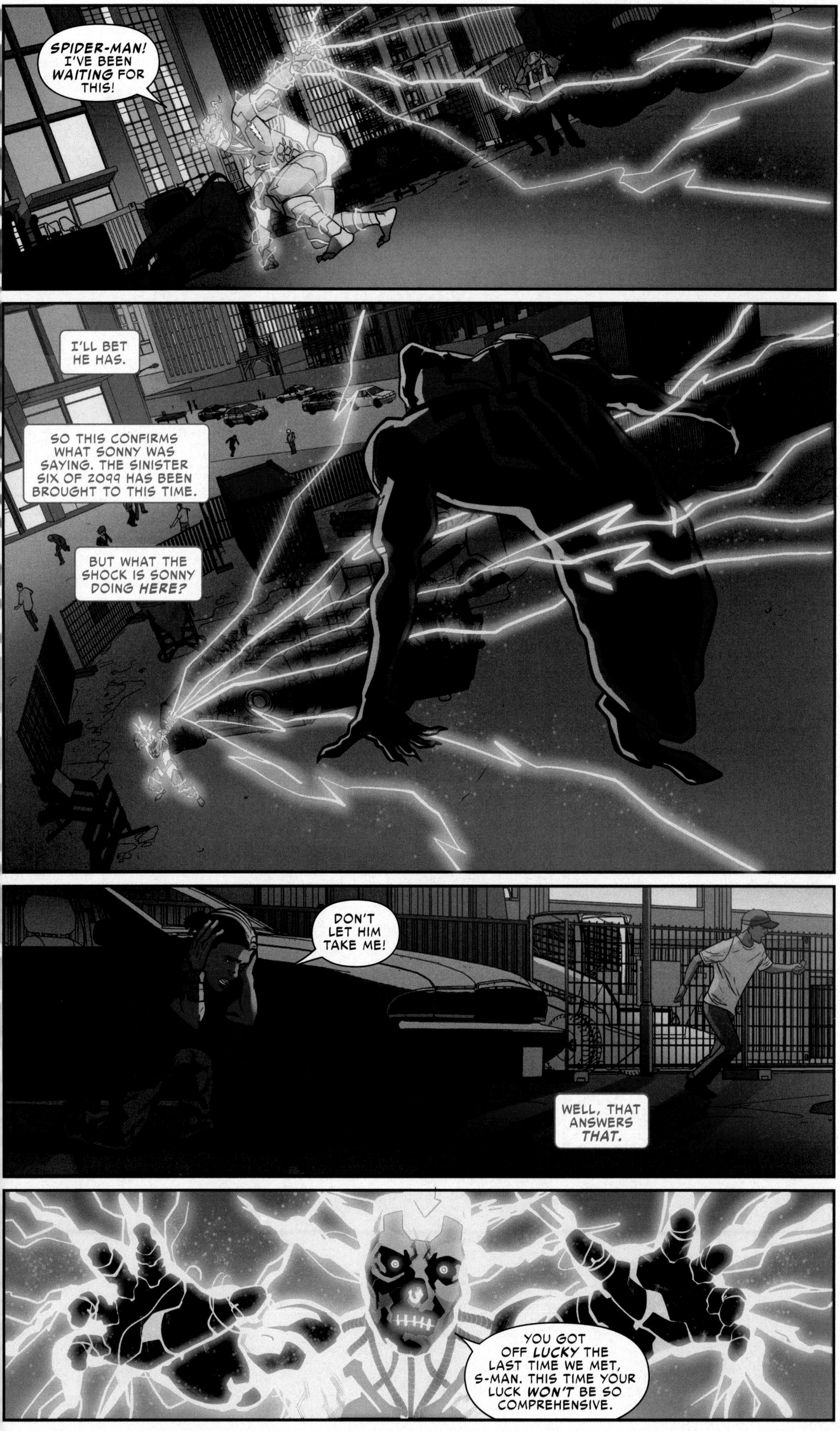
SPIDER-MAN! I'VE BEEN WAITING FOR THIS!
I'LL BET HE HAS.
SO THIS CONFIRMS WHAT SONNY WAS SAYING. THE SINISTER SIX OF 2099 HAS BEEN BROUGHT TO THIS TIME.
BUT WHAT THE SHOCK IS SONNY DOING HERE?
DON'T LET HIM TAKE ME!
WELL, THAT ANSWERS THAT.
YOU GOT OFF LUCKY THE LAST TIME WE MET, S-MAN. THIS TIME YOUR LUCK WON'T BE SO COMPREHENSIVE.

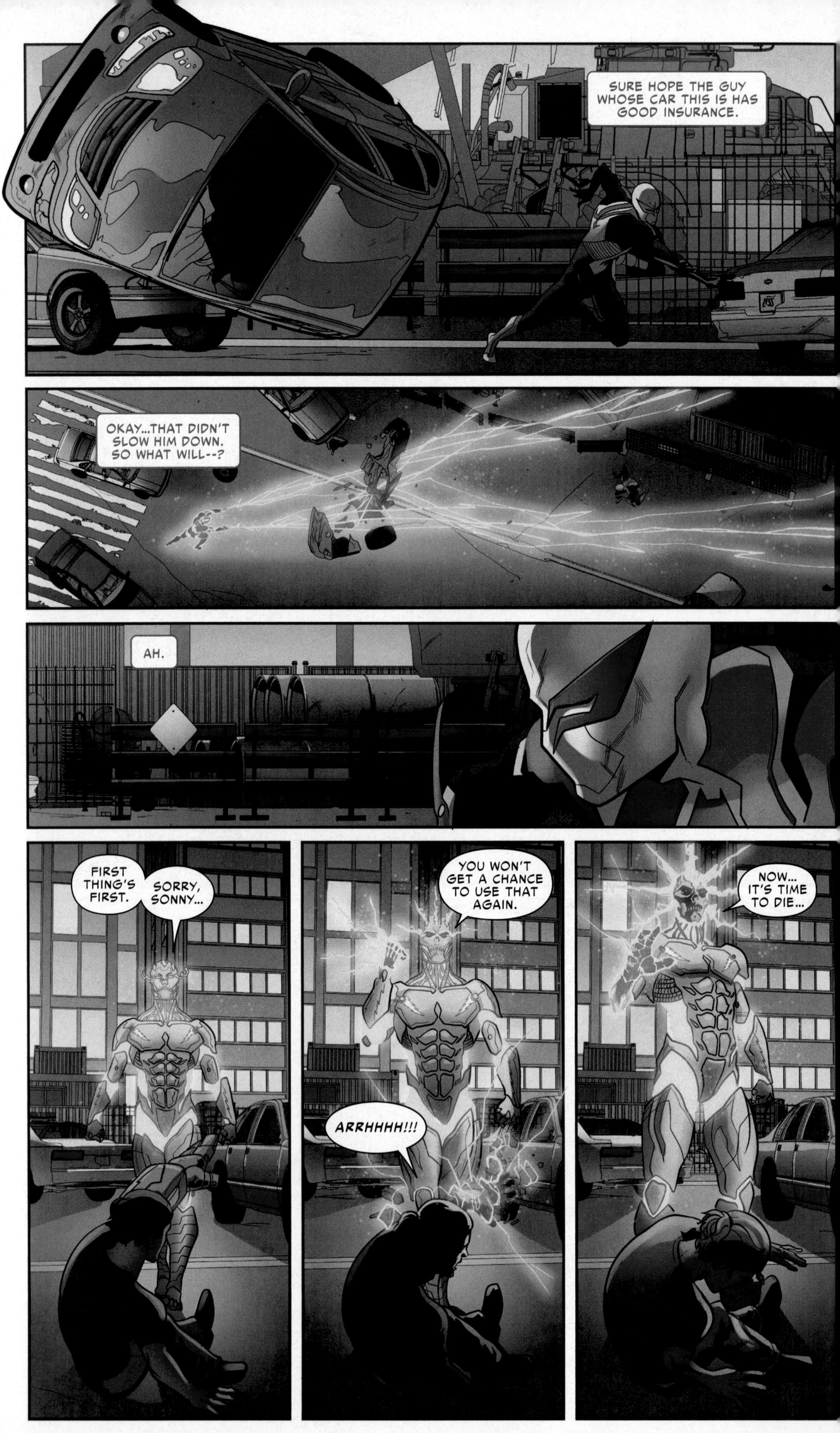
SURE HOPE THE GUY WHOSE CAR THIS IS HAS GOOD INSURANCE.
OKAY...THAT DIDN'T SLOW HIM DOWN. SO WHAT WILL--?
AH.
FIRST THING'S FIRST.
SORRY, SONNY...
YOU WON'T GET A CHANCE TO USE THAT AGAIN.
ARRHHHH!!!
NOW... IT'S TIME TO DIE...

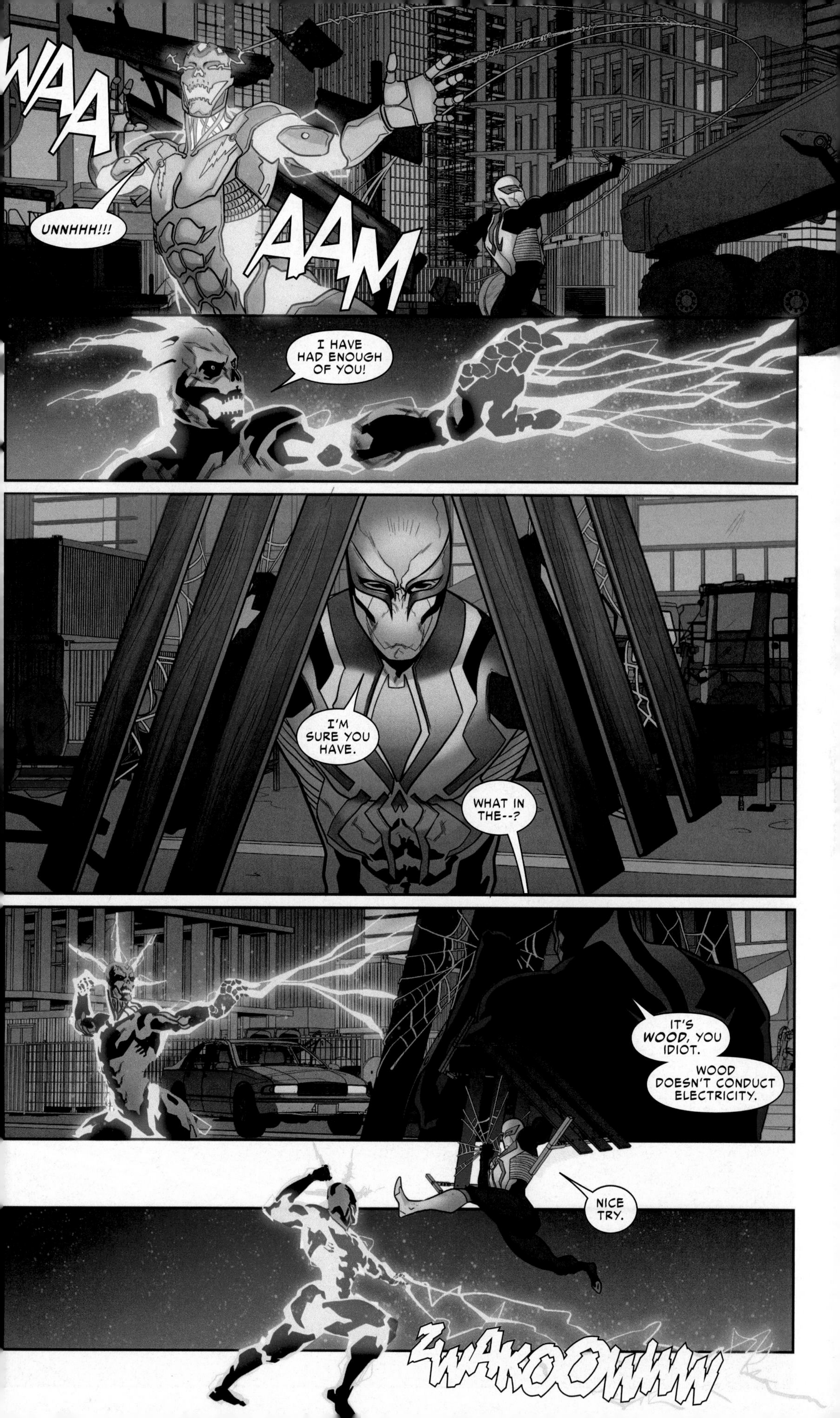
WAAAAM
UNNHHH!!!
I HAVE HAD ENOUGH OF YOU!
I'M SURE YOU HAVE.
WHAT IN THE--?
IT'S WOOD, YOU IDIOT.
WOOD DOESN'T CONDUCT ELECTRICITY.
NICE TRY.
ZWAKOOWWW

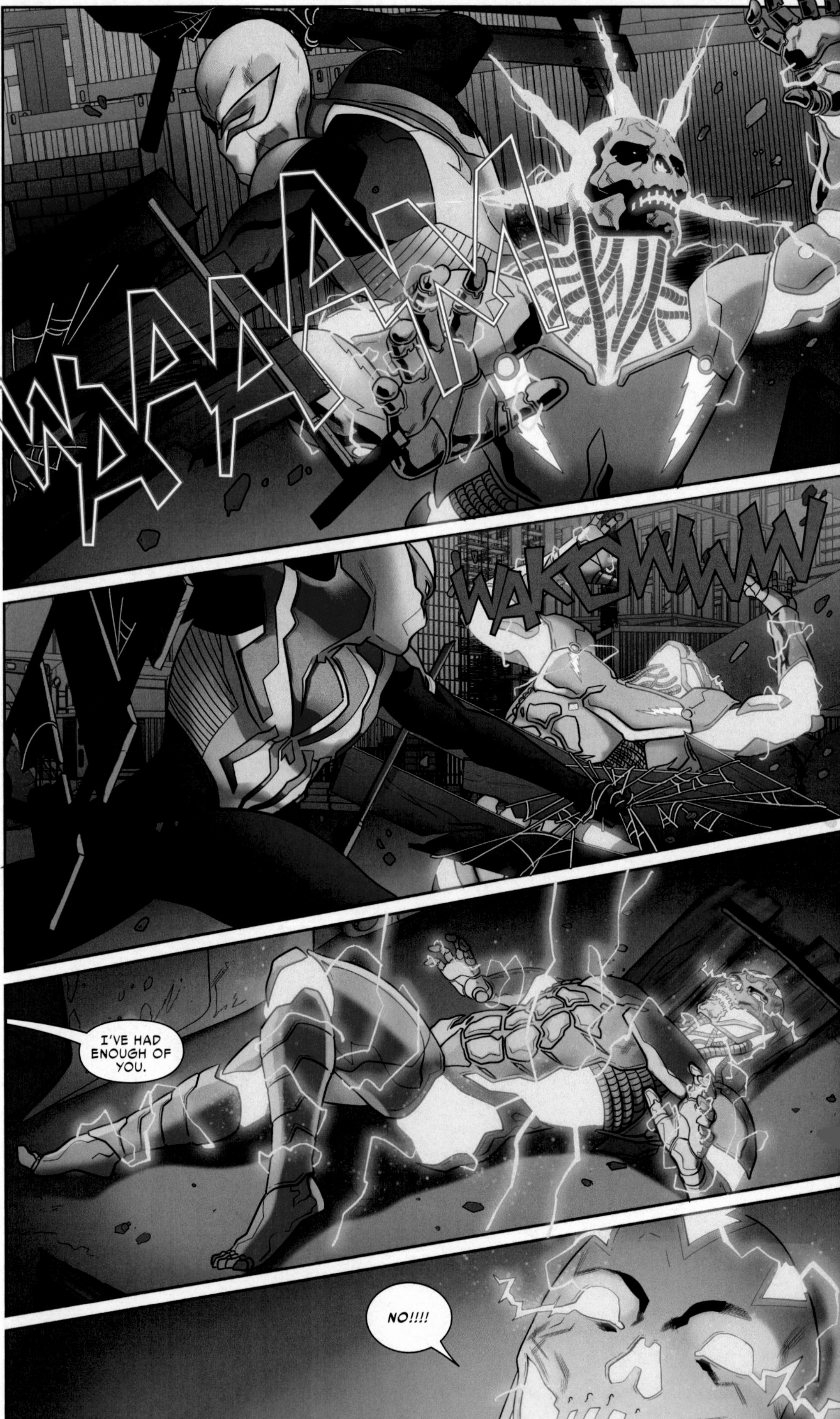
WAAAAM
WAKOWWW
I'VE HAD ENOUGH OF YOU.
NO!!!!

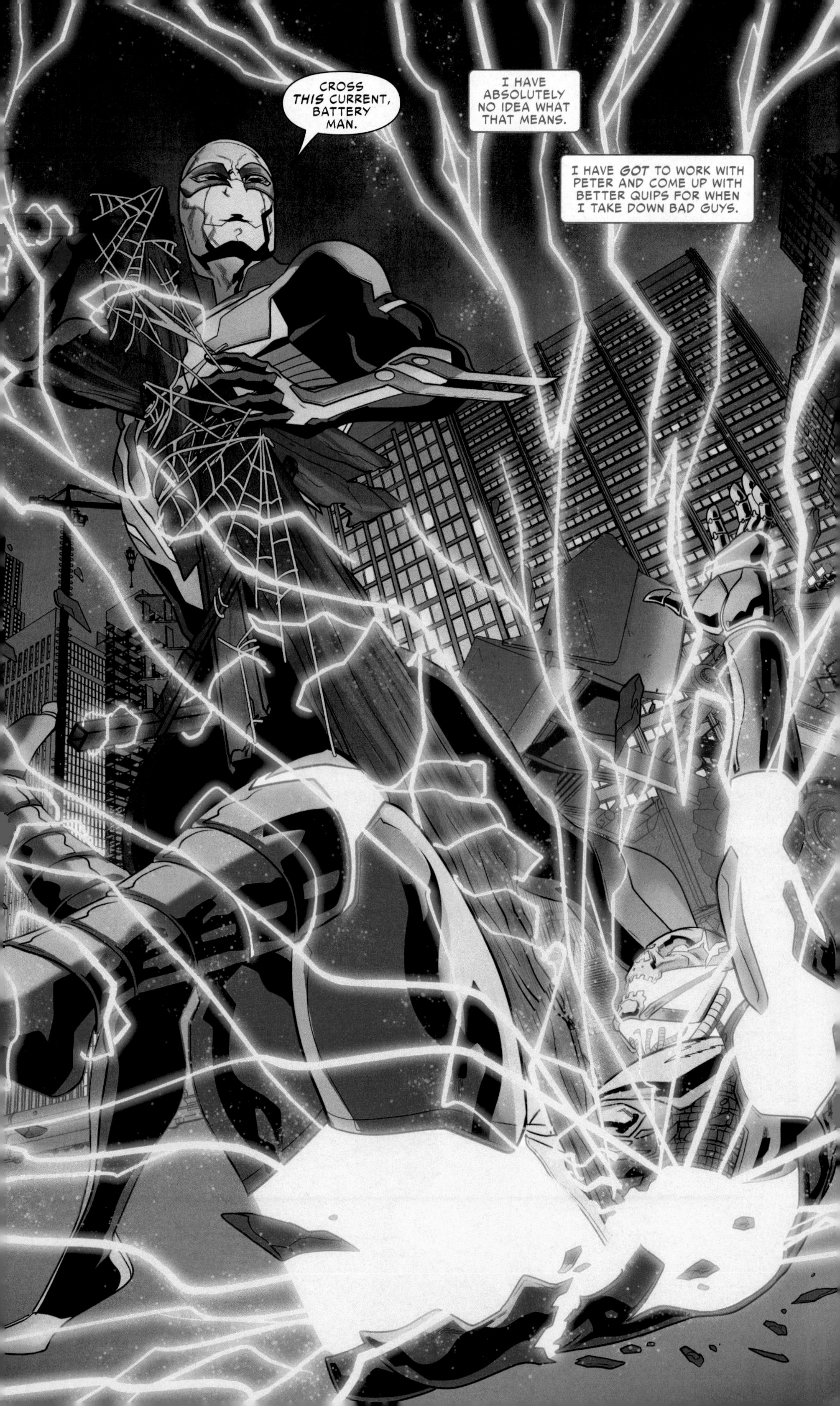
CROSS THIS CURRENT, BATTERY MAN.
I HAVE ABSOLUTELY NO IDEA WHAT THAT MEANS.
I HAVE GOT TO WORK WITH PETER AND COME UP WITH BETTER QUIPS FOR WHEN I TAKE DOWN BAD GUYS.

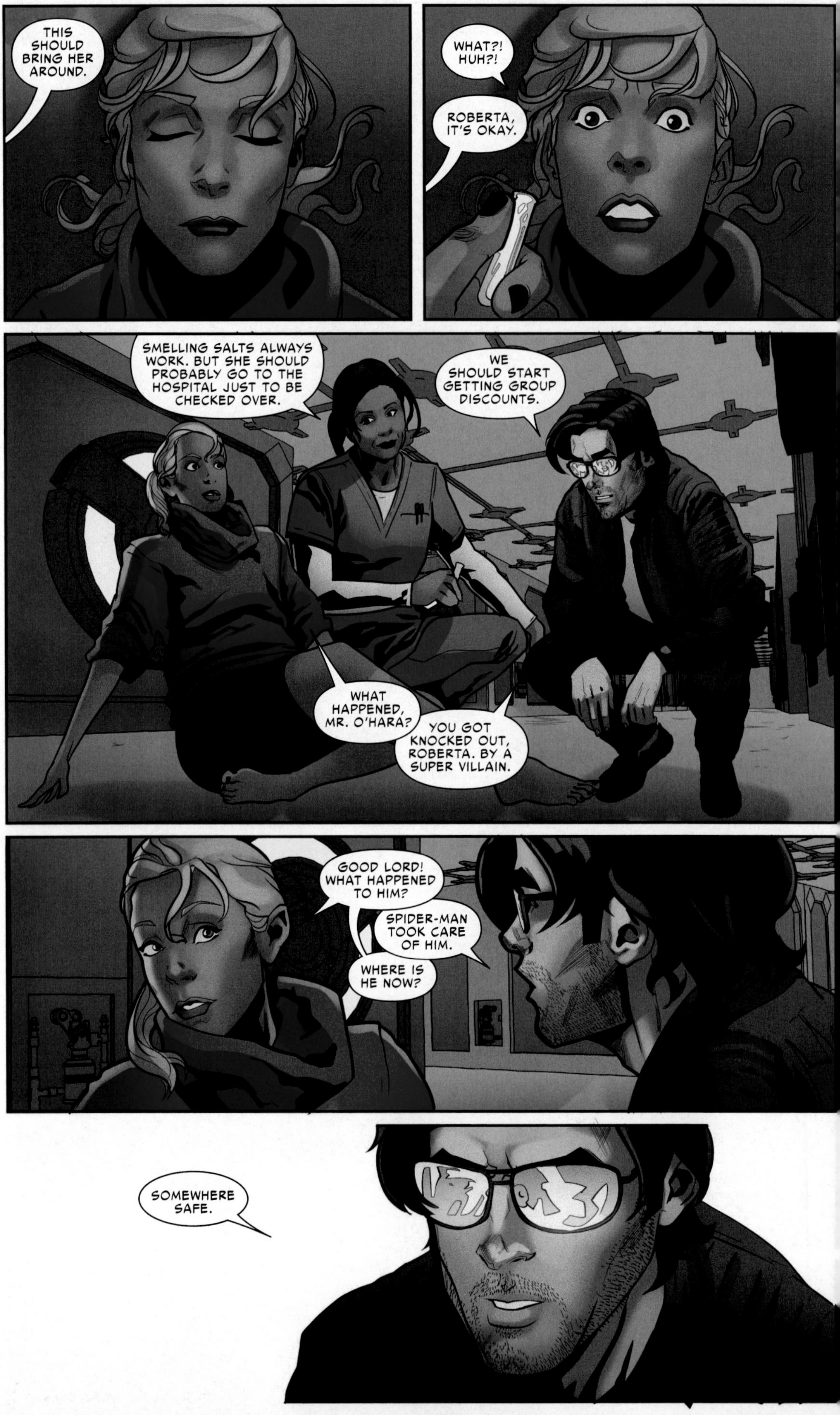
THIS SHOULD BRING HER AROUND.
WHAT?! HUH?!
ROBERTA, IT'S OKAY.
SMELLING SALTS ALWAYS WORK. BUT SHE SHOULD PROBABLY GO TO THE HOSPITAL JUST TO BE CHECKED OVER.
WE SHOULD START GETTING GROUP DISCOUNTS.
WHAT HAPPENED, MR. O'HARA?
YOU GOT KNOCKED OUT, ROBERTA. BY A SUPER VILLAIN.
GOOD LORD! WHAT HAPPENED TO HIM?
SPIDER-MAN TOOK CARE OF HIM.
WHERE IS HE NOW?
SOMEWHERE SAFE.

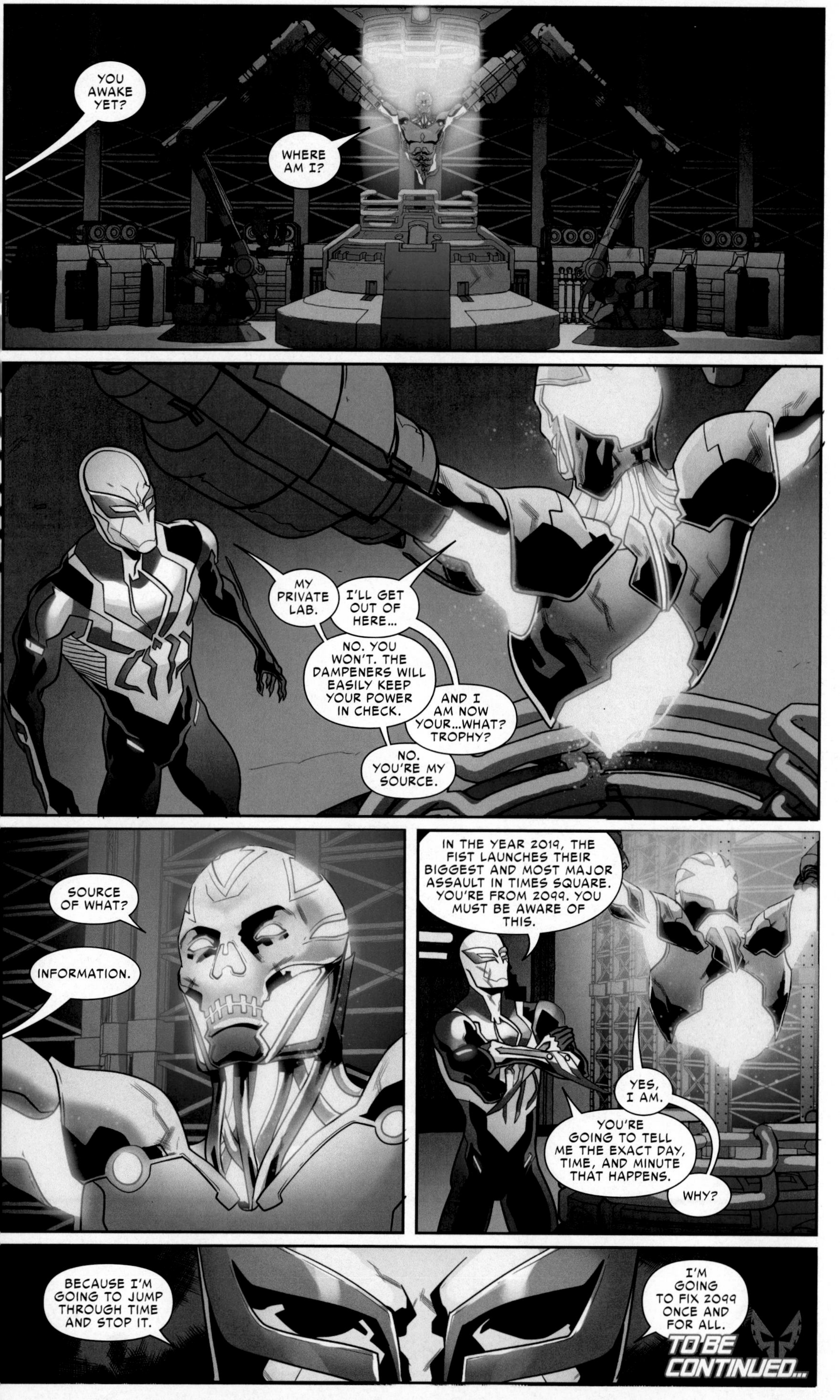
YOU AWAKE YET?
WHERE AM I?
MY PRIVATE LAB.
I'LL GET OUT OF HERE...
NO. YOU WON'T. THE DAMPENERS WILL EASILY KEEP YOUR POWER IN CHECK.
AND I AM NOW YOUR...WHAT? TROPHY?
NO. YOU'RE MY SOURCE.
SOURCE OF WHAT?
INFORMATION.
IN THE YEAR 2019, THE FIST LAUNCHES THEIR BIGGEST AND MOST MAJOR ASSAULT IN TIMES SQUARE. YOU'RE FROM 2099. YOU MUST BE AWARE OF THIS.
YES, I AM.
YOU'RE GOING TO TELL ME THE EXACT DAY, TIME, AND MINUTE THAT HAPPENS.
WHY?
BECAUSE I'M GOING TO JUMP THROUGH TIME AND STOP IT.
I'M GOING TO FIX 2099 ONCE AND FOR ALL.
TO BE CONTINUED...

#20, Page 4 art by WILL SLINEY

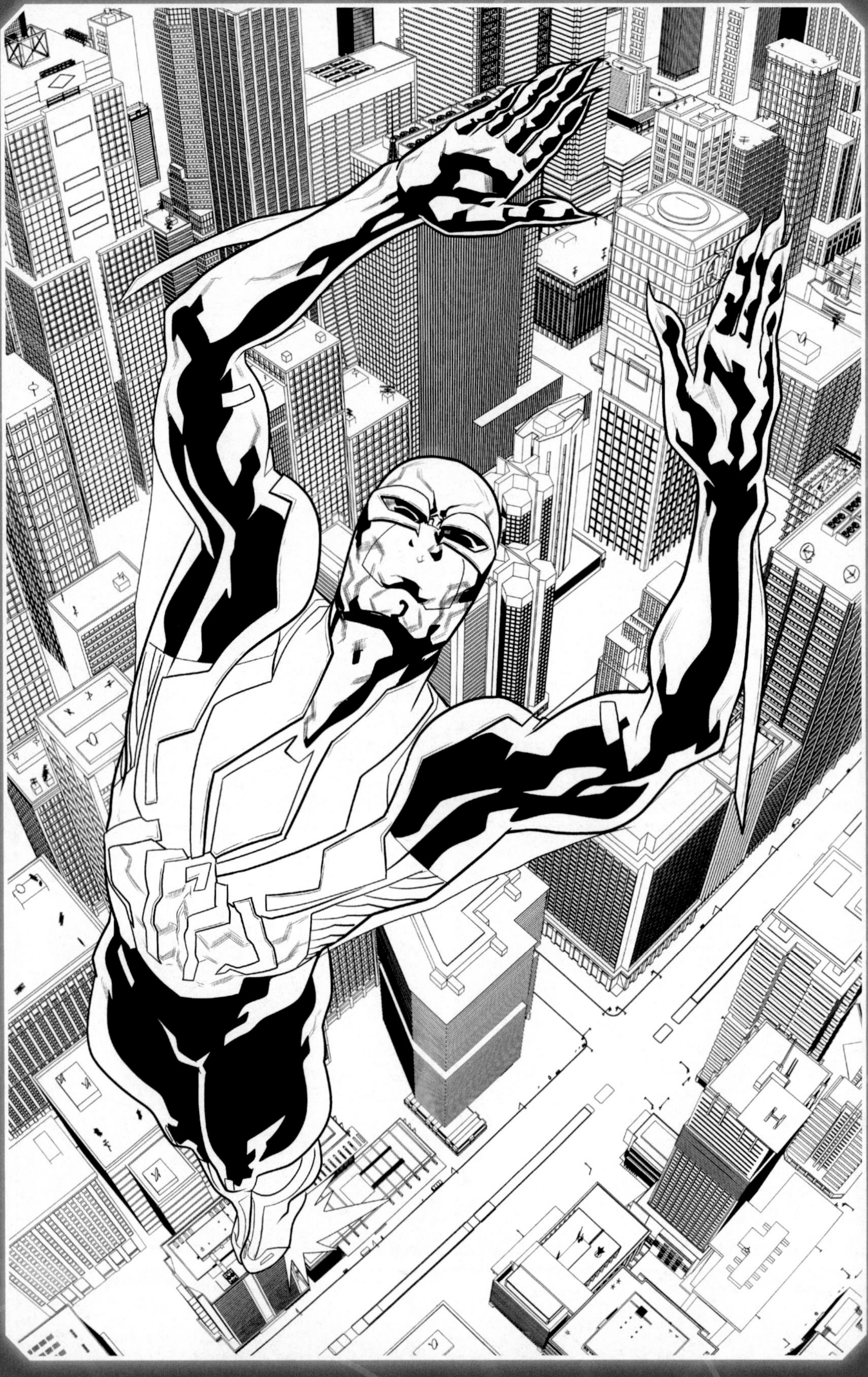

#21, Page 5 art by **WILL SLINEY**

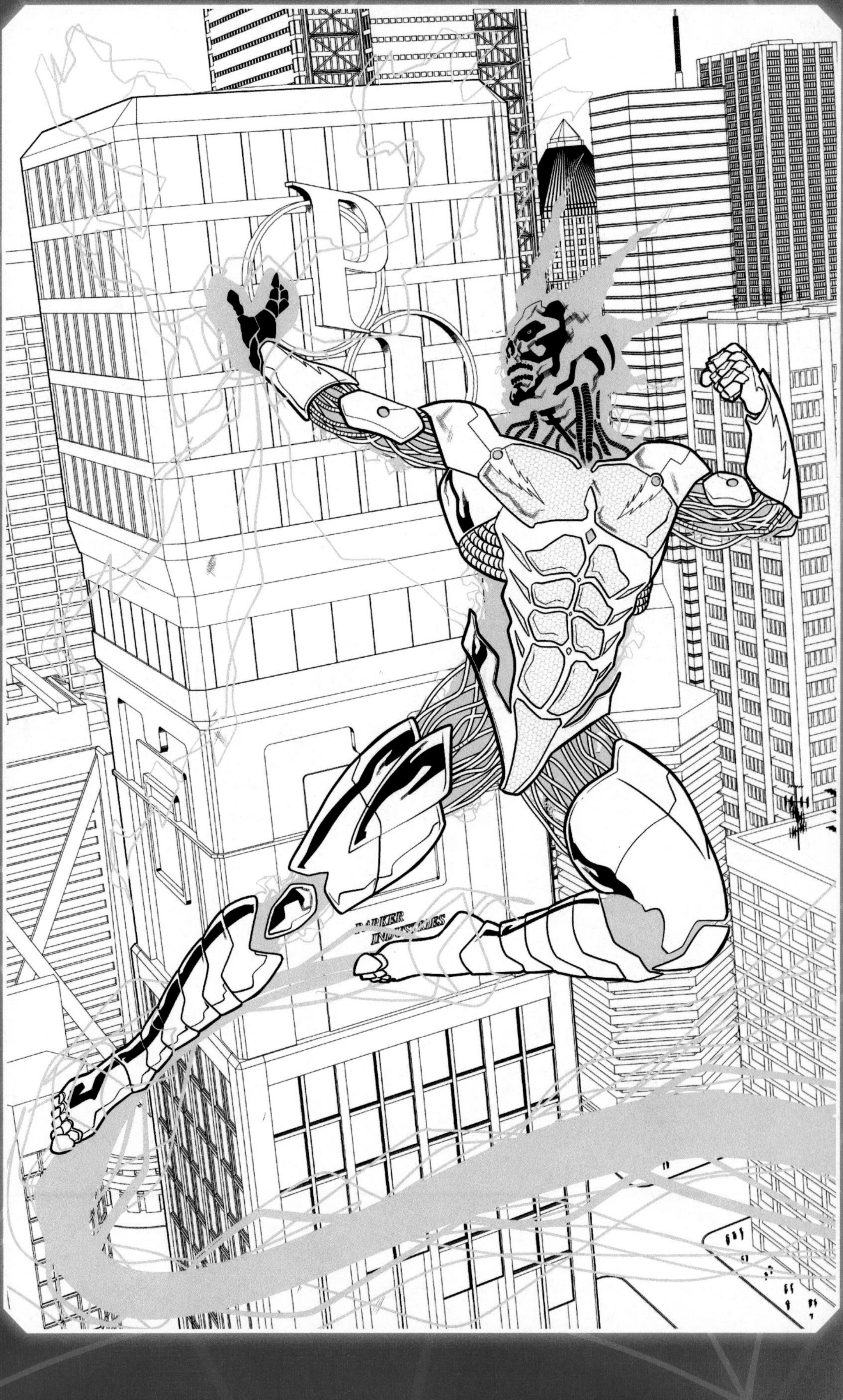

#21, Page 18 art by WILL SLINEY

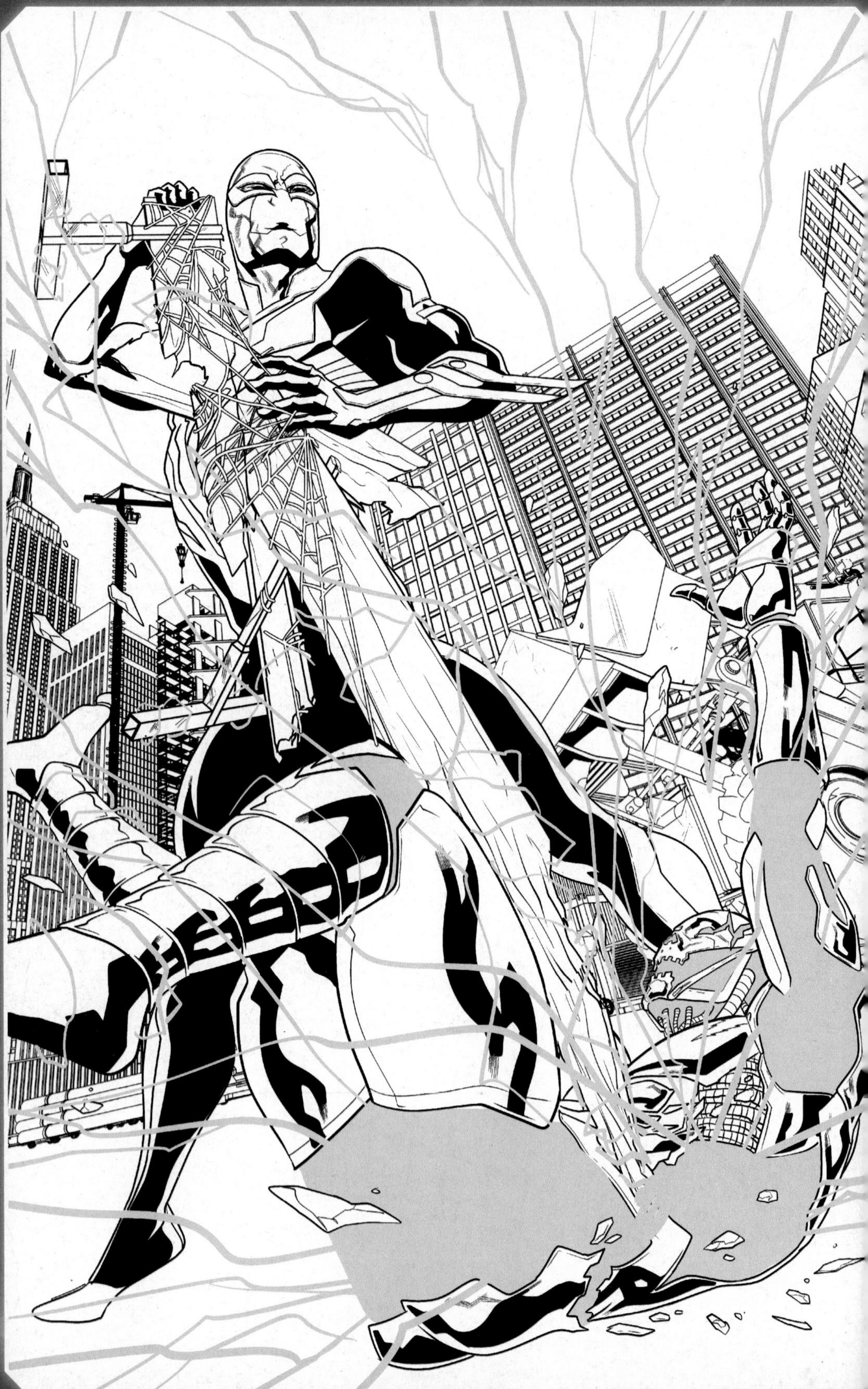